'MODERNIST' WOMEN WRITERS
AND NARRATIVE ART

Also by Kathleen Wheeler

SOURCES, PROCESSES AND METHODS IN COLERIDGE'S
BIOGRAPHIA LITERARIA

THE CREATIVE MIND IN COLERIDGE'S POETRY

ROMANTICISM, PRAGMATISM, AND DECONSTRUCTION

'Modernist' Women Writers and Narrative Art

Kathleen Wheeler
Fellow of Darwin College and University Lecturer
University of Cambridge

NEW YORK UNIVERSITY PRESS
Washington Square, New York

© Kathleen Wheeler 1994

All rights reserved

First published in the U.S.A. in 1994 by
NEW YORK UNIVERSITY PRESS
Washington Square
New York, N.Y. 10003

Library of Congress Cataloging-in-Publication Data
Wheeler, Kathleen M.
"Modernist" women writers and narrative art / Kathleen Wheeler.
p.   cm.
Includes bibliographical references and index.
ISBN 0–8147–9275–8 — ISBN 0–8147–9276–6 (pbk.)
1. American fiction—Women authors—History and criticism.
2. English fiction—Women authors—History and criticism.
3. Modernism (Literature)   4. Women and literature.   5. Narration
(Rhetoric)   I. Title.
PS374.W6W44   1994
813.009'9287—dc20   93–45749
                                                          CIP

Printed in Great Britain

Contents

Preface		vi
Acknowledgements		viii
1	Introduction: The Dragon of St Cyril	1
2	Excavating Meaning in Willa Cather's Novels	19
3	Kate Chopin: Ironist of Realism	51
4	The Attack on Realism: Edith Wharton's *In Morocco* and 'Roman Fever'	77
5	Style as Characterisation in Jean Rhys' Novels	99
6	Dramatic Art in Katherine Mansfield's 'Bliss'	121
7	The Multiple Realities of Stevie Smith	141
8	Jane Bowles: That Modern Legend	162
	Conclusion: The 'Voice of Silence' Speaks	182
	Notes	189
	Bibliography	207
	Index	216

Preface

In a collection of essays, Eudora Welty remarked that fiction is often 'brought off (when it does not fail) on the sharp edge of experiment'. She added that 'mystery waits for people wherever they go, whatever extreme they run to', and that even in realistic fictions, the reality is mystery. In the following sentence she clarified her insight when she explained that 'the mystery lies in the use of language to express human life'. The transformation of words into fiction is said to be a leap in the dark which brings writers and readers into 'the presence, the power, of the imagination'. Welty maintained that without its interpretation, without its artist, human life or experience – the 'so-called raw material' of fiction – is 'the worst kind of emptiness; it is obliteration, black or prismatic ... meaningless'. Before there can be meaning to human experience and life, there has to occur some 'personal act of vision' which is continuously 'projected as the novelist writes and the reader reads'. She then concluded:

> If this makes fiction sound full of mystery, I think it's fuller than I know how to say.... In writing, do we try to solve this mystery? No, I think ... we rediscover the mystery. We even, I might say, take advantage of it.
>
> As we know, a body of criticism stands ready to provide its solution, which is a kind of translation of fiction into another language ... the critical phrase 'in other words' is one to destroy rather than make for a real – that is, imaginative – understanding of the author.

In this study of seven women fiction writers, an effort has been made to avoid translating their fiction into another, less imaginative language. The mystery of the transformation of human life into words remains, as we explore the territory of fiction and seek to experience it more deeply through increased, more intimate acquaintance with the fiction, rather than through reductive generalisations or discursive accounts. In a sense, most criticism seeks to avoid such reductiveness, but by paying close, scrupulous attention to that 'sharp edge of experiment' which the texts exemplify, and attention to the 'personal acts of vision' they express, we hope to gain a better sense of the 'degrees and degrees and degrees of communication ... possible between novelists and ... readers'. An effort is made to respect and understand these elements of mystery, of vision, and of art as experiments in original, individual personal acts of imagination, which seek to interpret human life and make it meaningful. The artistic products of that power of imagination (which is 'above all the power to reveal, with nothing barred') reveal themselves to readers who seek 'no explanation outside fiction for what its writer is learning to do'. These statements, far from rejecting criticism *per se*, encourage a more imaginative response from readers, as Welty's prolific criticism shows. What is at stake is a respect for literary experiment and for the mystery of putting life into words, a respect which if cultivated, leads critics into creative articulation of experiences of reading which are their own 'raw material'.

K.M.W.

Acknowledgements

My sincerest thanks go to Anne Rendell, whose initiative and determination got this book into legible form. I am also grateful to my editor Margaret Cannon whose interest in and enthusiasm for the project rescued it from oblivion. Many students, both graduate and undergraduate, contributed unawares to the book, both with specific ideas and approaches, and with their fascination for the modernist period as evinced in supervisions, seminars and lectures. To Gillian Rogers, the Librarian of the English Faculty, Cambridge, I owe much gratitude, not only for an unusually well-stocked library of women's texts, but also for helpful advice over the years about general matters to do with the book. To the Librarians of the University Library I am also grateful for help whenever needed. To the Master and Fellows of Darwin College thanks are due of a general kind for the congenial surroundings in which the writing of this book occurred.

1

Introduction: The Dragon of St Cyril

In *Mystery and Manners*, a book of essays on the writing of fiction, Flannery O'Connor referred to the responsibility she felt as a writer to her readership, when she remarked: 'I hate to think of the day when the Southern writer will satisfy the tired reader.' She further explained that stories of any depth tell the tale, in an endless variety of disguises, of the mysterious passage past the dragon of St Cyril of Jerusalem, continuing: 'it requires considerable courage at any time, in any country, not to turn away from the storyteller.'[1] A few decades earlier, the American philosopher John Dewey had made a not unrelated observation, first paraphrasing a remark of John Keats: 'no "reasoning", as reasoning, that is, as excluding imagination and sense, can reach truth.... Reason must fall back on imagination – upon the embodiment of ideas in an emotionally charged sense.' Dewey then concluded:

> Ultimately there are but two philosophies. One of them accepts life and experience in all its uncertainty, mystery, doubt, and half-knowledge, and turns that experience upon itself to deepen and intensify its own qualities – to imagination and art.[2]

The intensifying and deepening of experience – even if the empirical qualities of that experience are 'uncertainty, mystery, doubt and half-knowledge' – occurs, Dewey said, by means of 'imagination and art'. They make possible intelligent reflection about the experience which leads to enrichment and to a kind of wisdom ('understanding' or 'knowledge' would not be quite the right word). Reason, then, is placed firmly under the control of imagination. O'Connor's more imaginative, metaphorical description (quoted above) communicates Dewey's idea forcefully, as she invoked images of 'mysterious passages' past dragons and spoke of the courage required by readers and listeners to face up to the

1

irresolvable mysteries that the story-teller reveals. The strong emphasis of both these writers on the need to respect mystery, the role they and such earlier writers as John Keats gave to imagination and art as preservers and enrichening forces of that mystery, and the reference to a mysterious passage, act as apt indications of a fruitful spirit in which to approach the writers discussed and referred to here.

The image of the 'mysterious passage' has strong reverberations of meaning for many of these writers, in its multiple significance as journey, as maturation, as initiation, and as a complex anatomical image. Travelling and journeys are evidently still an effective and exhilarating metaphor for imagination and aesthetic experience, as well as 'soul-making' or self-development. This is especially the case for writers like Jane Bowles, Stevie Smith, Katherine Mansfield, Jean Rhys, Willa Cather, and Edith Wharton; the latter noted joyously in 1917 that no guidebook for her destination, Morocco, was obtainable anywhere.[3] These women's fictions are magic carpets which testify not only to the author's imaginative journey into the exotic and unknown territories of innovative art. These novels are also vehicles for readers on which to pass into the uncharted and unexplored realms of imaginative mental life. Writers such as Smith, Bowles, not to mention Margaret Atwood, Rachel Ingalls, Doris Lessing, and Djuna Barnes, have exploited the journey metaphor in all its richness.[4] They and others have emphasised specifically its power as an image for expressing exploration into the realms of the unconscious and the unknown, whether in life or art. Travel is also a metaphor for the passage from childhood to adulthood, from life to death, and from sanity to madness. The metaphor of the journey also expresses the process of the discovery of love and sexuality, their relation to art and culture, energy in general, and its role in violence and in loving relationships. Closely related to these interests are concerns which Bowles, Smith and Charlotte Perkins Gilman, among others, specifically scrutinised in their novels, namely the relation of logic and reason to imagination, the illogical, and insanity. Other writers, such as Virginia Woolf, Katherine Mansfield, Hilda Doolittle, and Stevie Smith, explored the nature of the self, emphasising the multiple, ever-changing selves which inhabit the mind. Many of their novels portray the difficulty of creating an individuality genuinely distinct from the stereotyped social roles imposed from an early age. Other writers, such as Jean Rhys, Virginia Woolf, and Jane Bowles stressed the importance of individuality as something to be striven for and to be created through imaginative living and artistry. Thus, the journey or passage metaphor takes on further connotations as an image for an existential striving to raise oneself above lifeless role-playing. Genuine individuality is established through creative acts of the imagination and the will.

The problem of how to strive for and achieve individuality as a person was reflected in the struggle to develop an originality as an artist-writer. Many writers used the metaphor of the passage (or of travel beyond the familiar everyday world into exotic realms) as a description of the process by which an author could search for and find a voice and style of her own. That is, the familiar world became a metaphor for familiar literary conventions, themes, narrative strategies, and language, while the passing beyond these to an unknown world meant breaking the boundaries of literary convention, in order to have new experiences and to find new and stimulating forms of expression. Shelley had argued in *A Defence of Poetry* (1819) that imaginative writers have the invaluable function in culture of revitalising old metaphors and of creating new ones. Language (and literary conventions), he explained, degenerates through custom and familiarity, losing its power to stimulate the reader's or writer's imagination:

and then if no new poets should arise to create afresh the associations which have been thus disorganized language will be dead to all the nobler purposes of human intercourse.[5]

Few twentieth-century writers experimented more imaginatively with fiction than the women discussed here, and while they made many similar experiments in disrupting literary fashions and traditional conventions, each of them achieved a striking individuality. They made use of narrative and other conventions for purposes of parody; that is, they ironised the hidden assumptions underlying literary conventions, such as 'objectivity' or neutrality of point of view, transparency of language, hierarchies of privilege, and the hegemony of reason and logic. These women writers also exploited traditions of the baroque and gothic, the grotesque and picaresque, folk-tales and fairy-tales, legends, and medieval and gothic romance. They also adapted traditional imagery and metaphor (like the journey metaphor), traditional narrative techniques or structural devices, and other familiar conventions for new ends or in innovative ways in order to refashion experience itself. They could thereby make literature more expressive of their own unique experience, both as women and as artists. Into their experiments with narrative themes, forms and style, such writers as Woolf, Barnes, H. D., Rhys, Bowles, Smith, Dorothy Richardson, May Sinclair, and Gertrude Stein wove passionately articulate critiques of prevailing ideologies, whether social and political patriarchy, medical mistreatment of women, economic exploitation, racism, homophobia, or literary ideologies, such as realism. No convention of society or of fiction was left unexamined. Stock-in-trade devices involving stereotyped imagery, worn-out 'dead' metaphors, character types, notions of the role of plot, dialogue, and description, styles of language, and formal structures or modes of organisation, were boldly exploited for new ends. Language and form were pulled, stretched, distorted, parodied, and disrupted in innumerable ways into innovative and witty transformations, which embodied new conceptions of life and art while questioning prevailing values.

The narratives of these women writers pushed the limits of twentieth century fiction deep into new territory, influencing many later writers. Another way of describing the effects of such writers' experiments in fiction is to say that each of them, in her own unique way, multiplied still further the possibilities for viewing ourselves and our worlds. Such new points of view lead to new worlds of perception and experience. Some used familiar modernist 'disruption' techniques and their counterparts, namely constructive innovation; others used realist gestures and then built into the subtext a 'deconstruction' of that very realism (a more recent example being Doris Lessing's Golden Notebook).[6] These newly created worlds of perception and experience extend our consciousness as the landscape of experience changes; depending on the point of view from which we look at life, society, and the individual, new possibilities for how we live emerge. Hence, our most basic values and beliefs are shown to be subject to examination and change. Indeed, not only our most cherished values may have to change; the very facts of experience change too, under imaginative scrutiny. The novels and short stories of these women portray many of our ideals, our aspirations, and the things we seek to preserve, as destructive fantasies, hypocrisies, cruelty, and exploitation at the worst, and harmful sentimentality and folly at the best. Both values and facts are transformed by these novelists through artistic innovations which frequently mirror, or are analogies for, the thematics of the texts. Fine, precise congruence between form and content is thereby achieved, a congruence in the sense that forms of art, language, and thematics coincide, reinforcing each other as well as the belief that there is always more than one valuable way of seeing the world, of thinking, feeling, or living.[7] Exploration of the points of view which madness and dreams offer, or the points of view of freaks, outcasts, children, women, certain 'unacceptable' men, and other types of 'outsiders', like tarts and criminals, lead these writers to a rejection of the adequacy of so-called normal attitudes, beliefs, and behaviour. Such exposures of convention in life and in literature become the main themes and structuring principles of these novels, whether overtly or whether subtly built into an ironic sub-text.

One of the most striking characteristics of these modernist and 'pre-modernist' texts is the extent to which the authors' fictional exploits anticipate and enact present-day theories of art and literature, by means of techniques of metadiscourse, self-conscious writing, and self-consuming artefacts. Related matters such as the centrality of rhetorical devices, levels of self-commentary by means of ironic sub-texts, extended metaphorical levels of meaning, and complex imagery referring both to the reading and the writing of the text abound in the fictions of the women writers studied here, not to mention many of their contemporaries. For example, overt modernists like Stevie Smith, Jane Bowles, Jean Rhys, Katherine Anne Porter, and Katherine Mansfield use familiar modernist techniques for such ironic, metaphoric, mirroring designs. Yet, as is shown below, Edith Wharton, Charlotte Perkins Gilman, Willa Cather, and Kate Chopin also wove ironic, systematically detailed and precisely constructed 'looking-glass' levels into an only superficially realist or 'straight' narrative form. These writers' novels and stories make it evident that much fiction has a sophisticated, distinct layer of critical commentary built into its fabric. Such criticism woven into the fictional design of texts acts to criticise the implicit 'ideology' of the surface thematics. That is, the sub-text reverses the values and facts the overt thematics appeared to support and condone. A level of criticism also functions as a self-conscious commentary on textuality – on the status of the text as fiction, its relation to 'reality' – to the author, the world, and especially to the reader in the act of the reading, interpreting, and making sense of the text. In such a level of self-criticism, the nature of an artist's relation to her literary predecessors is also variously explored: *Wide Sargasso Sea* is only the most parodic, overt example, while Kate Chopin less overtly – but no less ironically – 'deconstructed' the main planks of realism, and Willa Cather explicitly and avowedly threw out its props and furniture. Charlotte Perkins Gilman personified the realist in her male characters and showed the madness to which such men could drive an original mind. Edith Wharton, on the other hand, like Jane Austen before her, tamed realism to suit her own ironic predilections. She disrespectfully dismissed what did not please her, by means of queenly reversals of life–art relations and ironic, detached 'hidden' narrators who adopt 'knitting', for example, as a parody of realist literary proprieties.[8]

In 'disestablishing' their supposed relation to their literary precursors, whether through indirect allusion or overt reference, these women emphasised the way novels can be designed to adopt, adapt, tease, mock, ironise, and reject traditional literary devices and conventions. An awareness of such a level of criticism in fiction, regarding both thematics and formal elements, leads to the question of the relation of fiction to criticism, or fiction to any other non-fictional form of writing. Both implicitly and explicitly, such writing suggests that the relation between fictional and non-fictional writing is more complex than a simple 'difference' understood as a dichotomy. Other related questions arise about the nature of the relationship between art and reality, fiction and reality, and language and reality. Any reader familiar with Gertrude Stein, Woolf, Bowles, Smith, or Rhys, not to mention more recent authors such as Angela Carter, Marguerite Young, Leonora Carrington, Doris Lessing, and Louise Erdrich, will realise immediately that for these artists, such apparent dichotomies as language–world, art–reality, and fiction–history are functional and relative.[9] That is, these dualities are examples of conventional modes of reflecting about experience; the relationship of such dualities becomes problematic only if we mistake the dualities as a fundamental character of experience, and not the product of reflection and socialised learning. One of the dichotomies these writers are most concerned to expose as functional and relative, rather than as a 'given' of basic experience, is that supposed duality between articulation and experience, between linguistic expression and feeling.

For many of these writers, there is no such thing as self-conscious, human experience antecedent to the articulation of it, however underdeveloped and blunt that articulation may be. As is clear from the complex ironies of their textual fabrics, language is the means of organising chaos into a conscious awareness which is the only awareness worthy of the name, experience. As John Dewey, Derrida, or Heidegger would argue, experience is not even 'had' until it is articulated, however crudely. As that articulation is cultivated and sharpened, experience becomes more sophisticated, more qualitatively meaningful, and even more 'real'. To put it in another Deweyan way, mind emerges, as does self-conscious experience, concurrently with emerging language use.[10] Each one of the women authors discussed here, from Chopin and Wharton to Bowles and Smith, depicts in new and imaginative ways the saturation of experience by language, and the linguistic character of all experience. Relatedly, one of the most common general themes (often reflected in the formal structures) of these and others such as Stein, Woolf, Dorothy Richardson, May Sinclair, H. D., Djuna Barnes, not to mention Ellen Glasgow and Rebecca West, was to expose duality itself,[11] and its resulting hierarchies, as defunct, as a delusion resulting from mistaking a product of reflection for the nature of reality. Through fiction, these women writers broke through the boundaries such dualities set up, not only to rewrite the dual elements as functions of each other and interdependent, but also to expose them as mere conventions, not truths once and for all. We, as readers, are shown that, valuable as dualistic conventions may be, they need constantly to be disrupted if the imagination required to see new possibilities is to be kept alive.

Moreover, such conventional dualities are nearly always imbued with unequal, hierarchical values. Rhys and Wharton in particular expose these inequalities as ideologies devised to maintain privilege and prejudice. Imaginative reversals are invoked to debunk the 'reality' of such inequable valuations; the resulting two sides of the duality are shown to be conceptually and empirically interdependent for existence and for meaning. Indeed, not only are they interdependent 'in reality', and not opposed to each other (except ideologically), their very existence is shown to be a product of reflection, a way of looking at the world, not a fact of reality. Finally, these women's texts show that meaning or value is itself conventional and subject to change. For example, not only is gender shown to be a social construct; sexual, biological difference itself is equally a way of structuring experience. Every human being differs from every other human being; but as Jean Rhys, for example, insisted, we can focus in on any difference we like. Yet if we turn that chosen difference into a category for placing people into pecking orders of value, we dehumanise ourselves and them. To focus on certain differences, and not others, and to raise them to the level of some supreme importance, some 'biological fact', is to interpret the world ideologically. For Rhys we are all first and foremost human beings, to be treated as individuals, not to be categorised, classed, and labelled with price tags of our worth. Katherine Mansfield also knifed through the facade of the pretensions and hypocrisies which allege categories to be realities and not ideologies. Other writers such as Djuna Barnes, Radclyffe Hall, Jane Bowles, Gertrude Stein, and H. D., to take only a few obvious examples, debunked the notion that while gender may admittedly be a social category (to determine specified social roles which have little, strangely enough, to do with our genitalia), sexuality at least is a fact. Like gender, these texts confirm that biology is interpretation too, and is in as much need of examination of its premises and presuppositions as science is of its methods and aims.

Whether we read Gilman or Bowles, Cather or Smith, Wharton or Mansfield, the levels of multiple critical commentary, embedded like a beautiful design in each text, alert the reader both to the general, theoretical issues touched upon above, and to the more immediate, phenomenological moments of reading itself. Questions about the nature of reading, interpretation, and the 'extraction' of meaning from texts, questions about the reader's role – as passive receiver of someone else's artistry, ideas, and acts or as active participant in the aesthetic experience of art – questions about the nature and role of imagination, reason, desire, will, expectations, opinions, and so on, all such questions are not merely implied by these texts. These matters are 'figured' into the designs, the formal structures, and the thematics of the texts. Sometimes they are displayed by means of familiar symbolic emblems, as with Willa Cather. Other times, they are 'knitted' (as in Edith Wharton's 'Roman Fever') into the text by semantic levels of analogy. Such analogy is drawn to the reader's attention by repeated, recognisable gestures of imagery, pun, or self-referentiality (through, for example, self-conscious narrative frameworks). Jean Rhys achieved a (typically) fine congruence when she repeatedly mentioned the racial issue of white–black and depicted racism in nearly every character except 'the tarts' – especially excepting Anna. Then, through repeated insertions into the textual subject-matter of comments about reading, books, and words (in *Voyage in the Dark* and *After Leaving Mr MacKenzie*), Rhys punned on the words 'black and white', implying not only racism, but also words typed in black on a white page.[12] Such witty, authorised gestures for constructing mirroring situations in which the reader is 'caught in the act' of reading permeate nearly every text discussed here. To use a conventional metaphor from the rag-bag of critical discourse, such novels and stories are distorting mirrors ('looking-glasses' as Rhys, Porter, and others like to call them) in which we readers get the chance to view ourselves from many perspectives and in a whole variety of different mirrors. Rhys and Mansfield exposed our prejudices, Chopin and Cather our destructive fantasies, Gilman and Wharton our inadequate understanding of the reaction of a 'sane' individual to an 'insane society'. Bowles showed us our unfounded preconceptions about morality, sex, homophobia, and religious strictures; Porter laughed at our self-importance and Stevie Smith at our *naïveté*.

Innovations in style, imagery, characterisation, structural unity, narrative strategy, and thematics are often overlooked if we read lazily, without the scrupulous attention to detail that each one of these exquisitely unique texts deserves. Their potential to provide aesthetic experiences of beauty and insight – of what it feels like to be an imaginative reader – is lost unless we as readers cultivate an almost mystical respect for these texts as individuals. Their unique character and originality set them off from every other text, no matter how much they share in articulating the issues discussed above. These texts can be treated as possessing a particularity much like that of any human individual. Hence, they should never be treated mechanically, as objects, but as living things which, together with imaginative critical response, will reveal their inner structures. The aesthetic experience they engender, moreover, is their meaning as works of art, and aesthetic experience occurs in the interacting of a text with a writer or a reader. The reader is, through beautifully designed settings in the narrative, aroused to demandingly complex levels of response, to an awareness of second- and third-order significances and meanings. Of course, the novels and stories are, at a thematic level, fascinating and provocative critiques of society and individuals; though even on this level they may turn out to have complexities which force us to reject or reverse our initial interpretations. These texts are intensely meaningful as works of art when their formal, artistic qualities create a congruence with the thematics. They create such a congruence, which is almost a definition of art, by being both overt and covert meditations on the ways fiction is produced by an individual, yet in a tradition. They meditate upon the relation of a work of fiction to the world or the reality it is supposed to 'reflect', a relation which is far from a simple representation or allegory.

Such metadiscourse, such second- and third-order levels of self-reference, are not purely formal. For these modernists, such literary and artistic formalities are themselves substantive. Without them, the so-called content or thematics would have no shape and hence no being. Moreover, these formal qualities, distinguishable only, not divisible from the thematics, are designed by such writers as Chopin, Rhys, Wharton, Bowles, Cather, and Smith, to show how central art and imaginative activity are to our ordinary, everyday lives. These levels of textual meaning reveal that the alleged dichotomy between creativity or imaginativeness and 'mere' perception or ordinary everyday life is itself only relative. Ordinary life and basic, 'mere' perception are themselves rich with imaginative character, if only we would activate our imagination. They seem different because custom and familiarity blind us to the art of living, the beauty of the world around us, and the imaginative character of simple perception. According to these modernists, the latter is at the basis of artistic creativity, that power of stripping away the veil of familiarity which hides the beauty, and the ugliness, of the ordinary world, and of ordinary perception itself.

All the writers discussed here offer opportunities for imaginative response of a sophisticated kind, opportunities for an unusual degree of self-awareness concerning the possible ways in which reading can presume upon, distort, and even imprison, as well as liberate, a text. Contrary to the covertly conservative presuppositions of much of what is misnamed 'New Historicism', each of the levels of meaning touched upon above (and discussed more fully in the following chapters) are significant and valuable. The women writers discussed here, as well as many of their contemporaries, clearly refuted by example the simplistic notion that literature is somehow secondary and supplemental to a prior reality, to history, to context. They rejected the notion that literature is a mimetic or even critical representation of these prior givens. William James brilliantly exploded this delusion by discovering an implicit human spectator unconsciously assumed in all such 'theories' which posit duality as the essential character of experience.[13] Literature may be 'like' history or life, and even a representation of it. Yet life and history are no less 'like' literature, that is, meaningful and intelligible only because engaged with by our imaginative response. Nature is not so much prior to culture or art as a product of it, as Edith Wharton (like Elizabeth Spencer in Italy) so eloquently and wittily displayed.[14] In her travel writings, Wharton constantly resorted to familiar paintings, poems, and novels by means of which she saw and enjoyed the landscape and villages of Morocco and Italy. Willa Cather's fascination with the cliff dwellings of the American Southwest arose because she 'saw' them as a metaphor, as emblematic of the congruence of culture and nature, or art and history. Then she used this nature–human, real, historical phenomenon as a simile for the nature of art itself. These incredible cliff dwellings in their magnificent setting became supernatural in import, models for the 'essence' of imaginative artefacts: the cliff dwellings in their natural setting are like the finest works of art, and as such reveal to us what art is. Isak Dinesen was another artist of the reversal of the nature – culture, reality, or history – art dichotomies. Her 'historical', Gothic tales-within-tales-within tales anticipate Jorge Luis Borges' incredible labyrinthine forking paths, illustrating the way culture is at the very heart of our conception of nature, and, correspondingly, that art and story-telling constitute the very essence of our lives, our history, our reality.[15] This is not merely to say that histories are also stories or narratives told from a limited point of view: rather, the reality history purports to refer to or describe is itself not some 'other', not some real world, but only more history, more stories, more interpretation – interpretations of other, prior interpretations. The literal, scientific, rational, logical language of truth is shown by Rhys, Cather, Bowles, and others to be a 'dead metaphor';[16] it is just our familiar way of seeing the world. As Nadine Gordimer put it, rationality, logic, the literal, and the true are simply the most familiar form of the irrational.[17]

Priorities and hierarchies are arrived at only by 'forgetting' (to use Heidegger's Freudian word) or repressing the functional and dynamic nature of all such dualities and oppositions as literature–history, language–world, art (or fiction)–reality, word–thing, male–female, black–white, and so on.

For Stein and Woolf, as for Chopin and Gilman, Bowles and Smith, Barnes and Sinclair, our world is not a single world, but a variety of greatly differing, mutually existing worlds. This variety of worlds is structured and constructed in part by the various discourses, languages, and vocabularies relating to them. There is not a Reality, a History, or a Context. There are many competing and co-operating realities, histories, and contexts, just as there are many styles, literatures, and languages, and they are not irreducibly dichotomous or hierarchical. These modernist and pre-modernist writers questioned the meaning and relation of the real and the non-real, in such a way that neither the 'unreal' nor the real could any longer be taken for granted. Modernist writers took realist assumptions and ideologies and turned them inside out, partly to expose their inherent prejudices and assumptions. Such reversals could open up new ways of legitimising and authorising the experiences of people that had been denied validity or importance. Modernism attacked the very notion of a dichotomy in literature between, for example, romance and realism, or modernism and realism. It showed that realism was just another form of experimentation with art, language, and story-telling, and not 'The authorized version' of literature; whereas for realists, language used properly was naïvely assumed to be a transparent medium of reality. The realist sought to communicate directly with the reader by means of true description. No interpretive, subjective point of view interfered with the objectivity of the account.

Yet, for the women writers discussed here, the realist notion of the Real, the Literal, the True, was the most pervasive delusion of all because of its denial of fantasy, desire, and the unreal inherent within it. Reality, as Marquerite Young argued,[18] has to be imagined, and thus is inherently, conceptually involved in the notion of the imaginative. The fantastic plurality and multifariousness of reality, life and art is envisaged by these writers as they experiment constantly with new forms and themes. They avoid as deathly any gesture of resolving ambiguities, complexities, and indeterminacies into readily available, univocal meanings, or single realities with pre-ordained hegemonies and preferred, 'objective' points of view alleged to be neutral. Cather waged war on the mediocrity such realism breeds, while Mansfield and Wharton ruthlessly exposed its hypocrisies and pretensions. Porter portrayed us all as 'fools of life' and Bowles turned proprieties on their heads to devise a 'downward path to wisdom'. In Smith, Barnes, Stein, and H. D., formal chaos and confusion proliferate and disseminate in Nietzschean, Dionysiac fecundity, while Woolf (and, later, Marguerite Young, Carter, Carrington, Frame, and Bessie Head)[19] celebrate a corresponding flux, fragmentation, and surface disorganisation of thematics. A rich profusion of dreams, memories, fantasies, and hilarious conversational or tragic hallucinogenic digressions preclude the progressive development of any single plot in many texts, or any single meaning to the plot in others. Similarly, time fragments into subjective measures; for example, Miriam Henderson in *Pilgrimage* becomes intoxicated with lager and words, and her companion intoxicated with her visions, which stretch seconds into long descriptive metaphors. While some of the plots of the novels and stories discussed here 'progress' in labyrinthine meanderings through multiple time–space dimensions, resembling nothing so much as Blake's *Four Zoas* or *Jerusalem*, other novels maintain a surface appearance of order, with proliferations of meanings and indeterminacies of interpretation worked out in palimpsest sub-texts of ironic commentary upon ironic commentary. Neologisms, puns, witty allusions, and etymological or proper-name jokes abound in the text of Smith, Barnes, H. D., and Stein, to create a rich materiality of style which directly challenges any intelligible notion of 'ordinary language', a notion at the basis of realism. Other texts, like those of Jean Rhys, Katherine Anne Porter, and Willa Cather, are extraordinary for their carefully crafted, calculated simplicity, and unpretentious clarity of style which nevertheless leads to complexity of structure and meaning. Still others, like Jane Bowles or Charlotte Perkins Gilman, borrow from the grotesque and picaresque to give their language its distinct, fantastic character, which still has a purity of style and diction in many cases.

Chopin and Smith overtly exploited the forcefully subversive elements of fairy-tale, folklore, and mythology, as did H. D., not to mention later writers like Atwood, Eudora Welty, and Angela Carter.[20] Combinations of these familiar genres, along with mixings of the fantastic and the real, are modes of subjecting powerful traditional, cultural forms to astute criticism, satire, and ironic reversals of meaning. Thus, patriarchal attitudes to sex, work, art, and play are questioned by submerging ourselves into the forms which unconsciously structure and 'people' our imaginations from our earliest childhood. One of the results is a celebration of a sexuality liberated from patriarchal conventions and preferences, a central aspect of these feminist critiques of social stereotypes and unquestioned imposition of desires by one group of human beings upon another: the claiming of the priority of one reality over another.

One of the conventional sources of imaginative power fully exploited by writers such as Wharton, Gilman, Cather, Rhys, Chopin, Woolf and Dorothy Richardson is 'the power of the place', as Eudora Welty described it in *The Eye of the Story*. Landscape and nature, city and houses or rooms, are all sources of symbolic enrichment of the narrative, and often almost become central characters, or at least embodiments of the heart and soul of a central character. Jean Rhys mirrored Sasha's mental state in her description of the hotel room in the opening to *After Leaving Mr Mackenzie*. Wharton and Elizabeth Spencer use Italy, Kay Boyle Spain, and Cather the magical presence of the American Southwest to enrich their narrative meanings. Houses and rooms can become intense allegories for states of mind, social edifices, ideologies, or formalities that imprison, as in May Sinclair and Gilman. In Rhys and Chopin, houses and rooms are left behind like clothes that no longer fit the emerging personality. The most notable examples of this power of the place occur in some of Mansfield's stories and in Wharton's novels, *The House of Mirth*, and *The Reef*, or in Jane Bowles' *Two Serious Ladies* and Cather's *The Professor's House*. The house can, then, be a metaphor for a person's spiritual being, and, as with Cather and Chopin, the leaving of the family home signifies destruction of an old way of life for the creation of a new way. Sometimes the new way, which disrupts the deadening routine of the old, leads to suicide (as with the professor, Lily Bart, or Edna Pontellier). Destruction is always ambiguous in meaning, however, and this ambiguity is the theme of many novels or stories. Such ambiguity takes the form of the destruction of dehumanizing respectability, the breaking out of imprisoning relationships, and overcoming 'sane' forms of behaviour which, however, cripple the imagination. Moreover, old literary conventions are disrupted to show how they inhibit originality, while restrictive sexual behaviour, intolerably stultifying social roles, and even readers' expectations are disrupted because they lead only to banality and stereotyped response. Destruction and disruption are portrayed inevitably as ambiguous in values and meaning, then, because they are, in certain forms, the necessary, creative preconditions for overcoming mediocrity, passivity, and submission to harmful conventions and ideologies. Blakean wars, 'battles between the sexes', battles between mediocrity and imagination, between propriety and the *demi-monde*, between human 'progress' and the preservation of natural beauty, between living and suicide – these battles are never portrayed in simple dualistic allegories, since, like love and hate, imaginative innovation and traditional art, these dualities of creation and destruction are shown to be intertwined. Disruption and destruction are often portrayed as necessary conditions for creativity, though wanton destruction is shown to be as mediocre as any form of stifling conventionality. Indeed, astute social critiques often form the backdrop for certain kinds of institutionalised destruction which have nothing to do with the disruption allied with imaginative innovation. Gilman, Rhys, Wharton, Smith, and others portray scathingly the tragic and wanton destruction that a patriarchal society can perpetrate on individuals in order to maintain the hold on power, money, culture and sex of the privileged élite.

The problematic relationship between destruction and creation often becomes the locus for the effort to express the inexpressible, that mystery 'at the centre of things' and ineluctable for language. Yet, for most of these writers, this mystery, metaphorically at the heart of things, was seen to be the very life and vitality of art, language, and life. Its intractability to the reason, hence its mysteriousness – emblematic of that most mysterious experience of all, imagination – refers, for none of these writers, to some orthodox religious reality or ideal. Such an idea of mystery relates to the experience of any artist or scientist – or any human being who has ever had aesthetic or loving experiences – and is a practical acknowledgement that reason, logic, and the discursive understanding are only one small, albeit vital, aspect of human life. Reason must co-operate with and complement, not tyrannise over, the mystery which is imagination itself, whether in art, science, or personal relationships.

The idea of mystery was evoked at the beginning of this introduction in the form of the journey metaphor. Now it can be seen to refer to the aesthetic issues discussed above, as meanings elude us, allusions proliferate, sources enrich to excess the content of the text, value judgements are suspended, and events, characters and utterings have multiple, indefinite interpretations which characters are shown straining to pin down (often in mock reflections of the reader's struggles). All the writers discussed here, and many of their contemporaries, tried to dissuade the reader, through irony and indirection, from expecting to be able to dissolve mystery and indeterminacy into univocal, rational, logical, known, visible, or concrete definites. Nevertheless, through their art they demonstrated without exception that to respect the inherent mystery in life (embodied in the imagination) means, paradoxically, precisely to cultivate the concrete. The concrete embodiment of this mysteriousness and indeterminacy is essential to art for the (albeit partial) expression of the ineffable – concreteness of theme, style, imagery, language, characterisation, unity, and structure. Each of these writers shows us that the senses are involved in all our experience, including our so-called rational, intellectual, knowledge-experience. The senses are involved in experience in a direct, not an indirect way, as traditional (dualistic) philosophers assumed. For these modernists, there is no dichotomy between the intellect and the senses, for the eye, the ear, the nose, the body are portrayed as themselves intelligent processes of discrimination and organisation. The dualistic division between the senses and the intellect is simply another importation from an unimaginative analytic tendency, which ascribes to reality what it itself projects. The paradoxical relationship between concreteness and the ineluctable is evident everywhere in the stories and novels of many twentieth-century women writers, from Cather and Chopin to Erdrich and Janet Frame today.

For many of these writers, the ideal of embodying imagination and mystery in concrete art form is a challenge to the very notion of the real, and of realism in literary terms. Flannery O'Connor argued explicitly that the real is conceived of too superficially, too much as a matter of surface fact and information.[21] The real, she (and Ellen Glasgow before her)[22] argued, reaches into the depths of concrete life, precisely into its mystery, its inexpressibility, the latter being a residue or excess of meaning always present in every word, sentence, event, or experience. There is an excess, a residue everywhere for O'Connor because, as for Keats, life is unfathomable; individuality (the self) and personal identity are incomprehensible; imagination and creativity are beyond the conceptual grasp of logic or reason. Carson McCullers, in a similar vein, exhorted her readers to accept the need for a 'divine collusion' between imagination (the 'dream' as Anaïs Nin would put it)[23] and reality, in the exploration of the mystery surrounding, for example, human self-conscious existence and the resulting spiritual isolation and knowledge of death.[24] Both the effort to overcome isolation through shared experience and mutual respect, and the complete failure to do so (due often, if not always, to egotism, greed, and mediocrity), are dramatised in the writings of most of the writers discussed here, but in their own unique, individual, imaginatively original ways. Spiritual isolation and inadequacy are often expressed by means of the conventions of the *demi-monde* or the grotesque. Writers thereby seek to gain a knowledge of human experience from the perspective of marginalised people, whose view is different from the prevailing ideology of mediocrity. Many of these writers make it pellucid that they consider their freaks, outsiders, tarts and perverts to be far more imaginative and 'normal' than apparently normal, superficial people. The latter live like mechanised stereotypes of conventional attitudes, who, in Angela Carter's words, are 'in trouble with their souls'.[25] Rhys exposed the prostitution of the soul in ordinary, bourgeois lives as a dehumanisation and loss of fellow-feeling, in contrast to the 'prostitutes' of the body, in her witheringly ironic portrayals of social outcasts. Stevie Smith constantly reversed the values between normality and madness, while Barnes and Bowles used the convention of the 'freak' or 'degenerate' as symbolic not only of the downward direction of the path of wisdom, but also as a metaphor for the ordinary mortal's spiritual and moral deformity.

For many of these writers, there is a belief in a need to shock readers out of their 'mind-forged manacles' so that they can be surprised into seeing, into envisaging the possible. Art is not so much conceived of as a revelation of the ideal (though ideals may be implied), as of the way we are at any given time, in all our spiritual and imaginative-artistic limitations. The unexpected mirrors (which the texts turn out to be) often show us views and traits in ourselves that we do not want to see. Hence we repress, ignore, and read over the details of the text to avoid a clear picture of the self-knowledge offered. Normal, acceptable behaviour is often revealed to be a perversion and a dehumanised selfishness, while 'normal' reading habits are also condemned as unimaginative perversions of the texts. O'Connor remarked that she hoped writers would never lose 'their ability to see that those gentlemen [in grey flannel suits] are even greater freaks than what we are writing about now' (*Mystery and Manners*).[26] Conventions of travel to foreign lands, of the circus, the theatre, masquerades, and parties are all exploited to express the way in which, in ordinary life, we all assume fictitious identities in the world of make-believe which constitutes our reality. In Bowles, Porter, and Smith overtly, and in Rhys, Cather, Woolf, Richardson, and Wharton more delicately, humour and tragedy are juxtaposed, as stories are insinuated into narratives and frames are woven around stories of stories to express both the indefinableness of meaning (the irrationality of rationality) in human experience, and to depict the endless regress of interpretation. For interpretation is based, it is shown, not on objective description, but only on other interpretations of prior interpretations. Monologue often becomes a prominent narrative technique as in *Over the Frontier*, Barnes' *Nightwood*, May Sinclair, and Gilman, to express through structural techniques the extent of the chaos and failure of communication and the rarity of co-operative, shared experience and imaginative community. Hackneyed speech, worn-out clichés, rule-bound game-playing, stereotyped, cardboard cut-out responses are ridiculed by these writers and shown to pervade all our speech and actions. Surrealism and grotesque effects are used to set the speech and actions of characters just off-centre enough to catch the reader by surprise, before the censoring reading faculty of reason can shut out the exposure or throw a veil across the mirror the text has become. Blends of realism and the grotesque, of tragedy and compassionate comedy, of the bizarre and the familiar, surprise the reader into glimpses of the self in the looking-glass of the text, and sometimes make the ugliness that is there bearable to behold, only because it can become a powerful incentive for change.

2

Excavating Meaning in Willa Cather's Novels

I PIONEER-ARTIST

Willa Cather was born in 1873 in Black Creek Valley, Virginia, in the house of her grandmother, her family having lived and farmed the region since the late eighteenth century. In 1883, her family resettled in a farm near Red Cloud, Nebraska, a small midwestern town of twenty-five hundred inhabitants, including many immigrants of Swedish, Russian, and Bohemian descent, with whom the young Cather identified. These often highly cultivated, educated immigrants provided her with experiences and memories that, much later, dominated many of her novels. These people came to represent the common ideal of the cultivated but vigorous, determined, and powerful pioneer spirit which bridged the gulf between East and West, urban and rural, physical and spiritual, natural and cultural.

Cather studied literature and classics at Lincoln before embarking in 1896 on a successful career in Pittsburgh, and later in New York (1906) as editor and arts critic of various magazines and newspapers. She met Sarah Orne Jewett during a newspaper assignment in Boston in 1908, and was influenced both by Jewett's writing style and by the force of her personality, dedicating her first novel, *Alexander's Bridge* (1912) to this great New England stylist.[1] Cather finally resigned from her work as managing director of the famous *McClure's Magazine* in 1912 to devote herself to writing fiction. Travels to Europe with her friend Isabella McClung and later with Edith Lewis perhaps affected her less than her trips to the magical American Southwest, which she discovered in the Spring of 1912 on a visit to her brother Douglas in Arizona. Her explorations of the sublimely inspiring ruins of the cliff-dwellers in Walnut Canyon, Arizona, were to haunt her for the rest of her life, and may have affected her work more deeply than any other personal experience.[2] *O Pioneers!*, her first full length novel, was greatly affected by the discovery of this almost supernaturally beautiful country, and two of her finest novels, The Song of the Lark (1915), and My Ántonia (1918) followed. In The Professor's House (1925) and in Death Comes to the Archbishop (1927), arguably her other finest works, the magnificent Southwest again plays a central role, and excavation of Cliff City becomes a metaphor for reading and for imaginative activity, and for the archaeological strata and layerings of the human mind and of language itself (and art generally), as Michel Foucault was to elaborate.[3]

As Cather's success grew, her disenchantment with 'modern' life and the world around her is thought to have increased. Her own values and beliefs seemed to her to diverge increasingly from the consumerism and material, machine-age advances of the post-war period. In England, E. M. Forster had been feeling similar reservations some ten to twenty years earlier. Oppositions that had been thematic aspects of most of Cather's novels provided the material for this later conflict, oppositions between country and city life, between society, or family, and the individual's need for solitude, between artistic genius and mediocrity, between nature and the urban, Europe and America, order and chaos, male and female experience, for example. Some of Cather's novels seem to suggest the possibility of finding a relationship between the spirit of the pioneer or conquistador (with all its physical courage, vigour, and elemental natural force) and the spirit of the artist–genius. The opposition for Cather both in her life and in her work was not, however, between nature and art or culture, not between the pioneer and the artist; these are spiritual relations. The most urgent conflict was between mediocrity and excellence, between the pretentious and the genuinely cultivated mind, between the imprisonment of the human spirit in small, mean, petty concerns and the fulfillment of the human spirit by releasing the elemental, creative forces within it, whether through art, nature, religion, or loving human relationship. The enemies of art and of fulfillment she saw as greed, fear of the unconventional, passivity, and mediocrity. Cather explored in her novels the effects of these enemies of creative energy in several different areas: in close human relationship, in art, and in social intercourse.

Cather's interest in the novel as novel (a work of art), and not merely as a document or repository of ideas, led to an emphasis upon the intricacies and techniques that constitute Cather's art, and which make her novels artistic in the fullest sense of the word.

Among the many 'literary' aspects of her novels, the use of land-scape as a principle of artistic unity, her use of complex narrative techniques and personas, her sophisticated emblematic imagery, her foregrounding of story-telling, and her original style stand out as major devices of central importance in appreciating her art. It is well known that, deeply impressed as Cather was by the realism and, later, naturalism, of Flaubert, Balzac, Maupassant, Zola, and others, she, like Chopin and Wharton, eventually reacted against these as a model for her own writing. Widely read in the literature of many languages, familiar with Greek, Latin, German, French, and English classics as well as with American literature (such as Jewett, Emerson, Freeman, Poe, Hawthorne, Crane, Wharton, James, Gilman), Cather came early in her career to reject realism as restricting the imagination to the ordinary and social superficial-ities of life. Cather, like Hawthorne, embraced what she termed the romance 'as the highest form of fiction', and emphasised the great value she placed upon the elemental force of the creative imagination. By 'romance' Cather anticipated Flannery O'Connor with the idea that at the basis of all spiritual achievement is a thoroughgoing commitment to the physical, the sensuous, and to nature and the natural within humanity itself.[4] For Cather, as for Blake and Coleridge, the forces of life and artistic creation are one.[5] Both are natural forces of a powerful and mysterious nature, which Cather explored in order to find ways of opening out, to herself and to others, its energy and restorative vitality for constructive pur-poses. For she knew that, undirected and unshaped, such powerful natural energy could destroy everything.

Cather, then, rejected what she saw as the contrived artifices of much writing, the 'over-furnishing' of the novel that realism and naturalism had turned into a cult.[6] She sought rather to simplify, to sweep away old props which had lost the power of novelty, and to reveal nature's fundamental life forces operating in humans through the creation of living characters in ordinary situations.[7] She wished, moreover, to free the novel into the open spaces she had experienced in the stupendous and overwhelming landscape of the Great Plains and the magical southwestern United States. Con-sequently, she emphasised the idea that art 'should simplify. That, indeed, is very nearly the whole of the higher artistic process; finding what conventions of form and what detail one can do without and yet preserve the spirit of the whole'.[8] Cather explained that art must simplify by compression, not simply by excision. The artist simplifies by compressing many subordinate elements into a few main elements, yet the subordinate elements remain hovering in the background or atmosphere by means of suggestion. Coleridge had argued for 'compression' in similar terms, shortly after writing 'Kubla Khan' in 1797.[9] For Cather, the many good conceptions which are finally sacrificed to the better conception still hover in the life of that conception by means of suggestion: 'All that one has suppressed and cut away is there to the reader's consciousness as much as if it were in type on the page'.[10] The reader then must excavate the novel, to find its details. Contrary to the realist and naturalist technique of detailed, explicit enumeration and cataloguing of gritty facts, Cather argued that

> whatever is felt upon the page without being specifically named there – that, one might say is created. It is the inexplicable presence of the thing not named, of the overtone divined by the ear but not heard by it, the verbal mood, the emotional aura of the fact or the thing or the deed, that gives high quality to the novel or the drama, as well as to poetry itself.[11]

The cram-jammed detail and enumeration of realism destroys such suggestion and compression, at the same time that it cramps and restricts imaginative forces to attention to the familiar and social. Cather's emphasis upon the 'spirit of the whole' and on compression in art are founded in Coleridgean and Romantic theories, and are related to Cather's preoccupation, of an almost classical kind, with what she saw in the landscape of the Southwest, with the exquisite, timeless, but human-made cliff dwellings so harmoniously set in the natural scenery. What she saw there was harmony, proportion, and the perfect integration of the human with nature. A novel, she thought, could, through the imaginative techniques of simplification and unity, achieve such proportion and harmony, by which she meant that the end is always kept in view, through understatement, restraint, and the control over the elements that make up the unity. Harmony further suggests the familiar technique of using contrasts and oppositions (one major mode of simplification and compression) to contribute to the clarity of the conception as a whole. Cather structured her novels with certain fundamental contrasts and oppositions that contain within themselves a whole array of specific issues. She then achieved continuity by raising these principal contrasts to the level of unifying structures, of stratifications of meanings, of emblems and symbols, or by using recurring imagery suggestive of elemental oppositions.

Finally, memory, and the excavation of the individual's past, plays the vital role in Cather's art of keeping her in touch with powerful early life experience, providing continuity with her present adult self.[12] The opposite, but not contrary force of imagination selects and shapes that material of life experience which memory provides but cannot shape without the power of a highly sophisticated and carefully developed imaginative genius. Through memory as intermediary medium and imagination as agent, adult and elemental childhood experiences are excavated and then shaped into a continuity and unity, which is the pre-condition of genius for Cather, as for Rhys and Porter.

Cather's idea of a 'magical memory', which she, like Porter and Rhys, so often extolled, is contrasted with the merely mechanical realist faculty of recall. Such a magical memory was, for Cather, a faculty integrated into imagination, and not something contrary to it. Indeed, such memory and remembrance are seen as powerful means of arousing their close relation, the imagination, into creativity. Moreover, both genuine memory as well as imagination, opposites though they may be in some sense, are the true contraries of all that is mechanical, artificial, and contrived. In her reflections on the relation between instinct, or intuition, and conscious craft, Cather concluded that the craft and techniques must be learned thoroughly, and then 'forgotten' or unlearned. Technique for Cather was always subordinate and indirect in its relation to the intuitive, unlike realist practices. Craft and technique become 'natural' to the thoroughly accomplished artist; they become a second nature always guided by that mysterious faculty, intuitive imaginativeness, that 'spirit of the whole'. Craft and technique are as essential as intuition, but, Cather argued, should never dominate it. This was one of the failures of realism for Cather. Cather portrayed the artistic process as something mysterious which cannot be fathomed or measured by the reasoning, conscious intellect. But she also made it clear that art is never merely a matter of spontaneous overflow, or untutored intuition. Thus, there is no simple dichotomy or opposition between those mysterious faculties, memory and imagination. Magical memory is for Cather a kind of imaginativeness. Yet without the greater creative and shaping power of imagination, memory can never produce works of art.[13]

Personified in Cather's narrative techniques, memory could be seen as a kind of astute observer and recoverer as well as preserver of one's past experience, and its importance for the imaginative shaping of its material is reflected in Cather's designing of complex narrative points of view expressive of these different faculties. In clearing away the furnishings of realism and even of the conventional romance novel, Cather sought, then, to express the complexity of the artistic process, and of human life. She insisted that art was not merely a repository of thoughts, or emotions or memories, but rather 'expression, always expression';[14] the artist must seek as her highest goal the ideal of keeping the thought, the idea, the emotion, or the memory alive in the articulation, expression, or embodiment of it. Since the mind, she argued, has more power to conceive than the hand has to create, the art lies in overcoming this imbalance. The artist must strengthen the hand – the technique, the craft – so that she can express those powerful passions of nature, and of human nature, which will then in turn be strengthened.[15]

Cather sought to escape what she and so many other artists saw as the imprisoning, confining effects of artistic forms that had become conventional stereotypes, such as the realist novel and even the form of conventional romance. New experiences, she argued, call for new forms of expressions, for new techniques, new crafts. She claimed to seek to avoid both the usual fictional patterns, of plots, of love, courtship, adventure, family conflicts, and so on, while she sought to use the 'details of everyday life', instead of these larger, more public issues to provide the material for her fiction. Yet she used those details sparsely, emblematically, even sometimes allegorically. Above all, she used them to re-create a 'powerful sense of place', as Eudora Welty has described this central element of fictional narrative. Locality and natural landscape become a Blakean metaphor in Cather's novels for imagination itself. Or rather, nature is the metaphor for imagination, hardly a surprising reversal of relations since, for Cather, as for Blake, imagination is the human form of nature's elemental forces.[16]

Memory, meanwhile, that close relation of imagination, plays, it was said earlier, the role of the recoverer and observer, or reflector, of experiences, or at least it can do so. For without the observer, whether within the psyche or whether as a separate person, there is no record of experience. In addition to narrative personifications of memory as a conscious artistic device, excavating past experiences, Cather used framework techniques, stories within stories, personas, and a 'nouvelle' within a 'roman', in the best Spanish and French manner, to express the metaphor of memory and imagination as observers and transformers of experience, both past and present. Cather also used metaphors of excavation and discovery in 'Tom Outland's Story' to represent the importance of memory (she also gently mocks the futility of realist cataloguing in Tom's rejection of his own catalogue of Cliff City). Excavation becomes, indeed, a multiple symbol for writing, reading, and experience of the past, as will be discussed below. While these strategies may complicate her tales at the surface level, they make possible both simplification and compression at deeper levels. They also make possible a level of critical self-consciousness within the text, which is the very essence of art, namely a self-watching, a self-awareness of the text's own artistry.[17] Cather achieved her goal without the realist's enumerating or cataloging, through the mysterious power of suggestion, that strange sense of things present, hovering above, without being specifically named. An atmosphere of openness, of spaciousness, of great vistas and distances, the very opposite of realism, is the essence for her of imaginativeness. She found in the vast, open landscape of New Mexico and Colorado an evocation of powerful forces and happenings by means of the barest, most meager traces in its geological history. Moreover, Cather's use of landscape and artistic strategies, of personas and frameworks, also provided the distance and spaciousness needed for the level of self-conscious criticism found in any work of art,[18] and which makes possible an artistic response more self-conscious than the merely sentimental and naïve subjugation of the artefact to the reader's unexamined, unconscious values, desires, and prejudices.

The complex methods and narrative strategies of Willa Cather indicate that experience is of several different kinds. Experience can be merely 'had', in which case it goes unnoticed by the conscious mind, though it may be stored in the unconscious. Experience can also be noticed and observed, and in that case it is raised to a second-order level of experience. It becomes known, conscious, and can be material for a third level of experience, namely, reflection upon conscious experience. At this third level, experience is now reflected upon, analysed, and, as such, yields further experience of a knowledge kind. Finally, one may reflect on the processes of seeing, observation, and even reflection or analysis itself. By this means, brute, 'had' experience is refined, by stages, into experience which eventually can lead to the production of works of art and science, or to imaginative living. Cather, through her narrative complexities, managed to convey these levels of experience, and to show that ignorance, passivity, and mediocrity, those primitive enemies of art, love, and life itself, result from a failure to go through these stages of rarefying experience into its highest degree of imaginative awareness, involving ultimately a detached self-consciousness.[19]

II PARODIC FORM IN MY ÁNTONIA

The literature on My Ántonia suggests that this novel has been poorly understood, though for easily understandable reasons. Its strategies of narrative personas, framework devices, and innumerable stories within stories have at times been accused of being artificial and unconvincing. Further, Cather has been repeatedly criticised for her portrayal of Ántonia as a kind of ideal woman, an earth-mother. The novel has been accused of having no integrity of structure; it is said to be merely a set of stories strung together. The sections on the hired girls and Lena are described as crippling and explicable diversions from the main issue of Jim's and Ántonia's relationship. These criticisms have had little effect upon the popularity of one of Cather's finest novels, demonstrably one of her finest, if the errors leading to these misreadings are uncovered.[20]

One of the great, unrecognised artistic achievements of My Ántonia is a distancing of the author from the text in order that Cather should portray not the ideal woman, but a male notion of the ideal woman. This is a shift that demands artistic detachment; Cather's text is designed such that one of its primary subject matters is an analysis of the male psyche and its fantasies about women, sexuality, and male–female relationships. Once the reader makes this artistically crucial shift, she can never read the novel again allowing Jim Burden's sentimental and nostalgic longings for the past and for a mother to dominate her reading. Otherwise, an uncritical reading blinds the reader to the realisation of the crushing indictment the text utters about destructive fantasies.[21] Hence the novel begins with a blatant and parodic framework, and a thoroughly fanciful narrative persona, all too often dismissed by critics as not to be taken seriously.[22] These satirical strategies are designed precisely, however, to be seen through by the reader, but in an artistically significant way. That is, they should alert her to the fact that the point of view is a male's fond but warped point of view on women. By shifting brazenly and artificially the authority of the contents of the novel on to Jim Burden, Cather makes *My Ántonia* into a 'masterpiece' of exposure of male idealisation of women, of male nostalgia, as well as exposing male attitudes toward sex, female independence, and toward other types of independent women. Such women as Lena and the young Ántonia are shown in the novel to threaten men and to thwart the realisation of their hopelessly unrealistic, immature fantasies of wife as mother.[23] As such, these sections on Lena and the hired girls are crucial to the text, not the digressions they are usually said to be.

Read this way, Cather's use of outrageously blatant, parodic artificialities, her phoney personas and contrived narrative accounts written on pretended journeys out West, her transparent claim to be only the editor of Burden's 'thing', his 'account', her feigned dislike of Burden's fictional wife, all of these parodies of earlier writers' devices are used in blatantly unacceptable, artificial, and totally artistically unconvincing ways, but not because Cather is a poor artist. They are used thus in order to shout to the obtuse reader that the following text is not the sentimental, nostalgic idealisation that it has, obtusely, been read to be. These ludicrous parodies by Cather of frames and personas are designed to tell the reader that the following text is a satire, exposé, and critique of such male fantasies. Cather was no doubt profoundly sobered, and at the same time challenged, by the difficulty of breaking down the stereotypes that prevailed then and still do today. Her only recourse against the entrenched views and determined blindness of her powerful male critics, publishers, and the reviewers was a covert humour, bordering nevertheless on the outrageous.[24]

That the fantastically nostalgic passage at the end of the novel, describing Jim Burden's disconsolate walk to the north of town on to the road from Black Hawk village to the old farm, is not often recognised as a rich parody of male yearning for the female that would have changed his life by fulfilling all his fantasies, is incredible. This 'girl', Ántonia, would have made him happy, he fantasises, if only he had had the wisdom twenty years ago that he has now. And to sum up his situation, he notes nostalgically: 'Now I understood that the same road was to bring us together again. Whatever we had missed, we possessed together the precious, the incommunicable past' (p.372). Such yearning for the past, such living in the past, is swallowed as an acceptable response by nearly all of us on a first, sentimental, uncritical reading. This initial response says something very frightening about the powerful hold of such sentimental male idealisations, which Kate Chopin, Stevie Smith, Virginia Woolf, Katherine Mansfield, and Jean Rhys all exposed ruthlessly from the female perspective. After twenty years, Burden has wandered around only to get back to the same old place, in full, uncreative circling. No sense of progress, change, growth, or development is evoked, only decay, the unproductive passing of twenty years of folly and wasted life. The idea that 'whatever we had missed' could be made up for by the transient sharing of the past in one brief afternoon is disingenuous in the extreme. Cather herself contrasted this with Tom Outland's comment in the *Professor's House*.

> All that summer, I never went up the Eagle's Nest to get my diary–indeed, it's probably there yet. I didn't feel the need of that record. It would have been going backward. I didn't want to go back and unravel things step by step. Perhaps I was afraid that I would lose the whole in the parts. At any rate, I didn't go for my record.   (p. 252)

Cather's novel is a crushing exposure of the destructive consequences of the kind of idealisation, fantasy, sentimentality, and sheer 'muddle', as E. M. Forster would describe Burden's state, a state which Outland utterly rejected.[25] That Jim Burden is portrayed as a relatively decent, moderately imaginative, kindly male makes his responses to women, from Lena and the hired girls to Ántonia, all the more inexcusable and depressing. And the crucial distance that allows, indeed, demands a more self-conscious critical reading is established by the very ironising strategies rejected as mere artificialities and contrivances by most critics.

Self-conscious story-telling, the dangers of idealisation and the sentimentality it involves, along with an ironic critique of nostalgia, are some of the main preoccupations of the novel. This novel is replete with innumerable stories told by many varied characters, male and female, many of them such memorable stories that the novel could easily be turned into an autonomous collection of short fictions. Cather, however, was aware of this and did not see it as a weakness: 'Any first-rate novel or story must have in it the strength of a dozen fairly good stories that have been sacrificed to it.'[26] Story-telling, with an implicit critique or ironising of story-telling, is the main form or structuring device of the novel. And what, in part, holds all these various stories in an integral unity is this ironising of story-telling, in general (with its fantasising or fiction-alising of history, the past, and experience).[27] In particular, the novel is a parody of the story of Jim and Ántonia's related lives, those parallel lives that, according to nostalgic critics, are like the two sides of one deeper personality, a more complete, 'ideal' per-sonality uniting the two characters.[28] One of the integral, unifying forces of the many stories and stories within stories is the exposure of the falsity of precisely such fantasies and ideals, and, more precisely, of the falsity of them as foundations for male–female relations. The harmfulness to both women and men of allowing men to indulge in their mother-fantasies is ruthlessly analysed by Cather. An analogous unifying force is, of course, the Porter-like exposure of 'truthful' accounts of the past as ever anything other than the creation of fictions, each with innumerable points of view.[29] Suddenly, moreover the large portions of the novel given up to Lena and the other hired girls, usually seen as disruptive intrusions, take their appropriate place. They are expressive of Jim's incapacity for equal and meaningful relations with independ-ent women who are unwilling to indulge his fantasies, crippled as he is by his unanalysed, 'unexcavated' yearnings for mothering relationships. Jim Burden cannot discard his patronising behaviour for a more equal, adult relationship. Meanwhile, his powerful, unconscious misconceptions of male–female relations make it impossible for him to achieve distance from his idealisations. Cather's art shows this critical distance to be essential to self-knowledge and to the evolution of human beings from mere stereo-typed, conventional, cardboard cut-outs of dehumanisation, into people who are genuinely individual and humane.[30]

By her prefatorial disclaimers, Cather was being overtly ironic, in the sense that she meant something other than what she said. She was trying to write a new kind of novel, without the conven-tional forms, arrangements, furnishings, patterns, structures, themes, or styles, of realist novels. She was both anticipating an incom-prehending readership and gently mocking it for its narrow, unimaginative, and stubborn concept of what the novel might be and what it might become (and, analogously, of what women might be and what they might become). By creating this frame, which in crucial ways enriches the book, she jokingly, ironically distanced herself from the content of the text, by making Burden a fictional counterpart to herself. She also made polemical aesthetic statements in her preface, as she called attention to central aesthetic issues of form, arrangement, memory, and how writing and reading take place. Basically, she called attention to the communicative situation involved in all story-telling: first, she referred ironically to Jim's making Ántonia 'come alive' for (the fictional) Cather on the train through Iowa by his 'relating stories' about her. Second, Cather emphasised the fact that she would now read his 'thing', his 'account', and presumably, edit it for us to read later. The import of these ironic, self-referential, framing strategies, though simple and easy to follow, has been neglected by readers. Yet they are crucial in leading to a realisation of a level of self-criticism embedded in the text, a criticism of reading, and a representation of the self-conscious nature of life, and art, as well as of the complex, mysterious relation between craft, imagination, and memory. These three latter elements become explicit parts of the subject matter of the novel, as are their interrelations. Memory, along with criticism embedded in art, is overtly an issue and is personified to some degree by Burden himself; additionally, artistic energy becomes a metaphorical subject as characterised by Ántonia. Her natural energy and vitality, and their relation to her womanliness and her idealness are an issue for the reader. Her energy and creativity are the source and the material for Jim's subsequent work of art. No single allegories are possible here, though the issues of relationship are clearly present. They are present, perhaps, but in the only sense acceptable to Cather, namely, hovering over the work, as overtones, as metaphors, 'on the page without being specifically named there'.[31] That 'inexplicable presence of the thing not named' is what provides much of the unity, the end which is always kept in view if a harmony of the elements and proportion of part to whole are to be achieved: 'that, one might say, is created.'

III THE FUSION OF ART AND NATURE IN
THE PROFESSOR'S HOUSE

In the above two sections discussing narrative strategies, ironic frameworks, and the artistic significance of personas, Cather's profound and continuous response to the sublimity and mystery of nature, with its twin life and death forces, has only been touched upon. Her response to the country of the cliff dwellers, like that of such great artists as Georgia O'Keeffe, permeates her work, even where it is 'absent', or rather, where it is only one of those over-tones or suggestions more 'inexplicably present' in the text than if landscape had been overtly invoked. Cather's fascination and re-spect for what one might call a naked, Blakean energy of nature, whether used for positive or destructive ends, has brought criticism from a number of critics.[32] Like Blake, however, Cather saw clearly that the most deadly enemy of fulfillment and creativity was not misuse of vital, powerful energy, destructive as it can be at times, so much as the passivity and mediocrity which stifles imagination hourly and daily. *The Song of the Lark* is a constant meditation upon the deadliness and suffocation of genius by convention and narrow-mindedness, which sees in all excellence danger and threat to entrenched ways of living. Like William Blake, Cather believed that the only 'truths' for human beings were this vital energy and its diminution, death. Yet, paradoxically, she saw death as a natural part of energy, so that the real death to be feared most is death-in-life, namely, the mediocrity of ordinary everyday life: it alone kills the spirit and leads to a death-in-life existence.

In the exquisite cliff dwellings, Cather was inordinately inspired to see nature inset with human life in the most harmonious, perfect proportion she had ever found:

> But the really splendid thing about our city, the thing that made it delightful to work there, and must have made it delightful to live there, was the setting. The town hung like a bird's nest in the cliff, looking off into the box canyon below, and beyond into the wide valley we called Cow Canyon, facing an ocean of clear air. A people who had the hardihood to build there, and who lived day after day looking down upon such grandeur, who came and went by those hazardous trails, must have been, as we often told each other, a fine people. But what had become of them? What catastrophe had overwhelmed them? (p. 213)

Life and death were at one in those canyons, while any duality between nature and art or nature and human life was overcome. There, she saw humanity and art as themselves natural, as in nature, continuous with and one with nature, not above it or outside it or alienated from it, as in modern city life. The abysses and the endless dualities that modern life created between art and nature, and between the spiritual and the physical, were overcome in those tiny, perfectly wrought cities set into the natural arches of the high cliffs in the canyons.

Nature, that most fully developed 'character' in Cather's novels (and personified explicity in Ántonia), not only provides a sense of the sheer immensity of space and energy surrounding life. Nature seems itself all alive, whether organic or inorganic, and death is portrayed as a natural part of a living nature. Absolute dualities between life and death are overcome for Cather through imaginative, relational apprehension. Nature also acts as one of the unifying principles of her novels, as Cather explores, time and again, as one of her central thematic preoccupations, woman's relation to nature and how nature's stupendous energies can be released by the human imagination for fulfillment and art.[33] Moreover, the unfathomable mystery and wonder of how nature could have come into being, of how it is that there is anything at all, informs most of her writings with a pagan, religious dimension, just as it permeated Dorothy Richardson's *Pilgrimage*.

Cather wrote in her preface to *The Song of the Lark* that style is the artist's very self. Some of her most exquisite prose occurs in the passages describing the canyons of the Southwest, where the cliff dwellings seemed more like outcroppings and outgrowths of nature itself, not intrusions into it, as the towns and cities of civilisation usually are. The naturalness, harmony, and proportion of those cliff cities became a kind of model, ideal, and inspiration for Cather, as she sought to develop a style of writing and a formal structure that were 'like' the cliff dwellings. Her rejection of realism, with its overcrowded furnishings, her rejection of the traditional romance with all its props of plot, drama, and thematics, and her craving for a spaciousness, austerity, and harmony in her style arose from her powerful response to the wild natural beauty she saw in the perfect congruence of humanity, art, and nature. Her forms and style, then, can be understood as an imaginative expression or representation of the cliff canyons, that is, as emblematic of them and as metaphors for them. Her style is a constant striving to re-enact in language the harmony, proportion, and integration of the congruence of nature, the human, and art which she experienced there. Moreover, her novels, as artefacts, also seek to emulate in their shape and form the exquisite, austere beauty and natural order of the cliff cities.

Cather's use of nature occurs in quite strikingly different ways, from its permeating utterly the atmosphere of *Death Comes for the Archbishop* (1927), to being an incredibly effective inset ('Tom Outland's Story') in *The Professor's House* (1925). Earlier, nature was used as a pivotal and recurrent force in Thea Kronberg's life (in *The Song of the Lark*, 1915), and it provided the entire background and much of the vitality of *My Ántonia* (1918) and *O Pioneers!* (1913). While in Cather's other novels nature impinges in less obviously powerful ways, it is rarely absent, whether the setting is the Great Plains and prairies, the Southwest, or Virginia. Even where events may take one of the characters to a large East Coast city like New York, or Washington, the deadly absence of the nurturing qualities of nature are a powerful, unnamed 'presence'. Those nurturing qualities still permeate the style of the novel, reminding the reader by suggestion and overtone that life-forces cut off from nature wither.

In terms of artistic craft, Cather's most strikingly successful, overt uses of nature may be the 'Tom Outland's Story' inset of *The Professor's House*, and in *Death Comes for the Archbishop*. Yet there are powerful sections in *The Song of the Lark*: Thea returns to the Southwest to revitalise her seriously life-endangering, failing energy. Powerful as nature is as an atmosphere, background, and even stage upon which the events of *My Ántonia* and *O Pioneers!* are enacted, the plains and prairies fail to provide the imaginative richness of the Southwest, where the integrated nature–art– humanity strides in as central unifying force. Hence, in *My Ántonia*, the force of nature is embodied in the central character. If we examine Cather's design in *The Professor's House* and her stylistic achievement in that novel, and, more briefly, style in *Death Comes for the Archbishop*, the emblematic quality of her structure and style as an attempt to a re-create the canyon-city perfection will become more evident, both in the novel and in the reading experience of the novel, where the reader is drawn into an excavation, like Tom Outland, of a work of art which turns out to be nothing other than a process of the construction of one's very individuality. Excavation, then, is a central, unifying emblem for both art and for reading or aesthetic response; it constitutes indeed a 'recipe' for reading imaginatively.

In *The Professor's House*, the 'Tom Outland's Story' turns the whole novel inside out by a stroke of magic, shifting the artistic emphasis to an apparently a-central, or, at least, supplementary element (to use one of Derrida's favourite techniques). Structurally, the novel is divided into three sections, vastly varying in length. 'The Family', book one, is some 165 pages; book three, 'The Professor', is only 26 pages, while the inset, book two ('Tom Outland's Story') is 74 pages. Outland's story is a stunning piece of prose, a priceless work of art, inset into a larger framework. What seems to be the novel turns out, in a sense, only to be the frame for (arguably) the most successful piece of prose writing Cather ever produced. This 'inversion' of novel into framework, and an apparent interruption or intrusion transformed into the centre-piece, suggests the role of disruption in imaginative creation. A kind of reversal of values is announced, whereby the novel becomes a mere setting for the story within the novel, the novel almost an annoying distraction from the real substance at hand, namely, the elemental forces of nature that nurture women and men and reproduce themselves in imaginative human artefacts.[34]

In *My Ántonia*, an explicit, ironised frame contains a central story, itself containing stories within stories, and this Chinese-box effect deliberately forces the reader's attention on to the art of story-telling and all its dangers and rewards. The reader is not encouraged to remain mesmerised by the overt content, but is pressed to seek out the stratifications of meaning that a work of art provides in order to induce greater awareness about social and psychological issues and about the processes of creation, reading, interpretation, and perception. In *The Professor's House*, Cather has found a still more impressive framework technique; a part of a triptych turns the whole novel inside out, forcing upon the reader the meta-fictional issues of novel-form, of unity, of story-telling, of figuration, or the making of metaphors, and of the nature of listening, interpretation, and making meaning out of words and stories, thus anticipating central 'post-structuralist' critical issues.

There are many complications in *The Professor's House*, which one can only mention in passing here. Issues regarding the relation of author to reader, creation to interpretation, and the problem of the nature of language and communication arise as a result of the story within the novel. Tom is the teller, allegedly, of the inner tale, while the professor is the chosen listener. Since Cather selects this 'tale within a tale' form of art, instead of giving us Tom's experiences 'directly', she is clearly, as in so many of her novels, making story-telling and listening overt subject-matter. To complicate matters, the professor is overtly the subject of the outer tale, the novel, but he is also made the transmitter to the reader of Outland's story. In *My Ántonia* Jim Burden allegedly 'tells' Ántonia's story (Cather transmitted it to us) and Ántonia is overtly the subject of '*My Ántonia*' (the Burden MS, not the novel). The doubling of characters in both novels suggests, however, not only fantasies of wholeness through love and affection, but also a more sophisticated suggestion of the collapse of absolutely distinct identities, so that teller is the listener's double. Jim and Ántonia, and the professor and Tom, lose their separate identities and merge into each other. The notion of an autonomous, discrete 'self', is parodied, while the identities and activities of the two corresponding processes (interpretation versus the creation of 'fictions' – themselves being interpretations) overlap and merge. The dualities of speaker – listener and story-interpretation show these opposite roles to be more alike than different; or at least their alleged difference (activity versus passivity) is shown to have been misrepresented as more absolute than it is.[35]

As in Coleridge's 'Ancient Mariner', the listener is carefully chosen. These tales of the Mariner's, and Outlands's, and Burden's can only be told to certain chosen people, perhaps even because the teller could not even tell the story without the stimulation or inspiration of having 'the right listener'. It is suggested here that landscape and persona devices, along with style, can select readers to whom Cather herself also tells various tales, the meaning of each tale being determined by the point of view from which the reader assumes Cather to be speaking. That is, the interpretations of readers vary decidedly depending on the point of view they themselves take, and the view they mistakenly ascribe to Cather. This in turn depends in part upon whether the irony (the framework of self-criticism) is recognised or whether it is repressed by the reader. One may deny the textual gestures of self-consciousness in these novels only by a determined blindness to the artistic facts. Note, for example, the humorous way Cather engaged in self-referential tactics shortly before and during the initial part of the Outland story. Tom is said to have 'always kept back' (p. 176) the story that he 'at last told' to St Peter. This is also the story that Cather kept back from her readers for 165 pages! Moreover, Outland begins his story by saying 'the thing that sidetracked me and made me so late coming to college was a somewhat unusual accident, a string of accidents. It began with a poker game' (179). Cather delighted in raising the issue of the role of blind chance and accidents in life, but what really makes one smile here is the ironic, indirect reference to the fact that the reader is now being 'sidetracked' from St Peter's story to Outland's, which also began with a poker game! Poker-faced Cather could also be said to have begun with a poker game with her readers: the novel began with St Peter's story masquerading as the mainline. It turns out to be itself a side-tracking from the Outland story.[36]

Further gestures toward self-consciousness and irony occur if we consider the names of Cather's characters. Jim 'Burden' unburdens his soul and his MS to a fictional Willa Cather. He becomes an awful burden to the reader, as well, who sees his male fantasies embarrassingly revealed. Tom Outland's name, on the other hand, suggests something beyond convention, unusual and exotic, though not without a touch of parody. The professor's name is the most parodic of all, Napoleon Godfrey St Peter, and to be forced to refer to him all the time as St Peter has a remarkably satiric effect. Named after warriors, crusaders, and adventurers, his life-work devoted to an account of *Spanish Adventurers in North America*, he seems an appropriate person to 'receive' Tom Outland's gift of the incredible story of the discovery and excavation of the cliff dwellings.[37] But we must not take him too nostalgically, too seriously, or we fail to see Cather's gentle fun-poking criticism, on the one hand of the 'burdens', and on the other hand, of the males who fantasise that a life of adventure would have been the key to happiness. Integration, balance, and the need to connect up our differing human needs, is emphasised: 'only connect' as Forster said.[38] 'Thea' 'Kronberg' in *The Song of the Lark*, has a doubly funny name, the use of the Greek word for goddess suggesting paganism, since the Christian myth, invoked in 'St Peter', always involves a male God. This use of names in fiction overtly to allegorise is a very conventional, but nevertheless effective technique of self-consciousness, much akin to Bowles', Chopin's, Stevie Smith's, Mansfield's, and others' puns on naming.[39]

Related, however, to the above-mentioned issue of author–reader, mainline–sideline interactions is the question of Cather's portrayal of the relation of imagination to perception. Coleridge described this as the relation of secondary to primary imagination, meaning that basic perception itself is imaginative, artistic creation being a secondary 'echo' of that primary form of human mental activity. Shelley followed Coleridge's insistence that the poet's mental activity is not a special kind of behavior, but the paradigmatic form of all human mental activity, namely perception itself.[40]

The latter, as Derrida has recently suggested, is not to be conceived of as a passive receptivity, but as active creativity (though the latter degenerates through time and custom into 'dead metaphors').[41] Cather's style, her use of landscape description, and her narrative techniques suggest the awareness that perception is imagination, and that the reader's perception must become, like the author's, imaginative and creative if the text is to be anything but a 'dead metaphor'. Cather's style, that is, revels the primacy of imagination in all perception, and the fact that interpretation, emblemised as excavation, is involved in what often passes for 'mere' description. Cather's meta-narrative devices show that fact and history are imbued with fiction, to use a familiar phrase; by taking fact and history literally, we forget, first, that any point of view is always only one possible perspective, and second, that truth is 'an army of metaphors', to use Nietzsche's phrase.

In 'Tom Outland's Story', other remarkable passages testify to similar preoccupations of Cather with the way language works preeminently figuratively to reveal that basic perception is essentially imaginative. The following passage demonstrates the perceptual creation of order out of chaos through metaphor, simile, personification, symbol, and allegory, as a process of excavating layers of meaning both in life experience, in language, and in art:

I happened to glance up at the canyon wall. I wish I could tell you what I saw there, just as I saw it, on the first morning, through a veil of lightly falling snow. Far up above me, a thousand feet or so, set in a great cavern in the face of the cliff, I saw a little city of stone, asleep. It was as still as sculpture – and something like that. It all hung together, seemed to have a kind of composition: pale little houses of stone nestling close to one another, perched on top of each other, with flat roofs, narrow windows, straight walls, and in the middle of the group, a round tower.

It was beautifully proportioned, that tower, swelling out to a larger girth a little above the base, then growing slender again. There was something symmetrical and powerful about the swell of the masonry. The tower was the fine thing that held all the jumble of houses together and made them mean something. It was red in colour, even on that grey day. In sunlight it was the colour of winter oak-leaves. A fringe of cedars grew along the edge of the cavern, like a garden. They were the only living things. Such silence and stillness and repose–immortal repose. That village sat looking down into the canyon with the calmness of eternity. The falling snow-flakes, sprinkling the pinions, gave it a special kind of solemnity. I can't describe it. It was more like sculpture than anything else. I knew at once that I had come upon the city of some extinct civilization, hidden away in this inaccessible mesa for centuries, preserved in the dry air and almost perpetual sunlight like a fly in amber, guarded by the cliffs and the river and the desert.   (pp. 201–2)

Phrases such as 'the face of the cliff', the 'little city of stone asleep', 'still as a sculpture', 'it was more like a sculpture than anything else', the 'solemnity', 'that village sat looking down into the canyon with the calmness of eternity', all these are gestures of personification, metaphor, and simile. Special to this passage is the way Cather both speaks of the scene as a still-life composition in painting, and then paints for her readers that very still-life composition in words. This is a technique she often used in the other novels. It is characteristic of her style, a characteristic that writers like Katherine Mansfield developed to a high degree of art. Yet all the while, hovering as an unspoken presence, is the metaphor that just such linguistic events of personification and figuration as occur in basic writing and reading also occur in perception itself: brute experience is raised to a high, imaginative quality by precisely these compositional, linguistic processes of perception which use metaphor, figures of speech, personification, imagery and symbol to layer, structure, and order the various elements of an experience so as to create a whole, unified effect. This passage is also a metaphor for Cather's ideal of the structure of her novels. Novels are compositions which for Cather are beautifully proportioned, with some one element or number of elements working, as does the tower in the cliff city to hold all the separate elements of the novel together and make them meaningful. Later passages reinforce the metaphor of the cliff-dwelling canyons as a metaphor for language and art, and particularly, to Cather, for her kind of art. The cliff cities combined artistic craft with domestic life in perfect integration, just as Cather sought to integrate her artistic structures with the thematics, namely the lives of her characters. Nature's relation to humankind is clarified in Father Duchene's insight that the cliff dwellers 'built themselves into this mesa and humanised it':[42]

Like you, I feel a reverence for this place. Wherever humanity has made that hardest of all starts and lifted itself out of mere brutality, is a sacred spot. Your people were cut off here without the influence of example or emulation, with no incentive but some natural yearning for order and security. They built themselves into this mesa and humanised it.   (p. 221)

'Tom Outland's Story' has a further significance in *The Professor's House*, which markedly enriches its aesthetic function for the reader as a story within a novel. The discovery of cliff City, along with Blake's and Outland's patient excavation of it, are described by Cather in such a way as to create a fascinating, complex analogy with reading. The tremendous efforts the two men have to make to get into the heart of the mesa at all become, for them, for the reader, and for the author, a rite of passage, an initiation into the mysteries of nature and imagination. The discovery of the completely unexpected magical hidden cliff dwellings add further layers of meaning to the journey metaphor. The men manage, moreover, only with great difficulty, to climb the canyon wall up to one of the cliff dwellings, Cliff City. There, the excavation of the incredible city in the sky and all its ancient, extraordinary furnishings turns Outland's story into an intricate, symbolic elaboration of processes of imaginative perception, writing, and reading. The details of Cather's own struggle to create her construction of this elaborate metaphor of imaginative activity in its three major modes of perception, artistic creation, and aesthetic response bear examination. For such details of the various phases of the journey reveal the methods of imaginative activity and, hence, are instructive as intimations to the reader of how to lift herself from a passive, 'lazy-onlooker' attitude into a more active, participatory response.

Cather begins her emblematic account of the men's sojourn near the fascinating mesa with a description of the mesa as monumental and impassable. In a characteristic gesture of irony, she has the foreman in charge of Blake and Outland issue a prohibition to Outland against trying to enter or climb the dangerous mesa:

Nobody has ever got into it yet. The cliffs are like the base of a monument, all the way round. The only way into it is through that deep canyon ... you can't get in by that, because the river's too deep to ford and too swift to swim ... if you boys try any nonsense of that sort, I'll fire you quick. You'd break your neck and lose the land for us.   (p. 191)

Outland, however, cannot resist the power of the great mesa:

The mesa was our only neighbour, and the closer we got to it, the more tantalizing it was. It was no longer a blue, featureless lump, as it had been from a distance, the sky-line was like the profile of a big beast lying down ... When I got up at daybreak and went down to the river to get water, our camp would be cold and grey, but the mesa would be red with sunshine, and all the slim cedars along the rocks would be gold-metallic, like tarnished gold-foil ... early in the afternoon ... the sunset colour would begin to stream up from behind it. Then the mesa was like one great ink-black rock against a sky on fire.
    No wonder the thing bothered us and tempted us; it was always before us and was always changing.   (pp. 191–3)

In this description, distinctions between the alive and the inert are completely abolished; nature is all alive, whether organic or inorganic, as it was for Coleridge. Moreover description and interpretation are indistinguishable; seeing is imagining, perception is itself visionary, as the light of imagination is projected into the verbal description of fiery nature. Personification, metaphor, metonymy, simile, powerful imagery, paradox, ambiguity, symbol, and allegory are all used by Cather in this passage to awaken the reader to imaginative participation, to 'seeing' imagination itself in action and thereby becoming imaginative.
    Further personifications, similes, metaphors, and other rhetorical devices follow, as Cather metaphorically depicts her own and Outland's increasingly imaginative perception, their 'humanizing of nature'. His eventual transgression of the prohibition expresses Cather's understanding of the role of disruption and disobedience in imaginative creation, while the apparent impassability of the giant mesa is an acknowledgement of the tremendous labour and courage demanded for imaginative undertaking, whether creation or reading. It is also a signal to the reader of the energy demanded of her, and Cather's step by step account of Outland's laborious undertaking becomes a symbolic recipe for the reader's struggle to penetrate into the text and discover its hidden beauties and its

'architecture'; to excavate its layers and strata of embodied artistry, not, however, to discover, hermeneutically, a hidden meaning. Rather, excavation is itself the goal – as activity of an imaginative, creative kind becomes not only the means of engaging with art, but the end itself. As Outland came to see, the value of the excavation of Cliff City was completely intrinsic to the process, as a metaphor for imaginative living.

Outland began by reconnoitering the mesa, first riding all the way around it, to get a sense of it, concluding that the only way into the mesa is via the dangerous river passing out of it. (Likewise, Cather showed the reader that she must climb back up the 'stream of narration' to get into the deeper layers of the text's existence.) Once Outland succeeded in fording the river, he made his way up the canyon, which, it turns out, has a well-marked trail! A sense of other-worldliness gradually entered into this multi-layered narrative, when Tom spoke of the air as the purest he had ever known: 'It made my mouth and nostril smart like charged water, seemed to go to my head a little and produce a kind of exaltation' (p. 200). For the water, he had a similar reverence:

> I've never anywhere tasted water like it; as cold as ice, and so pure … the water looked like liquid crystal, absolutely colorless … it threw off the sunlight like a diamond.   (p. 209)

After much 'rough scrambling' through the floor of the canyon which had become 'a mass of huge boulders, great pieces of rock … as big as haystacks' (p. 200), Outland stopped to catch his breath, and for the first time glanced up at the canyon wall: there he saw 'a little city of stone, asleep' (see quotation of full passage above, pages 37–8), and was so overcome with its magical presence that he hesitated to tell his comrade. Cather's breath-taking description of Outland's initial aesthetic response to Cliff City is a remarkable linguistic description of aesthetic experience itself, and as such is emblematic of imaginative reading, acting as a model for readerly participation. Yet she spared no detail in the narrative to emphasise the labour and determination Outland needed before he caught even a glimpse of the hidden city from the canyon below. And Cather indicated clearly, moreover, that Outland had not had the slightest knowledge of what he might find, if anything, once he penetrated the canyon.

Later Outland communicated his unexpected discovery to Blake, and they decided to devote themselves to climbing up the canyon wall to the cliff dwelling to explore it. After an arduous week, they made their way via a broken trail to the threshold, and 'stepped upon the ledge that was the floor of the Cliff City' (p. 207). Outland gave St Peter a detailed description of the architectural layout of the little cliff city and the innumerable household objects – the pots, jars, bowls, mats, baskets, clay ovens, implements – which they found lying about undisturbed. They spent weeks building a passable road before they started 'what we called excavating' (p. 211), another metaphor for excavating 'meaning' from the novel. Outland bought a book and wrote into it an exact description of each object found, and in another ledger he wrote an 'account of the day's work'. Later, he was to abandon this latter book which he came to call a diary, as antithetical to his eventual response and relation to Cliff City (p. 252 and see p. 223), a metaphor for Cather's rejection of realism.

It would be reductive and unimaginative to seek explicit allegories for Cather's careful construction of Outland's story, but the intricate artistry of his tale invites reading analogies and metaphors of imaginative activity which greatly enrich the text. Outland's arduous journey entails several more stages in addition to the one described above, each of which is instructive for the reader in Cather's marvellous allegory of the reading imagination: Outland journeyed to Washington to announce his discovery, but no one took any interest in it. He was devastated by the stupidity of the bureaucrats, and horrified at the regimented life of the hundreds of 'little black-coated men pouring out of white buildings. Queer how much more depressing they are than workmen coming out of a factory' (p. 236). Suffering from a 'low-spiritedness I had never known before' (p. 233), he 'wanted nothing but to get back to the mesa and live a free life and breathe free air again' (p. 236). He returned to New Mexico only to learn to his horror that Blake had sold the entire furnishings of the City to a German collector who had already shipped them to Europe while Outland was in Washington. He quarreled with his friend Blake, who departed deeply hurt and feeling gravely misunderstood, and Outland decided to stay alone in the mesa all summer. The writing and reading analogy now becomes explicit and pronounced:

that was the first night I was ever really on the mesa at all – the first night that all of me was there. This was the first time I ever saw it *as a whole*. It all came together in my understanding, as a series of experiments do when you begin to see where they are leading. Something had happened in me that made it possible for me to co-ordinate and simplify, and that process, going on in my mind, brought with it great happiness. It was possession. The excitement of my first discovery was a very pale feeling compared to this one. For me the mesa was no longer an adventure, but a religious emotion. I had read of filial piety in the Latin poets, and I knew that was what I felt for this place. It had formerly been mixed up with other motives; but now that they were gone, I had my happiness unalloyed.   (pp. 250–1)

'To co-ordinate and simplify', these are the words Cather used to describe the essence of creative activity, whether in writing or in reading. Up to this point in the narrative, analogies of different responses in reading and varied interpretations have been multifold: Father Duchene gave a long, detailed verbal interpretation of the furnishings of Cliff City (pp. 218–21), Blake and Outland's responses are contrasted – and lead to a terrible clash, the Washington bureaucrats don't care, but a German collector grabs up the valuable artefacts. After all these different responses to that work of art, 'Cliff City', are narrated, and after the multiple stages of Outland's imaginative activity are portrayed, Cather suddenly transmuted Outland's own aesthetic responses into another realm, as a mere 'adventure' has become a 'religious emotion':

I can scarcely hope that life will give me another summer like that one. It was my high tide. Every morning, when the sun's rays first hit the mesa top, while the rest of the world was in shadow, I wakened with the feeling that I had found everything, instead of having lost everything. Nothing tired me. Up there alone, a close neighbour to the sun, I seemed to get the solar energy in some direct way.   (p. 251)

Outland's rejection of his day-book and cataloguing follow this aesthetic experience of wholeness and of the primal energising effects of nature and the sun on the solitary mesa:

All that summer, I never went up to the Eagle's Nest to get my diary–indeed, it's probably there yet. I didn't feel the need of that record. It would have been going backward. I didn't want to go back and unravel things step by step. Perhaps I was afraid that I would lose the whole in the parts. At any rate, I didn't go for my record.   (p. 252)

Emblematically, this passage represents Cather's rejection of realism, its cataloguing and recording of detail, its 'props' and 'furnishings', and her commitment to something she saw as greater than such rational description, namely the aesthetic experience of unity and the imaginative creation of it. Nevertheless, there is a definite suggestion that this stage of detailed enumeration and intense familiarity with concrete particulars is a stage of experience that must be gone through, not skipped out. Had Tom not become intimate with the Cliff City's furnishings, he would never have been able to achieve the sense of wholeness and vision that he later gained. Similarly, author and reader must attend to detail, to concretes, in order to gain an experience of the whole aesthetic unit of an artefact. Later, Outland acknowledged the tragedy of the broken friendship with Blake over a disagreement about possession, over material objects, no matter how beautiful or valuable aesthetically and no matter how selfless his moral position. Cather thereby implied that imagination in art (or love in friendships) has, ultimately, little to do with possessions, as she forcefully argued in 'The Novel Démeublé', and as Outland came to believe by the end of his story. The interweaving of several distinct levels of thematics into Outland's story – developing friendship and its destruction, the relation of humans to nature, the nature of imaginative activity, and the essential quality of art as unifying – gives the text a powerful, multilayered complexity which is completed by Cather's inversion of history and fiction. St Peter's life-work was a 'historical' account of the exploration of America by the Spanish, while Outland's story was a living narrative of his own experience as a discoverer and explorer of the New Mexico cliff dwellings. Outland was making history while St Peter was writing about it; St Peter saw Outland as a personification of imagination, while Outland's narrative became for him a complex metaphor for the various stages of imaginative experience. As such, St Peter imaginatively identified with Outland, inspired as he was by Outland's story, and saw Outland as his ideal youthful self, as his own imagination in action. St Peter's ability to enter into Outland's story is a model for the reader, as is Outland's ability to enter into the beauty of the cliff dwellings and both excavate and appreciate them in a way such that aesthetic appreciation, through excavation, leads to almost religious fulfillment.

As in *My Ántonia*, the narrative of this novel is elaborately structured; indeed, it is Cather's most complex novel. Its Chinese-box structure is aesthetically unobtrusive (unlike *My Ántonia*), but irresolvably complex, as the central 'origin' of the story is a mystery, namely, the irrecoverable life of the cliff dwellers -- why they built such cities, and why they deserted them: 'What had become of them?' (p. 213). To sum, Cather's complex narrative involves the Professor, a writer of 'history' (fiction?), engaged in a powerful emotional conflict with life and death, as he struggled with *tedium vitae*. Within this 'framework novel' is set Outland's story, narrated to St Peter in the midst of the latter's struggle with the forces of death and suicide impulses. This framework about the failure of imaginative energies (one of Cather's central preoccupations throughout her writings) contrasts by opposition with Outland's story of adventure and imaginative living. But this centrepiece, the Outland story, is itself a story which gains its inspiration from another imaginative life – the past life of the cliff dwellers, who built their marvellous, awe-inspiring cities, and then mysteriously disappeared, leaving their work of art, the city, behind them, as a testimony and embodiment of their own imaginativeness. The city inspired Outland as an embodiment of his imagination, just as Outland himself, and his story, inspired St Peter. Cather was at pains to emphasise, moreover, that the city is a perfect integration of the natural and the human, this congruence constituting for her the definition of art. The city is a work of art, not a mere historical relic; it is an embodiment of the artistic power, the 'humaneness', of the people who built it and lived there. The collapse of the distinction between history and art is completed as Outland's account of his own history is the fiction at the heart of the novel. *The Professor's House* stands as Cather's most eloquent statement of the inadequacy of any notion which makes literature or art secondary to history and reality, such as 'new historicism' does. And her novels reject any hermeneutic interpretation of excavation as the relevation of hidden meaning. Excavation is valuable in itself. It is the intrinsically valuable activity of imaginative creation, both in artefact and in aesthetic response, but most especially in perception and life experience. The work-play is the écriture of Derrida, not the search for hidden, discoverable meanings of Ricoeur or Gadamer.

It is not exaggeration to suggest, then, again, that nature, understood as imagination, is the central character of Cather's novel, present even where it is not literally named in the pages of some of her novels.[43] Nature, Cather suggested, is the most elemental need of humankind; cut off from nature our spirit is lost. Deeper than family, Freudian, or Oedipal conflicts in the unconscious is the terrible deprivation and conflict that occurs in the spirit of humans when deprived of a close, nurturing, harmonious, and constant interaction with nature. For Cather, nature is our nature as humans, our living, vital, creative being. Without keeping in touch with nature (and our own nature, namely, imagination) we become dehumanised, denaturalised 'cogs in a machine'. Our speech becomes a series of dead metaphors, a string of parroted clichés; our feelings and thoughts borrowed, hackneyed, stereotyped, predictable reactions rather than individual, imaginative responses. Cather's novels show that our individuality never develops if we lose touch with nature and therefore with imagination. No amount of art, cultivation, or religion can stifle that need for creation, and without the constant restorative effects of nature, humans become unimaginative and dehumanised. Genuine humanity is in need of the sustenance that a relation with nature (that most fully drawn and living character of her novels) brings. This 'serious', almost religious attitude to nature (as imagination) which Cather's novels suggest should not, however, blind us to the playfulness throughout Cather's artistry. Nor should it make us insensitive to her irony and wit.

Cather, like Tom Outland and Jim Burden, seeks a reader sympathetic and imaginatively responsive to her unnamed 'presences' hovering over the page. The reader may realise that both she and her mode of reading are implicated in the tales. The experience, struggles, and conflicts of the protagonists are a depiction of each reader's psychological life-experience, not merely the struggle of someone else which readers passively watch. These struggles, when artistically portrayed in Cather's novels, always involve at some crucial level the effort to make meaning, to interpret, and to read actively. They involve universal conflicts, which unconsciously or consciously we all are undergoing. Thus, Tom Outland, the Professor, Jim Burden, Ántonia, Thea, and other characters are engaged in the struggle to make meaning of their lives. They must cope with the conflicting demands of the need for solitude and for relationship, the need for nature and for art. Those conflicts portrayed in the novels mirror our own, if only we are imaginative enough to experience that 'recognition' scene (so central a literary technique of Greek tragedy).[44] Moreover, Cather's style reveals the primacy of imagination in basic perception itself, as well as in the interpretation involved in apparently mere description.

IV IMAGINATIVE PERCEPTION IN *DEATH COMES FOR THE ARCHBISHOP*

The following long passage from *Death Comes for the Archbishop* shows Willa Cather at work in the effort to free the reader from notions of perception and reading as passive receptivity of already constituted external objects, on the one hand, and already fixed ideas, beliefs, and values of the author on the other. If we look closely at the following passage from *Death Comes for the Archbishop*, we can see how interpretation, perception, figuration, and communication, which are all issues at the heart of reading and writing, become metaphorical subject matter of Cather's novels. These texts are designed for the reader to use as mirrors in which to view one's own wakening into a greater imaginativeness about perception in general and reading in particular. They create the possibility for a greater self-awareness about the pitfalls that surround efforts to read and interpret, pitfalls such as the tendency to make reductive gestures aimed at increasing certainty and determinacy about textual meanings, and the tendency to read for fixed content, instead of for the awakening to active participation in the making of metaphors:

One afternoon in the autumn of 1851 a solitary horseman, followed by a pack-mule, was pushing through an arid stretch of country somewhere in central New Mexico. He had lost his way and was trying to get back to the trail, with only his compass and his sense of direction for guides. The difficulty was that the country in which he found himself was so featureless – or rather that it was crowded with features all exactly alike. As far as he could see, on every side, the landscape was heaped up into monotonous red sand-hills, not much larger than haycocks, and very much the shape of haycocks. One could not have believed that in the number of square miles a man is able to sweep with the eye there could be so many uniform red hills. He had been riding among them since early morning, and the look of the country had no more changed than if he had stood still. He must have travelled through thirty miles of these conical red hills, winding his way in the narrow cracks between them, and he had begun to think that he would never see anything else. They were so exactly like one another that he seemed to be wandering in some geometrical nightmare; flattened cones, they were, more the shape of Mexican ovens than haycocks – yes, exactly the shape of Mexican ovens, red as brick-dust, and naked of vegetation except for small juniper trees. And the junipers, too were the shape of Mexican ovens. Every conical hill was spotted with smaller cones of juniper, a uniform yellowish green, as the hills were a uniform red. The hills thrust out of the ground so thickly that they seemed to be pushing each other, elbowing each other aside, tipping each other over.

The blunted pyramid, repeated so many hundred times upon his retina and crowding down upon him in the heat, had confused the traveller, who was sensitive to the shape of things.

'Mais c'est fantastique!' he muttered, closing his eyes to rest them from the intrusive omnipresence of the triangle.

When he opened his eyes again, his glance immediately fell upon one juniper which differed in shape from the others. It was not a thick-growing cone, but a naked, twisted trunk, perhaps ten feet high, and at the top it parted into two lateral, flat-lying branches, with a little crest of green in the centre, just above the cleavage. Living vegetation could not present more faithfully the form of the Cross.

There is much wit and irony in this passage, a quite mocking irony, and also sympathy, of the tendency, when one has lost one's way, whether in nature or in reading, to make the strange and uncertain into something familiar and meaningful. An attentive reading of this passage, however, turns up some delightful metaphors of the processes of perception, of interpretation, and of making meaning of surrounding elements. (It is also a gentle parody of the enumerating and cataloging of detail of the realist.)

The solitary horseman has 'lost his way and was trying to get back to the trail', very much the feeling readers often have toward texts, the featurelessness of the landscape, which makes difficulties for the horseman, is suddenly changed to its opposite, and the landscape is now 'crowded with features all exactly alike'. Monotonous red sand-hills then become, under the solitary horseman's continuing gaze, likened to haycocks, this change being a clear move toward metaphor. The whole landscape is then described by means of another metaphor, namely, a 'geometrical nightmare', and the haycocks become mathematical cones. Next the observer decides they are not, after all, haycocks or geometrical cones so much as Mexican ovens, 'yes, exactly the shape of Mexican ovens'. His efforts to make sense of and interpret the landscape take him to another extreme. He identifies the red sand-hills with the contrasting yellowish-green juniper trees: 'And the junipers, too, were the shape of Mexican ovens.' Cather wittily confronts her reader with this quite incredible resolution of yellowish green, living juniper trees and red sand-hills into the identical interpretation of not haycocks, not cones, but Mexican ovens. Now everything in the landscape, whether green junipers or red hills, is like a Mexican oven. The narrative persona seems openly to intrude, in the next line, as simile, pushed to metaphor, gives way further to personification: 'The hills thrust out of the ground so quickly that they seemed to be pushing each other, elbowing each other aside, tipping them over.' This example of 'humanising nature' (as Coleridge liked to describe one of the primary activities of imagination) is yet another example of imaginative perception seeking to establish order in the midst of chaos and unfamiliarity, by means of similes and metaphors.[45] The hills, after this personification of the landscape, now become blunted pyramids, another geometrical metaphor, and in a gesture of gentle wit, the narrator humorously remarks, in justification of all the previous metaphors, that 'the traveler was sensitive to the shape of things.' Pyramids unobtrusively give way to triangles, and, finally, to crown the passage, one juniper stands out from all the 'featureless' hills and trees, in the form of the Cross!

This passage is a humorous and remarkable exemplification of the various processes of 'meaning-making' involved in perception and interpretation in general, and is characteristic of Cather's novels. Cather's metaphors, similes, and personifications show that perception is not merely a 'passive beholding of already constituted entities'. Rather, it involves imaginative activity at its most basic levels. The 'description' of this landscape, like Cather's other landscape descriptions, is shot through with self-referential depictions of the imaginative perception, or figuration, involved in both writing and in efforts to read meaning into the text. Metaphors, similes, personifications, and, finally, gross allegory are shown to be a part of all such 'description'; realist notions of the possibility of objective description collapse, as Cather exposed all description to be interpretations of a highly subjective kind. The final, delightfully parodic religious allegory gently satirises and exposes the superstitious tendency to reduce nature to religious iconography and artistic, imaginative play to familiar, recuperable, or univocal meanings.[46] The passage, while overtly serious, sets imaginative art and genuine spirituality against allegorisation, and proceeding in a dead-pan, poker-faced tone, eventually releases humour and irony about the priest's final allegory. For that final allegory is an 'emblem', a type, a metaphor for unimaginative reading and allegories unconsciously imposed by readers on to texts, as, for example, the systematic idealisation of Ántonia, and others. Cather ironically exposed idealisation for what it is, namely, a crucifixion of imaginative response, and the surest means to dehumanisation and death-in-life through reducing the human spirit to mediocrity. All her novels, without exception, depict, through sophisticated techniques, the struggle between mediocrity (the life of passive fantasy) and imagination, by confronting the reader directly with parodies of reductive readings and with models of imaginative perception.

3

Kate Chopin: Ironist of Realism

Katherine Chopin (née O'Flaherty) was born in 1851, in St Louis, Missouri, of a French Creole mother and an Irish immigrant father. She died in 1904, in St Louis, of a brain haemorrhage. Chopin received a strict Catholic education, was an excellent pianist, and was fluent in French. In 1870, she moved to New Orleans with her husband and had six children before returning, upon his death fourteen years later, to St Louis to take up the serious writing career interrupted by marriage. An early novel, *At Fault*, said to be derivative of Charlotte Brontë's *Jane Eyre*, numerous short stories, and a second novel (destroyed by the author), *Young Doctor Gosse*, preceded the 1899 publication of *The Awakening*. An insanely hostile critical reaction followed, along with her publisher's refusal to publish the third and final collection of short stories. Only sixty years later was her work rescued from oblivion with the 1969 Per Seyersted edition of the *Complete Works*.

Chopin's reading of Spencer, Darwin, Huxley, and other Victorian thinkers led her privately, at least, to renounce much of Catholicism. Her intimate knowledge, as a pianist, of music influenced her style and content, as did her close study of Maupassant and other French realists and naturalists. *The Awakening*, far from being a departure from Chopin's early stories, a little patronisingly described as 'delightful sketches', was the obvious continuation of themes of self-discovery and self-creation that had explicitly shaped her earliest stories and poems, many of which reached national publication in magazines such as *Harper's*, *Vogue*, *Century*, and others. Her handling of controversial themes such as sexual, financial, and emotional independence for women led to considerable critical neglect of her remarkable style, with its Maupassant characteristics of condensation and understatement, economy and clarity, and constant use of irony either as undertone or as explicit narrative stance. Similarly, her ability to capture local intonation and dialect and to portray folk humour gained her recognition as a local colourist but obscured the universality of her literary achievements.

Chopin, herself, awoke to the liberation in style and subject matter that European realism (the 'poison of Europe') offered her as an artist – material too strong, apparently, for her then rather sheltered American audience. Realism initially provided an alternative to the crippling sentimentalism of writers who had idealised marriage, family, and female dependence. Chopin's own style lacks the harsh pessimism and stark bleakness of other local colourists, such as Sarah Orne Jewett, Mary Wilkins Freeman, and McEnery Stewart, enriched as it is with intense and varied symbolism, eroticism, and sensuality (as she explored, for example, the sexual sublimation evident in Catholic rituals). Metaphors of light and warmth, lush visual settings, and colourful surroundings characterise her portrayals of poverty and ordinary life. Even by her most hostile, bullish critics, Chopin was described as 'a writer of great refinement and taste', and Willa Cather called her style 'exquisite and sensitive'.[1]

Chopin's own gradual awakening, however, from the restrictive realist, male techniques (which kept her 'landbound') to the unique and individual style that evolved most fully in *The Awakening*, is dramatised thematically in this last novel as a woman's (female artist's) struggle for her own identity and a self-realisation that undercuts the authority of male (literary and social) conventions.[2] Chopin's ability to create an astounding network of interwoven symbols, images, and metaphors (forming a tight and intricate narrative texture) is surpassed only by her fine use of Sophoclean irony built into the most apparently innocent 'realist' gestures to undercut that very realist authority. As with Jane Austen, the narrative stance is intensely ironic, as is to be expected in a writer seeking to challenge tradition and authority. The simple elegance and severe economy of this novel, where every episode contributes to a final, total effect, are exhilarating as the reader perceives the metaphorical drama of the woman/artist struggling to leave behind imprisoning literary forms, acceptable subject matter, and realist language. Chopin's last, exquisite, and liberating touch in *The Awakening* is her modernist gesture of a refusal of finality at the end of the novel:[3] even into the literal level of the narrative, an uncertainty as to the meaning and value of Edna's action is reinforced by the symbolic and metaphorical implications of her journey as the journey of the soul into the realms of the 'impossible'. Regenerative and 'vital' imagery, along with the indirect appeal to the Aphrodite legend, side by side with indications of fatigue, drowning, death, and hopeless defeat, create an unresolvable ambiguity between victory and defeat. Edna's voyage into the ocean, away from the solid stolidity of the shore, resembles the poet in Shelley's *Adonais*, where 'the spirit's bark is driven / Far from the shore, far from the trembling throng/Whose sails were never to the tempest given; / ... I am borne darkly, fearfully afar ... where the Eternal are'. The drowning and death may be more a symbolical death of the convention-fearing, time-bound ego – the self imprisoned by the morality and convention of its own time and place – to bring about the birth of a self freed from fear and egotism, as in Shelley's poem.[4] Such a theme has applications beyond the liberation of women from male traditions, whether social or literary, to the liberation of the human spirit from the crippling constraints of fear of social condemnation, as well as the recriminations and conflicts within one's own psyche. Other interpretations of the ambiguity of the novel's ending (discussed below) will suggest, however, that any simple account of Edna's death as symbolic of rebirth is misleading and to some extent inconsistent with the details of the text.

The Awakening becomes for the alert reader a literary autobiography, and a tragic prognostication of things to come in Chopin's life. For the novel was a literary suicide: Chopin's admirers viciously turned against her 'obscenities'. As a literary autobiography, it portrays Chopin's own awakening from a passive, submissive mother and wife to a woman with autonomy, as she asserted her right to become a fully alive human being (in her case, as an artist). Yet the novel also metaphorically dramatises the related struggle of both the woman artist (and all genuine artists) to break with artistic traditions and conventions in order to create new forms of expression that seem bizarre, offensive, immoral, and ugly to a contemporary audience. For Chopin, every artist is original only to the extent that she can adapt old forms and then create new ones more congruent with the new perceptions and experiences that she needs to express. Chopin showed that to remain within traditional conventions and accepted forms is tantamount to drowning one's individuality, originality, and creativity in a sea of banalities. Indeed, one's identity remains unformed and immature as a result, if not actually non-existent.

To sum, European realism gave Chopin one of the keys to moving out of the sentimentality and crass idealisation of much nineteenth century writing. Yet, after familiarising herself with that form, Chopin found it entirely inadequate to her needs as an artist and as a woman-artist. In her artistic struggle to free herself from these (in part, male) literary constraints, she discovered that she could turn realism against itself, by ironising its own limitations, while using its liberating capacities for her own effects. Chopin's narrative voice has its genius and originality precisely in this fusion of realism and irony, while her style achieved a union of realism and lush, southern symbolism that gives it its unique flavour. By ironising realism, she paradoxically exposed it as itself a decadent and, indeed, nonsensical concept.[5] That is, by her rich symbolism and use of complex imagery and extended metaphors, Chopin undercut realism's most central concept of language as transparent (as directly representative of 'reality'), showing that observation and description are never objective, but always interpretation. Consequently, 'reality' turns out to be plural, always: that is, a reality from a point of view, not the reality from the point of view. *The Awakening* depicts the struggle to establish an individual woman's right to her point of view in both life and art. As such, it explores thematically, at a literal level, the life aspect, while exploring thematically, at a metaphorical level (and through style), the possibility of an art and language more congruent with women's ways of seeing and living than are the styles, forms, and languages established by men. Overt subject matter is, then, a sustained metaphor for Chopin's (and for women-artists') efforts to find languages and forms expressive of their values, beliefs, and experiences. As such, it prophetically reveals the rewards of challenging the male prerogative and the deadly penalties that any woman and any woman artist who dares to do so, will pay.

The Awakening is a relatively short novel of 140 pages, divided nevertheless into thirty-nine sections of varying lengths.[6] The movement from section to section is often abrupt, with little effort to smooth by transitions the gaps in time, place, and mood from one to another. Indeed, the gaps seem deliberately to be emphasised, giving the reader a sense of profound urgency, as if in the inexorable march toward the conclusion no trifles or literary superfluities can be spared. Yet within the sections themselves, continuity of time and place is almost always strictly and fastidiously maintained. This sectional continuity makes the discontinuity between sections even more noticeable, and more powerfully effective in giving the reader a sense of being propelled toward some dreadful end. Alternation between continuity within sections and discontinuity between often very short sections (less than half a page sometimes) has much the same effect as May Sinclair's use of spacings between paragraphed sections which, in *Mary Olivier*, become shorter and shorter as the book nears its end, seeming thereby to rush headlong toward a powerful finality. In *The Awakening*, however, no speeding up occurs as the novel progresses; rather the speed keeps changing – a slow, emphatic, almost, stately, forward progression within each section, a sudden leap often to the next stage in the new section. This aspect of Chopin's narrative technique creates a potent sense of the subjectivity of time. For while she seems thus to respect the typical realist's objectivity of time within chapters, she rejects realist organisation with her sectionalising of the novel into what are not at all typical length chapters, but short, often choppy sections, mere fragments of narrative in fact (no section is longer than six pages, some are two or less, two are less than a page). Thus, Chopin's narrative 'fragments' are already a step towards modernism, towards liberating herself from the imposition of a false order to human experience characteristic of much realism, as Virginia Woolf was to complain later. The careful, scrupulous even, adherence to 'order' within sections is mocked gently, then, by the fragmentary narrative form that Chopin had selected instead of chapters. However, superimposed on these numerous fragments is a larger whole, structured into three major portions, or, rather, two main portions and a short conclusion. This fragmentation unified by a larger structure is comparable to Jean Rhys' structural technique in *Voyage in the Dark*, not to mention a number of other modernist texts. These various narrative strategies enable Chopin to create a Katherine Mansfield-type dramatic sense, a 'drama' of, roughly, three acts, with the same intense emphasis upon inevitability and inexorability that often occurs in dramas, and which helps to make it 'dramatic'. The first act takes place on Grand Isle, during the summer, and consists of sixteen sections, the second, in the city, taking up the next twenty-one pieces, and the third, only one brief fragment of a scene, occurs back at Grand Isle. A further Mansfield-like effect, that familiar Sophoclean irony, reinforces the sense of dread, with its prognostication of things to come and hidden significances studded throughout the novel like carefully placed gems.

Another narrative technique which Chopin employed within her sections, which also acts to reinforce a sense of the rapid acceleration of events, involves a favourite avowed modernist emphasis on understatement, that is, introducing major occurrences, decisions, and discoveries without any build-up or preparation. For example, in fragment twenty-six, Edna suddenly announces to Mlle Reisz, 'Mademoiselle, I am going to move away from my house on Esplanade Street' (p. 134). This is the first the reader has been given any inkling of such a momentous decision. Mlle Reisz is unimpressed, in contrast to the surprise Chopin springs upon her audience. Nor are we prepared for Edna's presence back at Grand Isle, in fragment thirty-nine, with no decision to go narrated, no description of journey, no preparation for Victor, who complains: 'By gimminy! Women have no consideration! She might have sent me word' (p. 174). Expressive also of the reader's response, such self-referral is characteristic of Chopin's ironic style. Equally, the ending of the season at Grand Isle in Part I is dealt with in a boldly perfunctory manner, as is the sudden relocation in New Orleans, which begins Part II. These artistic gestures of impatience with expected, realist transitions to new scenes and with accepted literary conventions requiring smoother development of plot are reinforced with a rare precision, however, in the thematics of the novel: Edna is hurt and outraged to learn of Robert's sudden decision to, and actual act of, departing. In one short six-page sequence, the reader is equally briskly informed of Robert's decision, presented with his and Edna's painful parting, and, presto! He is gone. Edna, likewise, treats her husband to a parallel briskness: in a letter out of the blue, she informs him of her decision, and, before allowing time for him to answer, she has accomplished her move. This element of surprise, rare in Chopin's novel, is used carefully and only for 'important' events, unlike Jane Bowles, for whom surprise is a major stylistic as well as structural device. Another example of understatement and surprise is Mlle Reisz's sudden revelation to Edna (in fragment twenty-six) that Robert is due back soon. Edna is shocked and desperate to know exactly when he returns, yet, contrastingly and perversely, their reunion is not only delayed until fragment thirty-three, but the meeting is another surprise, an accident. And they meet one another briefly and unexpectedly at Mlle Reisz's while she is out. The 'deferral' of reunion maddeningly continues and suspense mounts until section thirty-six, since until then Robert has refused to declare his love and Edna is in a torture of uncertainty. Curiously contrasting with these *faits accomplis* and arts of surprise and understatement is the preparation, exaggerated importance, and grand build-up given to the 'last supper' in the old house, which, in the event turns out to be a non-event, at least on a surface level. While carrying, no doubt, symbolic significances, the supper party hardly does anything to add to or advance the narrative, or to enhance the dramatic quality. Indeed, this section seems curiously loosely constructed, lacking the economy and pregnancy of meaning of many of the other sections. Much like Mansfield's dinner party in 'Bliss', this 'centrepiece' of the novel falls utterly flat at the level of thematics, so flat that one senses an artistic decision and deliberateness, as if Chopin used its surface meaninglessness to foster a symbolic significance – and that indeed is surely the case, as Sandra Gilbert has convincingly argued (see below, however, for discussion of the limitations of this view).

The dinner party, strategically poised as it is in the narrative between Edna's discovery of Robert's imminent return (xxvi) and her first accidental meeting with him (xxxiii) is in itself of little significance. After a tremendous build-up, Chopin designedly bored her reader with this uneventful evening in order to draw attention to certain qualities in the setting, and especially in Edna, that are maturing into full development:

There was the occasional sound of music, of mandolins, sufficiently removed to be an agreeable accompaniment rather than an interruption to the conversation. Outside the soft, monotonous splash of a fountain could be heard; the sound penetrated into the room with the heavy odor of jessamine that came through the open windows.

The golden shimmer of Edna's satin gown spread in rich folds on either side of her. There was a soft fall of lace encircling her shoulders. It was the color of her skin, without the glow, the myriad living tints that one may sometimes discover in vibrant flesh. There was something in her attitude, in her whole appearance when she leaned her head against the high-backed chair and spread her arms, which suggested that regal woman, the one who rules, who looks on, who stands alone. But as she sat there amid her guests, she felt the old ennui overtaking her; the hopelessness which so often assailed her, which came upon her like an obsession, like something extraneous, independent of volition. It was something which announced itself; a chill breath that seemed to issue from some vast cavern wherein discords wailed. There came over her the acute longing which always summoned into her spiritual vision the presence of the beloved one, overpowering her at once with a sense of the unattainable.

The moments glided on, while a feeling of good fellowship passed around the circle like a mystic cord, holding and binding these people together with jest and laughter.   (p. 145)

The last sentence of paragraph two is one example of many occasions when Chopin loaded the narrative with ambiguous, Sophoclean prognostications of both heroic and tragic endings, and a careful look suggests precisely the ambiguity found at the end of the novel. Edna is described as 'the regal woman, the one who rules, who looks on, who stands alone' (a far more apt description of Mlle Reisz, the pianist, in fact), yet, simultaneously, a sense of the unattainable is said to overpower her with hopelessness.

Chopin's abrupt handling of the penultimate dramatic moment – Robert's second desertion of Edna and his brief, pathetic farewell note – combines once again surprise and understatement with a number of ambiguous intimations preceding his largely unexpected flight from Edna, who, during their only love scene, has shocked him with her dismissal of respectability and convention ('I am no longer one of Mr Pontellier's possessions to dispose of or not. I give myself where I choose', p. 167). Sandwiched between their love-making (and that is unconsummated), is the scene in which Edna is called to attend the birth of her friend Adele Ratignolle's baby, which she had casually promised to do at the beginning of the section in which she and Robert met accidentally at Mlle Reisz's (xxxiii). The tragic consequences of this promise allied with the studied casualness on Kate Chopin's part are exemplary of her dramatic genius, for this casualness is in appalling contrast with the dire results. For in the midst of Edna's and Robert's long-awaited (literally) endlessly deferred union, Edna is forced to leave Robert to attend the birth, in spite of his pleadings that she should remain. Nevertheless, the narrative seems to assure the reader that Lebrun will await Edna, deprived as he is said to be 'of every impulse but the longing to hold her and keep her' (p. 168). Edna's faith in him adds to this unfulfilled expectation, and to the shock of his desertion shortly after. Towards the end of the birth-scene, Chopin introduced hints of possible trouble, as well as loading the narrative with symbolic meanings: the birth of the child is a metaphor for Edna's birth into a new life; the birth is shockingly painful and tortuous, as her own is becoming; insinuations of

the meaningless transience of life, of a Nietzschean horror at the
wanton profligacy of Nature, and of the futility of bringing children
into a world of suffering are implanted in the space of a brief
paragraph. Edna is 'seized with a vague dread ... with an "inward
agony, with a flaming, outspoken revolt against the ways of Nature",
[as] she witnesses the scene of torture' (p. 170). A brief, but
symbolically revealing conversation with her friend Doctor Mandelet
adds to the forebodings, as Edna remarks 'perhaps it is better to
wake up after all – even to suffer, rather than to remain a dupe to
illusions all one's life' (p. 171).

Edna's illusions are shown by Kate Chopin to be more complicated, however, than Edna realises consciously; Edna, and the
reader, are led for a time to believe the illusions to be marriage,
children, and conventional prosperity as sources of fulfilment. Yet
Chopin insinuated into the narrative, with admirably subtle artistry,
other more fundamental illusions which will confront Edna
eventually; namely 'she could picture at that moment no greater
bliss on earth than possession of the beloved one' (p. 172); earlier
Edna had an acute longing for the presence of the beloved one (see
pp. 57–8 above). A leering irony peers out at the reader from the
first quotation: *possession* of the beloved one'? This clearly is the
most destructive illusion of all, as Edna herself had known when
her husband treated her as one of his possessions, his 'household
gods' (p. 99; a play on words for 'goods'). Yet now, apparently,
Edna thinks of Robert that way, but fears he is 'unattainable',
another ironic word suggestive of the illusion of possession. Thus,
Edna's profoundest, most destructive illusion is also revealed in the
love scene with Robert, when she cries:

'It was you who awoke me last summer out of a life-long, stupid
dream. Oh! you have made me so unhappy with your
indifference. Oh! I have suffered, suffered! Now you are here we
shall love each other, my Robert. We shall be everything to each
other. Nothing else in the world is of any consequence. I must go
to my friend; but you will wait for me? No matter how late; you
will wait for me, Robert?'

'Don't go; don't go! Oh! Edna, stay with me,' he pleaded. 'Why
should you go? Stay with me, stay with me.'

'I shall come back as soon as I can; I shall find you here.' She
buried her face in his neck, and said good-by again. Her seductive voice, together with his great love for her, had enthralled his

senses, had deprived him of every impulse but the longing to hold her and keep her.   (p. 168)

For Chopin, Mansfield, Rhys, Richardson, Woolf, and many other women writers, the dream we need to be awakened from is not just that of the (questionable) possibility of complete fulfilment in marriage, child-bearing and mothering alone. Like Rhys, Chopin's novel and stories portray individual, existential self-development as a pre-condition for fulfilment from other spheres. We do not wake from the profoundest dream by embracing 'free love', unconventional relationships, much less promiscuity. We awake only through existential acts creative of individuality. The dream which women must awake from is the myth that fulfilment lies outside themselves, the illusion described in the above three quotations, or as Katherine Mansfield said,

> It is the hopelessly insipid doctrine that love is the only thing in the world, taught, hammered into women, from generation to generation, which hampers us so cruelly. We must get rid of that bogey – and then, then comes the opportunity of happiness and freedom.   (*Journal*, May 1908)[7]

Throughout the novel, metaphors of sleeping, dreaming, and awakening are used by Chopin to symbolise psychological imprisonment or liberation.[8] Chopin's irony, like that of Jane Austen, however, penetrates more deeply into the text than is at first apparent. Throughout the novel, 'the awakening' is, on the level of surface events and thematics, made out to be, as in 'Bliss', an awakening to sexual love, to passion of the body united with love. (It is never a question of mere lust, as the scenes between Edna and Arobin show.) This surface interpretation of 'awakening' as an opening up to sexual desire united with love is strengthened in the narrative on numerous occasions, as for example, when Edna asks Robert, 'Are you asleep' and he answers 'No', after which they embrace for the first time (p. 166). This contrasts (while reinforcing the more apparent meaning of awakening) with Edna's sleep in section thirteen and the narrative comment later that 'Robert ... did not know she was awake and up' (p. 85). Yet, in spite of this clear thematic interpretation of 'awakening', Chopin used powerfully ironic narrative techniques to construct the entirely different, indeed to some extent contradictory interpretation of awakening described in the Mansfield quotation, namely, the shattering of the illusion that sexual and romantic love can 'be everything', that 'nothing else in the world is of any consequence' (p. 168).

In order to develop this sub-textual meaning of awakening, Chopin created a foil for Edna in her characterization of Mlle Reisz, the name playing on the word 'rights', as is ironically indicated by Chopin in her description of the pianist: 'she was a disagreeable little woman, no longer young ... self-assertive and [with] a disposition to trample on the rights of others' (p. 70). The character of Mlle Reisz has rarely been accorded the attention she deserves. This neglect of Mlle Reisz's central place in the novel has led to a certain blindness to the crucial sub-text of *The Awakening*, which transforms the novel into a more sophisticated literary achievement than is usually realised. That is, once we 'awake' to Mlle Reisz's dramatic importance, we awake not only to a consciousness of a double, ironic text – sub-text construction. We also sophisticate our understanding of the double-awakening in the novel. The ambiguity of Chopin's ending is also better understood. Let us examine, then, Chopin's subtle construction of this alternative sub-text with Mlle Reisz as the central character, a sub-text wherein the meaning of awakening is different from the sexual liberation of the surface text with Edna as the protagonist.

Like Edna, whose sanity is seriously questioned by her husband (p. 108) when she begins to search for a self which is independent of her role as wife or mother, Mlle Reisz is said by Arobin to be 'partially demented' (p. 138; Edna finds her 'wonderfully sane' in reply to Arobin). On the other hand, while Edna overcomes her fear of swimming after hearing Mlle Reisz play the piano (section ix) – the pianist singling Edna out as the 'only one worth playing for' (p. 72) – Edna then makes swimming into an obsessional passion, incurring Mlle Reisz's disapproval. After Robert departs for Mexico (section xvi, last scene at Grand Isle), Edna is said to spend much time in the water 'since she had finally acquired the art of swimming' (p. 95): 'She felt that she could not give too much time to a diversion which afforded her the only real pleasurable moments that she knew' (p. 95). Since Mlle Reisz is the first of the characters to know Edna's love for Robert (indeed, she also is the only one to learn of Robert's love for Edna), Edna wants Mlle Reisz to come and swim with her, now that they share this knowledge and Robert is gone. Mlle Reisz rudely rejects the invitation, however, whereupon Edna remembers the pianist's 'aversion for water' and 'avoidance' of the sea (p. 97). Insinuations of danger from the sea were slipped unobtrusively into the text by Chopin, as she had Mlle Reisz watch over Edna's swim; ironically Edna wishes she would not wait, but Mlle does wait throughout the interminable bathe in a dogged, protective way, as if she senses Edna is in some danger from the water. Later, these sinister forebodings are borne out by events, as the water imagery takes on unexpected significance.

Mlle Reisz is also the object of many ambivalences on Edna's part. Edna is drawn to the pianist, yet finds her unbearably disagreeable at times (pp. 98, 114, 133), especially when she seeks to reveal to Edna aspects of Robert's character that are not flattering (pp. 98, 136).[9] Upon closer scrutiny of the structure of Chopin's plot, it becomes evident that she has woven two separate, but artistically complementary stories into her text to correspond precisely to the two contrasting meanings of 'the awakening'. The surface text involves, first, Edna's and Robert's discoveries of their love for each other, then Edna's awakening to sexual and emotional freedom from marriage and from enslavement to husband, children, and conventions, and, finally, Robert's cowardly desertion. The sub-text, which corresponds to the ironic, 'hidden' interpretation of an awakening out of that partial awakening (really another kind of sleep, or, rather, a delightful dream in contrast to the sleep of mediocrity and convention), involves Edna's relationship with the only other major character in the text besides Edna and Robert, namely Mlle Reisz herself. Indeed, the novel in its depth structure, resembles in certain respects, Bowles' *Two Serious Ladies*, with its division into two distinct but not entirely separate plots. Robert and Edna form the main focus of part I (sections i–xvi), while Edna and Mlle Reisz form the main focus of Part II (sections xvii–xxxviii). Part I attends to Edna's awakening from the sleep of repression into sexual fulfilment; part II attends to her failure to 'get rid of that bogey' that 'love is the only thing in the world', to use Mansfield's phrase. It is Mlle Reisz, not Robert, who is presented to Edna as the key to emotional liberation through independence. Part III illustrates the drastic consequences of that failure, but is also a celebration of Edna's success in escaping, at least, the prostitution of mediocrity.

This hidden sub-plot is an ironic commentary on the surface thematics,[10] with Mlle Reisz acting as a detached, critical, authorial observer over the entire sequence of events. Like Lily Briscoe in Woolf's *To the Lighthouse*, Mlle Reisz, an artist of great accomplishment, represents a kind of consciousness which is that other 'awakening' – the genuine independence and autonomy which Miriam Henderson in *Pilgrimage*, or Thea Kronborg in *The Song of the Lark*, or Mary Olivier painstakingly achieve. This autonomy is equated with the status of 'artist' by Kate Chopin, not because only artists can achieve such genuine self-development. For Chopin, the idea of 'artist' applies to the person who has created herself into an original individuality. Genuine autonomy and personal independence is a creative endeavour, and such a person is both a work of art and an artist who achieves that self-creation. By profession one may be a prostitute, as Jean Rhys showed, but self-creation by anyone is the fullest meaning of the word 'artist', and Chopin, like Rhys, thereby fuses art and life in an imaginative stroke. Mlle Reisz is, then, a critical, detached, indeed disturbing and disruptive point of view built into the narrative. It is her point of view which adds the sustained level of powerful dramatic irony to the text, while Kate Chopin wove an intricate pattern of carefully crafted tensions and oppositions throughout the novel with marvellously delicate imagery, to enrich and embellish her multiple, complex design. These oppositions work at the structural level (sub-text versus text, Part II versus Part I), at the thematic level (two types of awakening and the failure to awaken), at the level of character (oppositions between Robert and Edna, Robert and Arobin, Robert and Victor, Arobin and Victor, Edna and Mlle Reisz, Edna and Adele), and at the stylistic level (realism and the ironisation and transformation of realism into a distinct original style). Oppositions at the detailed level of imagery and tone further enrich the texture of the narrative and lead to sophisticated transvaluations.

More precisely, on Grand Isle (Part I) Edna awakens to her infatuation with Robert, as it is called, and begins a quest for fulfilment of it (p. 94). Chopin's narrative emphasises frequently that Edna's feeling for Robert was a childish infatuation, fast becoming an obsession much like several others Edna had felt as a child and young girl. Yet, the reader, trapped in her own dreams of true love, ignores these danger signals. In Part II, in New Orleans, Edna is, surprisingly, described as having 'started on her quest for the pianist' (p. 109). Throughout Part II, a powerful conflict develops between the two plot levels, with Edna enthralled by her dream of union with Robert as the illusory means of self-fulfilment, at the same time that her deeper self is drawn inexorably on a quest for the, at times, disagreeable and even offensive Mlle Reisz, who can set Edna's spirit free:

There was nothing which so quieted the turmoil of Edna's senses
as a visit to Mademoiselle Reisz. It was then, in the presence of that
personality which was offensive to her, that the woman, by her
divine art, seemed to reach Edna's spirit and set it free.   (p. 133)

Mlle Reisz is ambiguously portrayed by Kate Chopin as a pro-
tectress, yet with undertones of a dangerous sorceress. The latter
aspect is, ironically, Edna's projection of her own fears of what it
would mean to wake up – not only from her conventional sleep as
wife and mother, but also from the dream of true love as the source
of all meaning in life. This fantasy she clearly shares with Robert;
indeed, he is shown to encourage and embellish it. Chopin's text
ruthlessly but subtly undermines Edna's dream, and even exposes
it on a number of occasions as nothing more than the absurd
fantasies of a child, indeed, of two children, Edna and Robert, as in
the following two passages:

> When Edna awoke it was with the conviction that she had slept
> long and soundly ....
>   'How many years have I slept?' she inquired. 'The whole
> island seems changed. A new race of beings must have sprung
> up, leaving only you and me as past relics. How many ages ago
> did Madame Antoine and Tonie die? and when did our people
> from Grand Isle disappear from the earth?'
>   He familiarly adjusted a ruffle upon her shoulder.
>   'You have slept precisely one hundred years. I was left here to
> guard your slumbers; and for one hundred years I have been out
> under the shed reading a book. The only evil I couldn't prevent
> was to keep a broiled fowl from drying up.'   (pp. 84–5)

> Yes. On the twenty-eighth of August, at the hour of midnight,
> and if the moon is shining – the moon must be shining – a spirit
> that has haunted these shores for ages rises up from the Gulf.
> With its own penetrating vision the spirit seeks some one mortal
> worthy to hold him company, worthy to being exalted for a few
> hours into realms of the semi-celestials. His search has always
> hitherto been fruitless, and he has sunk back, disheartened, into
> the sea. But to-night he found Mrs Pontellier. Perhaps he will
> never wholly release her from the spell. Perhaps she will never
> again suffer a poor, unworthy earthling to walk in the shadow of
> her divine presence.   (p. 75)

These two episodes could be read as nothing more than the playful banter of two lovers, but they are too carefully constructed as fantasy and fairy-tale not to suspect that Chopin meant them ironically, that is, as parodies of the folly of such a dream of love as Edna and Robert have. Repeatedly throughout the novel, Chopin parodied Edna's love as a pure, childish fantasy, the description of which Edna herself gave most succinctly and most damningly at the first dinner party, for her father: 'She had [a story] of her own to tell, of a woman who paddled away with her lover one night in a pirogue and never came back ...' (p. 123). The narrator ironically comments 'It was pure invention ... perhaps it was a dream she had had' (p. 124). In a further gesture of supreme irony at the expense of the gullible reader, Chopin wrote:

> But every glowing word seemed real to those who listened. They could feel the hot breath of the Southern night; they could hear the long sweep of the pirogue through the glistening moonlit water, the beating of birds' wings, rising startled from among the reeds in the salt-water pools; they could see the faces of the lovers, pale, close together, rapt in oblivious forgetfulness, drifting into the unknown.   (p. 124)

Like the listeners to Edna's story, that story of pure invention, a mere dream, Chopin's readers fall under the spell of the story Chopin wrote: 'every glowing word seemed real to those who listened' (p. 124). Only Doctor Mandelet seems to penetrate some distance into the mystery. Indeed, he, like Mlle. Reisz, is another example of a relatively detached point of view – but he never sees Edna as clearly as Mlle Reisz does. For, although he is a type of artist, he is not portrayed as the supremely accomplished artist of life as well as music that the pianist became. Nevertheless, there are repeated suggestions throughout Part II of the novel that Mandelet is a man utterly unlike Robert or Edna's husband; he is a genuine friend, and might have been able to provide Edna with some support; yet somehow she does not let him. Throughout, Chopin relentlessly exposed Edna's dream of true love as a childish fantasy: she had Edna repeat to Adele Ratignolle her childhood memory (dream/fantasy?) of walking into infinity in a sea of grass (an ominous prognostication of things to come), and admits she was 'a little unthinking child ... following a misleading impulse without question ... I feel this summer as if I were walking through the green meadow again; idly, aimlessly, unthinking and unguided' (p. 61). Chopin, by a stroke of pure irony, has Edna unconsciously expose her own present, adult state as childish folly, albeit of a more deadly kind, and this irony is reinforced over the next few paragraphs as Edna remembers her previous, less dangerous infatuations (p. 62). All these men 'went the way of dreams', as will Robert, in the end, but with far more disastrous results. For her infatuation with Robert, being more emotionally, sexually intense, indeed, being the infatuation of 'true love' (that most dangerous illusion of all), constitutes the most dangerous hindrance to self-development, as the self is submerged in the loved one. Hence Mlle Reisz's hatred of swimming, as a symbol of submergence in emotional dependency.

The sea and the ocean become a metaphoric image of such all-consuming, drowning love, and, as such, they are a source of terrible danger and destruction; hence, Chopin made Mlle Reisz, who is free from such delusions, avoid the water. Over and over again, Chopin portrayed Edna's fantasies of love by means of images of the boundless ocean: 'Edna felt as if she were being borne away from some anchorage which had held her fast, whose chains had been loosening – had snapped the night before when the mystic spirit was abroad, leaving her free to drift whithersoever she chose to set her sails. Robert spoke to her incessantly; he no longer noticed Mariequita' (p. 81 and see p. 73, where Edna is likened to a child who 'grew daring and reckless, overestimating her strength. She wanted to swim far out, where no woman had swum before').

It quickly becomes evident that Chopin used the boundless ocean as an image of liberation only at the surface level of her story.[11] In the sub-text (the text describing the means of liberating oneself from not only the sleep of convention – as Edna does do – but also from the dream of true love as fulfilment – which she fails to do), the sea is, ironically, portrayed not as a state of mind of liberation, but as a state of totally blind, will-less immersion in fantasy, dream, and unreality. The sea is charged with sinister implications in Chopin's ironic, devastating sub-text: it is, indeed, contrasted with art, its opposite. Art is the activity of giving shape and order to oceanic formlessness. Art is a creative process, pre-eminently of the creation (through great labour) of a self which is genuinely original and individual. Art is structured through intelligent work, organised and articulated as a result of powerful imaginative gestures working on initially un-formed material. The ocean, on the other hand, represents a kind of primordial unity, a shapelessness, an unarticulated power, unformed force, which, as Willa Cather repeatedly wrote, may well be the source of all art and creativity, but remains beyond the control of the artist's imagination and will, without powerful, imaginative labour and systematic intervention by the human in such an otherwise oceanic, unbounded nature. Ocean and art are images opposed in Chopin's text, though they are not portrayed as contraries which exclude each other. The ocean is the symbol of creative nature in its Nietzchean original oneness and unity, a unity for which there is a powerful longing, and indeed, a death instinct, that desire for re-union into oceanic oneness, the desire to escape from the labour and suffering of individuality and life. Chopin's irony becomes a powerful tool, first, for imaging the sea as a world of partial liberation, then undercutting that image as Chopin deftly, unobtrusively portrayed the sea in her sub-text as the world of death. Twice, out swimming, Edna 'sees' death: 'A quick vision of death smote her soul, and for a second of time appalled and enfeebled her senses. But by an effort she rallied her staggering faculties and managed to regain the land' (p. 74). Frightened, Edna speaks of 'perishing out there', while the narrator describes her swim as 'an encounter with death' (p. 74).[12]

Chopin used the ocean as an image of danger because of its power totally to engulf one, as does love. She also frequently described the sea as seductive; as a force that will lovingly overpower Edna and totally drown her, as does 'love':

The voice of the sea is seductive; never ceasing, whispering, clamoring, murmuring, inviting the soul to wander for a spell in abysses of solitude; to lose itself in mazes of inward contemplation. The voice of the sea speaks to the soul. The touch of the sea is sensuous, enfolding the body in its soft, close embrace.

(p. 57, and see pp. 56, 81).

Not surprisingly, it was Robert who tried to teach Edna to swim, to love the sea, to venture out into such a sea of unbridled, uncontrolled, unbounded love, that 'mystic shimmer' of the Gulf, its waves like sinister white serpents (see also p. 23). On the final page of the novel, Chopin daringly plagiarised herself by describing the ocean in exactly the same sexual, sensuous words as she had used on p. 57, some hundred pages earlier. She also referred to Edna's childish fantasy of the fields like waves rolling into infinity, with 'no beginning and no end'. The deliberate narrative repetitions, which ironise spontaneity, also reinforce the voice of irony and its sub-text, in part by intruding upon the reader a realisation that the lines are not spontaneous outpouring of passion, but a deliberate authorial self-reference. As Edna swims out, on the final page of the novel, the reference to Mlle Reisz is illuminating – for it also is another deliberate narrative repetition of words of warning Mlle Reisz spoke to Edna:

> 'How Mlle Reisz would have laughed, perhaps sneered, if she knew! And you call yourself an artist! What pretensions, Madame! The artist must possess the courageous soul that dares and defies.' (p. 176)

In Edna's quest in the second half of the novel for Mlle Reisz, she is, at the narrative level of conflicting (or completing) sub-text, searching for herself – the 'artist' within herself – in the fullest sense of the word 'artist', as fully developed, original individuality, as a human work of art. Her efforts to sketch and eventually to paint lead her part of the way, to financial independence and setting up her own household. Her lack of further development as a better painter is less a cause than a metaphor, however, for her arrested emotional development as an individual: she wakes from the sleep of conventional notions of fulfilment, but is engulfed in the oceanic dream of love. Yet Mlle Reisz provides her with a model, one which, like herself, others see as mad, as 'imbalanced'. Edna has, both literally and figuratively, lost Mlle's address, lost touch with her, that is, and can only reach her through Mme Lebrun (Robert's and Victor's mother). When she goes to the Lebruns, Victor, Robert's brother, regales her with a story of lust and sexual adventure: Victor is not another Robert, for his role in the novel is primarily at the level of the sub-text. In the surface story, he makes little sense. But in the hidden, ironic sub-plot, where Mlle Reisz is Edna's potential self, Victor is Robert's 'reality' – a light, irresponsible sexual animal, hardly different from Arobin. It is Victor, not Robert, who meets Edna in the final scene, before her swim into oblivion; Victor, not Robert, who comes to her 'Last Supper'; Victor, not Robert, whom she meets on her quest for Mlle Reisz. Victor's presence in the surface plot is, dramatically, almost meaningless; any unrelated person could have served his function. Yet, when the sub-plot is attended to, he becomes a transparent 'figure' for Robert's hidden, actual character, a character only superficially different from Arobin (note the similarity of names: A-robin, not-Robert, yet

a variation on a Robert). Victor is exactly like Arobin in his amor-
ous, irresponsible seduction of women, yet he is also Robert's
'brother', indeed, he may be read as Robert's self, in important
respects. Robert has achieved a veneer of culture and a veneer of
maturity which Mlle Reisz appreciates, since so few achieve even
this. Yet Mlle Reisz does not delude herself about his moral being.
The novel suggests the possibility that he is a polished, cultivated
cad, but nevertheless still a cad, still Victor's spiritual and moral
brother. Indeed, his difference from Arobin and Victor may be only
a variation on a theme of a fantasy – a false veneer of superficial
cultivation passed over as moral development, whereas Victor and
Arobin at least have no pretensions. The ambiguity of Robert's
character is indissoluble. Nor is it important. Cad or 'sincere lover',
the dream of fulfilment through love rather than through self-
development is still a delusion. Indeed, Chopin's text suggests that
if the love is sincere, it can lead to still more damaging results,
especially if the lover lacks courage. Chopin's novel presses, with
its ironies, sub-text, and complex imagery, for a disruption of
fantasies of romantic love, however morally developed the lover.
While it offers Mlle Reisz, however, as an alternative, a more sure
basis for life, this does not suggest that Chopin argued for a single,
substantial self-identity independent of the world and an entity
unto itself. The self is understood as a work of art, as a text, with all
the ambiguities, uncertainties, and relativities of interpretation
involved in texts. Hence the impossibility of judging or evaluating
Robert becomes a code for the irreducible 'meaning' of the text.

Mlle Reisz accuses Edna gently of having pretensions (p. 115),
but she earlier referred to her as 'la belle dame' (sans merci?), suggesting imaginative possibilities. She, like the marvellous Doctor
Mandelet, sees Edna as awakening so far only from her sleep, but
not from her dream. She sees her as an animal almost (p. 114),
while the doctor describes her precisely as a 'beautiful, sleek animal
waking up in the sun' (p. 123). Yet Mlle Reisz seems, while fearing
for Edna, also to encourage her out of the dream, since she sees that
Edna has at least awakened from the sleep of repressed sexuality.
Already in section ix, Mlle Reisz had managed with her music to
propel Edna out of the common, mediocre response to art into a
realm where she was speechless with appreciation, while the other
listeners mindlessly babbled praise. Later, she speaks of the need to
be able to fly (not to swim!), and prophetically cautions Edna on
birds who seek to 'soar above tradition and prejudice' but, without

strong enough wings, fall exhausted back to earth (p. 138, section xxvii). The metonymic 'wings' are used as a traditional metaphor for imagination, rather than the bird itself. Chopin thereby emphasised that strength and development of one's powers, not just potentiality, are the crucial elements in becoming an artist. The repetition of the image of broken-winged bird (p. 175, near the end) is less crass than it seems. Although, it functions only as a poverty-stricken allegory in the surface plot as an emblem of why Edna failed, at the level of sub-plot, the image works as a viable convention rather than a cliché. The failure was one of strength, a failure on Edna's part to develop her capacities, before launching out into premature 'flights of fancy' which, if acted upon, lead to death.

Chopin's text is too rich to do more than mention a few more examples of her fine intricacy of imagery and narrative complexity, where each episode, each image is 'worked' for full effect. For example, throughout Part I, a pair of lovers appear in and out of the narrative; on most occasions they are followed by 'a lady in black' (pp. 44, 59, 66, 79, 80, where she is 'gaining steadily on them', pp. 81, 83; and pp. 63, 64, 73, where the lovers are mentioned without the lady in black, either several children or Robert literally come between them). This sinister image is an ironic device used by Chopin to image Edna's oppression, dread, and the 'fatality of love' and is similar to Chopin's repeated use of the garment as a metaphor for the conventional self. The garment, faded and unpleasant, Edna casts away to become naked, 'like some new-born creature' (p. 175). Chopin's sub-text has implied throughout that awakening to full self-realisation, to the self as an artist – individual, can come only through breaking the spell of the dream of love and sexual fulfilment as the ultimate source and ground of fulfilment. For Mlle Reisz, Edna is still submerged in this powerful fantasy, has not yet worked through it, is not yet strong enough to escape; yet, the pianist seems to feel that Edna has the chance, unlike most other people she knows. Hence the careful logic of numerous narrative details; for example Edna must go via the Lebrun's (via Robert and Victor) to fulfil her further 'quest' for Mlle Reisz. Chopin missed no chance to imbue her tapestry with rich emblems, as she sought on behalf of the reader to reveal the illusion for what it is. She also suggested the means by which one can 'avoid the terrible, seductive longing' for self-immolation into primeval nature: one must labour to strengthen the imagination, gradually to articulate into a work of art the self. Such articulation alone can give the ground and context for meaning in life. Unarticulated, abyss-like experience condemns the soul to solitary wanderings, to solipsism, to suicide, and to selfishness (pp. 57, 176). Edna's awakening is only a beginning, then, a beginning which is essential, absolutely necessary, in fact, to fuller realisation. But in itself it is quite insufficient as a basis for self-development:

> But the beginning of things, of a world especially, is necessarily vague, tangled, chaotic, and exceedingly disturbing. How few of us ever emerge from such beginning! How many souls perish in its tumult!   (p. 57)

Edna's throwing off of clothes, a metaphor for rejecting the conventional roles of mother and wife which enslave women, is not enough if one goes on dreaming the child-fantasy of submerging and drowning one's unindividuated self in an ocean of love (or sex, or anything else). Chopin's complex narratives, her ironic plottings, and her rich tapestries of imagery urge the reader to grasp the necessity for articulated, artistic experience, experience that is shaped and formed, not blindly felt like an animal. Chopin made Edna remark that expression is what men call unwomanly: 'but I have got in the habit of expressing myself' (p. 165). Yet, while having 'got in the habit', she had not yet learned to express herself articulately or artistically. Habit is animal-like; art requires something more than habit, though it is a start.

Chopin introduced, moreover, a powerful feminist theme which overshadows the entire novel.[13] It involves the critical, ironical, detached exposure of the destructiveness of seeing women as oceanic, as primeval oneness, as beings with those attributes given in the novel to the sea. Women, according to men (and to too many other women, like Irigaray)[14] are allegedly endowed with the 'essential feminine'. They are Nature itself in its primeval, mindless, unarticulated, procreation-seductive, engulfing, undifferentiated state. Pre-eminently, women are often viewed as essential Mother Natures, whose role and essential being is to procreate. That is, they create, but only in a bodily, sexual, animal way. Women are not supposed to move on from this primordial, animal-like, and primatively powerful stage. They are not to become language users – human beings, that is, much less artists. Many women are attracted to such a Mother-Nature role, partly out of instinct (Freud's combined life–death instinct, Nietzsche's urge for the primordial Dionysiac One), and partly out of a socialised belief that this can lead to fulfilment. It can, but only on an animal level, as Chopin demonstrated in *The Awakening*. To become fulfilled as an individuality (as opposed to a force of nature), as a human being, Chopin, Rhys, Richardson, and many other women writers suggested that women need to articulate experience, use art to become a work of art, not a mere blind product of natural forces. For, miraculous as nature is, as childbirth is, as all life is, art and humanity are something building on that specifically human capacity for self-conscious self-development.

The notion that *The Awakening* represents a celebration of the myth of Aphrodite rising from the waves is suggested by Sandra Gilbert, in her fine introduction to the Penguin edition (1983).[15] Clearly, the argument presented here would suggest, however, that such an interpretation is, in part, at least, an example of falling prey to the illusion or fantasy that the dream seductively offers, whether it be in the form of a dream of all-encompassing love or the analogous dream (fantasy) of returning to Oceanic Oneness. Gilbert's interpretation seems, unintentionally perhaps, to accede to Irigaray's naïve and even destructive celebration of an eternal, essential feminine essence. Aphrodite, Venus, is the Goddess of Love – the Goddess of Oceanic inarticulacy. It was, ironically, Victor, not Chopin, who envisaged and fantasised Edna as Aphrodite, in order to make Mariequita jealous:

> They had been talking for an hour or more. She was never tired of hearing Victor describe the dinner at Mrs. Pontellier's. He exaggerated every detail, making it appear a veritable Lucullean feast. The flowers were in tubs, he said. The champagne was quaffed from huge golden goblets. Venus rising from the foam could have presented no more entrancing a spectacle than Mrs. Pontellier, blazing with beauty and diamonds at the head of the board, while the other women were all of them youthful houris, possessed of incomparable charms.   (p. 173)

This, Victor's, view of women, Chopin painted as *the* male fantasy – what men want us to be, what men want us to see ourselves as. While Gilbert astutely realised the ironic undertones of the text which expose Edna's fantasies, her interpretation cuts somewhat short Chopin's critical, ironic exposure of Edna's 'retarded' emotional development. Gilbert is surely warranted in criticising Susanne Wolkenfeld's somewhat over-simplified account of Edna's situation as 'a defeat and a regression, rooted in a self-annihilating instinct, in a romantic incapacity to accommodate ... to the limitation of reality' (p. 31).[16] This, as Gilbert shows, is to miss Chopin's powerful analysis of the processes and stages of self-development. Far from regressing, far from being simply defeated, Edna has taken an enormously courageous step forward, more, as Mlle Reisz argues, than nearly anyone else. She needed to work through that achievement, however, to progress to the next stage, of becoming an individuality, a human work of art. This is the dramatic function of the carefully designed ambiguous ending, an ending which has created much critical controversy. Wolkenfeld's interpretation of Edna's end as essentially regression and defeat is consistent with the text only if one ignores the tremendously rich and subtle artistry of Chopin's complex plottings, ironies, imageries, and characters: all the details of the novel are working in the service of Chopin's analysis of the means and multiple stages toward self-realisation. Rather than simply holding up some distant, undefined ideal of self-knowledge, Chopin charted the way stage by stage, in so far as it can be charted. And of course she realised these stages in her own artistry, the complexity of which has been consistently, indeed systematically overlooked.[17] Readers and critics seem, in the main, unwilling to look at the details of the text – these 'minute particulars' which Blake claimed were all-important. To look at detail requires time and labour, but, as Chopin demonstrated, imaginative labour is precisely what develops one's strength, one's imagination. The neglect of such labour inevitably leads to the reader's becoming a victim of the text's irony. Yet irony and its sister, metaphor are the means by which the artist seeks to fashion her vision, and an awareness of these is crucial to seeing that vision.

Wolkenfeld's evaluation fails, in part, as Gilbert argued, in the face of textual detail, though, admittedly, it does express the spirit of destruction, one element of the text. Hence, it is not by any means entirely at odds with the text. It is, however, an account of one aspect of the text only, though in that capacity it makes a definite con-tribution. Gilbert's interpretation, though in some ways more subtle than Wolkenfeld's, is nevertheless (and paradoxically) still further at odds with the complexity of the text, for it seems inadvertently to be in the spell of the dream of love, the fantasy of romance and sexual freedom, in spite of perceiving the romantic illusion Edna labours under. That is, Gilbert's interpretation is inconsistent. The ironic sub-text acts contrary to Gilbert's conclusion of the novel as partly, much less pre-eminently, a celebration of Aphrodite, of Love, of Venus. The ambiguity of the ending is devised by Chopin not for this purpose, not to sustain this male fantasy of Victor's, of seeing Women as goddesses of love and romance. Chopin made her ending impossible to resolve into univocals, either negative or positive, because Edna's situation contains both creative and destructive forces. Edna has made a beginning – a heroic, admirable, rarely achieved beginning, and this partial progress and growth is sustained by the sub-text. The sub-text is, however, a further analysis of this progress as only partial; Edna did not get all the way – she did not succeed in flying, in articulating herself beyond the dream of love, beyond habit, and into the fuller self-development of human artistry: 'How few of us ever emerge from such a beginning! How many souls perish in its tumult!' (p. 57).

Edna, then, is both partially and imperfectly successful, and yet, crucially, she fails; hence the ambiguity of the ending of the book – its triumphant tone and its implication of failure, destruction, and death. Chopin had made indirectly two witty and ironic comments during the course of the novel about endings. Edna tells a story to her children:

> Then she sat and told the children a story. Instead of soothing it excited them, and added to their wakefulness. She left them in heated argument, speculating about the conclusion of the tale which their mother promised to finish the following night.   (p. 92)

Much later, Robert, Chopin wrote, tells Edna 'the end, to save her the trouble of *wading* through it, he said' (p. 166). This punning remark is within ten pages of Edna's last swim. Such overt irony is, one could argue, an effort on the author's part to 'awaken' the reader to the persuasiveness of the irony and of the wit of the book, by shocking her out of the fond, sentimental affection for the tale which blunts sensitivity to humour, irony, and to a critical awareness that the novel's analysis goes further than the reader could initially have perceived. Many of the other devices mentioned function with the same dramatic purpose of effecting a more complex, detached level of response in the reader. Such ironic devices often look like crass, rather stilted allegories, such as the broken-winged bird, or the lovers followed by the lady in black, and what can we make of the author's cynical repetition of an apparently spontaneous, 'moving and sensitive' passage on the final page – lifted word for word from page 57! 'The touch of the sea is sensuous, enfolding the body in its soft, close embrace', etc. (p. 176).

Gilbert's fascinating interpretation of *The Awakening's* ambiguous ending as expressive of the Aphrodite myth of rebirth is, then, based on a failure to perceive Chopin's portrayal of the Edna – Venus relation as ironic. That is, Edna is seen as an embodiment of Aphrodite not by Chopin, but by the superficial Victor. It is through Victor's eyes that we are presented with this equation; it is Victor's fantasy that Edna is a regal Venus goddess. Chopin explodes this fantasy as one of the most tragically destructive views of women, by narrating it to her readers as Victor's point of view on women.[18] This ironic commentary is a crucial part of Chopin's sub-text, as crucial as Willa Cather's portrayal of Ántonia as Jim Burden's fantasy of the ideal woman, or Virginia Woolf's ambiguous portrayal of Mrs Ramsey as the Woman — Mother. If we fail to see the importance of these authorial ironisings of male points of view, we end up seeing the women as Jim Burden, Victor Lebrun, and Mr Ramsey do, and we imagine that this view is the author's, when it is the view the author is brutally ironising.

In the first paragraph of the novel another of those apparently crass, over-obvious, belaboured images occurs, which bears inspection, placed as it is at the outset of the story:

A green and yellow parrot, which hung in a cage outside the door, kept repeating over and over:
'Allez vous-en! Allez vous-en! Sapristi! That's all right!'. He could speak a little Spanish, and also a language which nobody understood, unless it was the mocking-bird... (p. 43)

The parrot in the cage alone is a lamentable, over-used literary convention – all too worn-out and familiar to be very effective. What a poor, convention-ridden way to start a book that shocked the English-speaking world! Yet, closer scrutiny reveals an increment in complexity, a description of a 'mocking-bird that hung on the other side of the door, whistling his fluting notes out upon the breeze with maddening persistence' (p. 43). A mocking-bird, perhaps an image for the ironist, the two birds being images for the two-sided construction of the plot, for the double voice of Chopin the surface narrator and Chopin the voice behind appearance, ironising and criticising the surface. Such a beginning to a novel alerts the reader to irony, to wit, to double-edged meanings and two-sided texts or multi-layered texts. 'The language nobody understood' is suggestive of the language of Chopin the ironist, sensitive and open to humour even in tragic themes. The phrase also suggests Chopin's understanding of the need to keep an ironic perspective on life and on literature, pre-eminently through such humour as these bird images convey. Chopin did not speak the language of realism, nor that of romantic novels. Or rather, she spoke them both, and something more, an ironic, mocking criticism of both, which 'nobody understood, unless it be the mocking-bird'.[19]

4

The Attack on Realism: Edith Wharton's *In Morocco* and 'Roman Fever'

Marilyn French, in her introduction to Edith Wharton's short story collection *Roman Fever*, remarked that 'these stories are thus not just social commentaries but penetrating moral analyses'.[1] One could go further to say that these stories, like Wharton's novels and travel writings, are not just social commentaries or moral analyses, but works of art. While much secondary criticism has been devoted to the social and moral aspects of Wharton's writings,[2] a look at her works as artistic achievements is instructive. She marshalled complex narrative strategies, exploited carefully crafted imagery along with extended metaphor, developed Jamesian emphases on views and perspectives, and, in general, challenged realist notions of objectivity, representation, and transparent language.[3] This challenge involves techniques of reversal, comparing life and nature to art, for example, de-emphasising foreground to focus on background, and attending to frames more than to content. Wharton used sophisticated 'props' such as setting, lighting, colouring, and the Romantic technique of 'stripping the veil of familiarity' from things – 'tearing the gauze into shreds' (in Wharton's own words in 'Autres Temps … ').[4] In the following quotation from *Italian Backgrounds*,[5] Wharton expressed in admirably concise language some of the central issues of modern literature and literary theory today, simultaneously demonstrating her own literary strategies:

> As with the study of Italian pictures, so it is with Italy herself. The country is divided, not in *partes tres*, but in two: a foreground and a background. The foreground is the property of the guide-book and of its product, the mechanical sightseer; the background, that of the dawdler, the dreamer and the serious student of Italy. This distinction does not imply any depreciation

of the foreground. It must be known thoroughly before the middle distance can be enjoyed: there is no short cut to an intimacy with Italy.   (p. 183)

This quotation, a remarkably dense passage, is expressive of thematic issues and narrative techniques central to Wharton's fiction and travel writing. In the first sentence, Wharton upset the foundation of realism: art is not so much a representation or mirror of life, nature, or reality. Rather, life, nature, and reality are to be seen and understood by means of art. Henry James had built such reversals into his texts as a narrative principle and a systematic thematic dimension.[6] Edith Wharton, however, engaged in a systematic scrutiny of nineteenth century realism even more overtly than James. James and Dorothy Richardson, like Wharton, had laid claim to being realists, at least of a certain type. Yet their innovations, experiments, and challenges to traditional realist dogma are underestimated if one takes such claims at face value. If Wharton's texts are realist, then they are a very different realism from that of her nineteenth century predecessors. They are so different, indeed, as to challenge the meaning of realism other than as a brief historical moment of literary form. Wharton, in *The Writing of Fiction* (1925), complained of that 'constricting theory' of the realists, whose emphasis on a 'photographic reproduction' left out the 'larger whole'. Contemporaneously, Willa Cather was sharply attacking realism for similar reasons, while Virginia Woolf, Dorothy Richardson, May Sinclair, and Djuna Barnes were upsetting central planks of realist ideology with modernist techniques. For, example, to these writers the boundaries of each character or personality are not sharp; rather, each of us flows into the other and into our surrounding worlds. Wharton noted that realists had relied on a strong emphasis upon society and environment to express this fluidity of boundaries. She claimed, however, that the so-called 'new', modernist stream of consciousness method had superseded the realist technique, though it was not, she pointed out, so new after all. More importantly, Wharton further rejected realist ideology in insisting that all representation presupposed 'stylization' and 'transposition'.[7] Representation, she believed, could never be a neutral or objective mirror reflecting facts or objective traits in the world. For Edith Wharton, language was not a transparent medium of truth; rather, the language of the realists was itself a 'stylization', however ordinary it appeared on the surface.

Wharton's novels and short stories raise, by analogy with her more overt thematics, questions about the relation of artists to their predecessors and about the problematic relation of women artists to their male precursors.[8] Throughout her fiction, Wharton ironised and challenged the positions women were pressured into, both in society and in art. Her challenge by means of thematic content has been discussed repeatedly. Yet her contribution to this challenge by means of innovative and impressive narrative and other literary strategies has been somewhat overlooked, in part due to the unexamined assumption that she was using conventional, realist techniques with a few deviations derived from Henry James. Wharton's narrative strategies and use of style, image and metaphor, both in her fiction and in her travel writing, are sophisticated innovations moving away from realism and towards an individuality and originality which make her a writer much more interesting than a mere follower of Henry James. The quotation above depicts a number of Wharton's anti-realist gestures.

In the first sentence of the quotation, Wharton intimated that 'as art is, so is life', and stated that 'there is no short cut to an intimacy' either with Italy, books, or paintings. Indeed, Italy is treated as both a painting and a text – above all, as a work of art – but 'she' is also personified and shown to be in need of intimate study and interpretation. The audience's relationship to Italy involves intimacy, and Wharton argued that the reader/student/lover of Italy would have to work hard to get to know 'her'. Wharton elaborated this project with her characteristic reversal:

> Italy, to her real lovers, is like a great illuminated book, with here and there a glorious full-page picture, and between these, page after page of delicately pencilled margins, wherein every detail of her life may be traced.   (p. 185)

This simile, along with Wharton's description of two types of 'viewers', is repeated throughout her novels and short stories, as she contrasted those who are mere sightseers in Italy, Morocco, or in life, with 'the dawdler, the dreamer and the serious student'. In the first quotation above, Wharton's fine, characteristic artistry of condensation through imagery, metaphor, analogy, and suggestion is evident. Wharton evoked the nineteenth and early twentieth century mythic conception of Italy as a 'cultural construct' suggestive of passion, sexuality, freedom, imagination, and the fusion of the opposition of animal sexuality and cultivation in artistic achievement. She introduced, in passing, the powerful image or metaphor of the journey, of travelling, and distinguished between the phony traveller and the imaginative student, thereby raising Jamesian issues of the centrality of different views and perspectives. With her topological metaphor she connected up, as did Willa Cather, with Freudian psychoanalytical ideas of the mind, language, and art as comprised of layers of significance and, like Forster, implied that Italy could be that magical realm where unconscious, supressed passion and feelings would be allowed to breathe and live, as they did in 'Roman Fever'.[9]

Wharton essentially argued that there are a number of different Italys – that is, numerous possible interpretations of Italy. Italy, like paintings and art, is irreducibly ambiguous – she is creative and destructive, liberating and imprisoning. Wharton sought in her prose to rewrite and challenge earlier conceptions of Italy, of Morocco, of France, and of America, but especially of Italy, for it had become almost a fetish for the English-speaking world. Moreover, Wharton's evocations of such ideas as intimacy, the 'real lover', Italy as a book in need of study, suggest the intersubjective, even sexual nature of interpretation, response, and relationship.[10] Wharton's mode of approach is unashamedly a rejection of the objective, scientific, analytical, neutral, cold eye of the recording intelligence of the realist, that 'photographic' approach, a rejection not unlike her scathing rejection of the 'mechanical sightseer'. One can hardly think of anything more deliberately at odds with the characters portrayed by the realist, than 'the dawdler, the dreamer, ... the real lover'. Clearly, Wharton's idea of the artist as well as the reader is the latter, not the former.

Not only is Wharton's rejection of realism usually underestimated; her pervasive ironic tone and critical perspective is often overlooked. It is clearly evident in such stories as 'Roman Fever', discussed in detail below, as well as in her travel writings, whether in *Italian Backgrounds* or *In Morocco*. In the passage quoted above, a critical, detached tone creeps in at a number of points to pervade the whole with a gentle humour most akin to that found in the following ironic personification: 'the [Swiss] mountains present blunt weather-beaten surfaces rather than subtle contours, wrinkled as by meditation, of the Italian Alps'.[11] Such humorous, ironic touches are characteristic of Wharton's constant 'stylization' and personification of the landscape and the architecture she saw, and are expressive of her commitment to subjectivity and interpretive response, as opposed to descriptive, neutral enumeration. Her subtle irony is most effective in the quoted passage under discussion as one realises the folly of taking Wharton's statements literally. She denied that Italy is divided into three parts; yet by the end of the passage there are three parts. Moreover, the third allegedly non-existent part, the 'middle distance', turns out to be the most important, the most 'real': 'relegated to the middle distance ... is the real picture which has its birth in the artist's brain'. Additionally, Wharton casually reversed the conventional, relative value of foreground and background, arguing that the background is more valuable than the foreground, inconsistently denying any 'denigration of the foreground'. She then put in a completely ambiguous pronoun in the final sentence – 'it' – which could refer either to the foreground, the background, or the distinction between the two, leaving ambiguous '[What] must be known thoroughly'.

Wharton's topological metaphor of foregrounds, backgrounds, and middle is designed to distinguish relations among hypothetical parts, rather than to establish substantives which must then somehow be reintegrated into each other.[12] The latter is the method of all essentialist and dualistic philosophies, and the divided elements cannot, in fact, ever be reunited. Wharton's emphasis was on relations, not substantive, divisible parts. Her concern was to distinguish for the sake of greater understanding, without dividing, while preserving the integrity of the 'larger whole'. Her evocation of the image of the 'middle distance' was surely an attempt to show the inherent interdependence of foreground and background as relative functions of each other and not absolutely distinct entities. And the 'middle distance' is a rhetorical figure designed to represent this basic unity of difference – the 'middle distance' is not, properly understood, a *tertium aliquid*. It is, rather, a metaphor for the whole which is distinguishable into two relative parts, and is a metaphor for metaphor-making itself. Her irony resides in part in this apparent confusion of two and three, and in her casual reversal of the hierarchy which normally holds between foreground and background. Moreover, Wharton made it clear in this passage that Barthean enjoyment was the goal – the 'pleasure of the text' – and that her enjoyment was inextricably tied up with study and knowledge, understood humanely as 'intimacy' (not as scientific, positivist reasonings), whether about landscape, culture, society, or life.

Wharton was deeply impressed by the role of landscape and place in prose (what Willa Cather, Ellen Glasgow, and Eudora Welty would have described as 'the power of the place'),[13] as is evident in 'Roman Fever' and *In Morocco*, not to mention many other of her novels and travel writings. Her emphasis upon views and perspectives, which included a marked interest in the role of lighting to transform a scene, became a metaphor for imaginative perception, as Wharton showed how the perspective from (or light within) which one viewed any scene or object could have a transforming effect. In the little book, *In Morocco*, as in 'Roman Fever', Wharton made lighting a central feature of her descriptive imagery, and used light imagery in such a way that it became a metaphor for the power of imagination and imaginative perception, as in the following typical example:

> One day before sunrise we set out from Rabat for the ruins of Roman Volubilis. From the ferry … we looked backward on a last vision of orange ramparts under a nightblue sky sprinkled with stars … Dawn is the romantic hour in Africa. Dirt and dilapidation disappear under a pearly haze, and a breeze from the sea blows away the memory of fetid markets and sordid heaps of humanity. At that hour the old Moroccan cities look like the ivory citadels in a Persian minature, and the fat shopkeepers riding out to their vegetable gardens like princes rallying forth to rescue captive maidens.   (p. 43)

This passage is characteristic of Wharton's techniques especially throughout her travel writings, where reversals of the realist notion of art as a mirror of life are frequent and overt. In the novels and shorter fiction, this reversal is less overtly presented but everywhere implicit in the language, structure, and thematics, as Wharton rejected 'photographic', mechanistic description for overt 'stylization', 'transposition', and imaginative lighting, stressing points of views as relative and limited. Her other major mode of attack on realist ideology involved, in the travel writings, giving her readers historical accounts of Morocco, Italy, and so on as if they were fantastic stories, or fabricated, legendary myths. She thus completely debunked the realist and 'New Historicist' notion that history is factual, objective, neutral, and descriptive. History is not free from narrative views and figures of speech; it is simply often less self-conscious of them than is literature. Moreover, Wharton showed that history is often derived from art, overturning the realist and 'new' historicist notions that art is supplementary to history. Historical accounts are usually based on architectural remains and other artefacts as well as on literary texts. In many respects, history is more fictional than fiction *per se*, as Wharton ironically revealed in *In Morocco*. The following quotation is a characteristic example of her debunking of history as objective or neutral:

> Such were the wonders that seventeenth-century travellers toiled across the desert to see, and from which they came back dazzled and almost incredulous, as if half-suspecting that some djinn had deluded them with the vision of a phantom city ... 'the high Roman fashion' is visible in the shape and outline of the ruins. What they are no one knows. In spite of Ezziani's text (written when the place was already partly destroyed) archeologists disagree as to the uses of the crypt.   (p. 64)

Wharton made her readers acutely aware of the disorganised fragments and ruins upon which the weighty, pseudo-unified edifice of history is constructed.[14] She compared the fragile and disintegrating sandstone of Moroccan architecture to the more enduring, but nevertheless destructible, stones of Rome, and implied that in both cases, this great edifice of history is based on very flimsy fragments, indeed, mere traces of an irrecoverable past. Her fascination with ruins, fragments, and decay was rooted in her (Romantic) appreciation of ruins as metonyms and figures of speech for the past, and their metaphoric relations to the present.[15] For Wharton, the relation of past to present was a simile for the relation of art to reality, but, contrary to realist and historicist assumptions, no simple allegory exists, since the elements of each duality could relate to either element in the other. That is, the present is as fictional as the past, and the past is as real as the present. The ruins and fragments of past achievements acted for Wharton as words in a language from which stories, legends, and accounts could be constructed. As in 'Roman Fever', in *In Morocco* Wharton showed repeatedly and systematically how problematic the relation of past and present is, comparing it to the relation of art to reality and fiction to history. The following passage is exemplary of her problematizing of the present–past relation:

that afternoon ... the crowed roofs, terraces, and balconies packed
with women in bright dresses looked like a flower-field on the
edge of a marble quarry ... the scene seemed like a setting for
some extravagantly staged ballet ... the spectacle unrolling itself
below us took on a blessed air of unreality. In that unreal golden
light the scene became merely symbolical: it was like one of those
strange animal masks which the Middle Ages brought down from
antiquity by way of the satyr-plays of Greece, and of which the
half-human protagonists still grin and contort themselves among
the Christian symbols of Gothic Cathedrals.   (p. 55)

Reality and the present, in the golden light of imagination, become
'merely symbolical'. Wharton used such inversions throughout *In
Morocco* to query the simplistic, hierarchic, and dualistic notions of
realists and historicists. For her, the past and the 'real' are as much
in need of interpretation as are literature, art, and the present. They
become meaningful only when interpreted, that is, seen through
the eyes (or from the perspective) of some art or some culture.
Natural beauty, landscape, and scenery are overtly interpreted
through cultural lenses in all her writings, in such a way as to draw
the reader's attention to her own 'spectacles'.

Much of Wharton's travel writing, then, carries powerful
metaphoric implications for the writing and reading of fiction:
travel functions, as it has traditionally, as a complex suggestive
metaphor for, among other things, imaginative activity as a journey
into a realm of magic, exoticism, and mystery. The 'realm' of
imagination and art, like the realm of a foreign country, needs
exploration and leads to wondrous delights and discoveries, but is
also dangerous and fraught with risks and discomfiture. This
extended, traditional metaphor of imaginative activity as a journey
into an unfamiliar landscape (suggestive also of the unconscious,
and symbolic of the difficult 'rites of passage' into adulthood and
self-knowledge) is thoroughly exploited in Wharton's travel writings, nowhere more so, however, than in her little 'guide book', *In
Morocco*.

It is clear that both Henry James and his friend Edith Wharton
took delight in exploiting this literary figure of travel, which, in
spite of its commonplace familiarity, seems to retain immense
power for writer and reader alike. The convention of the adventur-
ous traveller, much like that of excavation in Cather, acts as
metaphor for both writer and reader as highly individual, original

adventurers into the unknown territories of new artistic modes and experiences. Not only writer but reader must undergo the journey. Wharton seemed particularly enchanted by the metaphor of travel for imaginative activity *a propos* her trip to Morocco (though travels to Italy, Spain, Tunisia, and Algeria had certainly been good metaphors in their own exotic ways). For she remarked, not without irony, in the first sentence of *In Morocco*, that

> To step aboard a steamer in a Spanish port, and three hours later to land in a *country without a guide-book*, is a sensation to rouse the hunger of the repletest sight-seer.
>
> The sensation is attainable by anyone who will take the trouble to row out into the harbour of Algerciras and scramble on to a little black boat headed across the straits. Hardly has the rock of Gibraltar turned to cloud when one's foot is on the soil of an almost unknown Africa.   (p. 21)

Wharton was delighted that no definitive 'guide book' existed to this realm of the imagination, that world of 'seers' (not, perhaps, sightseers, though the pun is evident) and visionaries, which nevertheless, is indeed open to 'anyone who will take the trouble'. Africa – that 'almost unknown' territory – becomes a symbol of imaginative landscape and its related mystery, the unconscious, throughout *In Morocco*. To summarise, Wharton's strategies in *In Morocco* involve a variety of metaphors, puns, and witty ironies as described above. That is, she challenged realism by reversing priorities, such as her systematic, ironic comparison of nature and life to paintings and fictional stories. Hence, her witty treatment of the history of Morocco as though it were some fantastic fabrication or legend, with no basis whatsoever in fact. She quoted chroniclers and travellers in the same ironic spirit as Shelley's authoritative traveller is quoted in 'Ozymandias', where not only the relations of reality to art, history to fiction, and nature to painting are reversed. Wharton also questioned constantly the relation of past to present, of the interpretation of ruins and fragments of earlier culture to life today. Pervading all her travel writings and many of her novels is a Willa Cather-like respect for the mystery of nature and the profundity of existence. She became deeply impressed by certain features of Moroccan life, art, history, and landscape which distinguish it from Europe, more specifically, or from Italy, for example. Its ruins, fragments, and decayed wrecks of earlier civilisations are different from those of Rome, she argued repeatedly. They are different, in part, because the materials used were less substantial – the solid stones of Greece and Rome versus the sand of Africa. The desert landscape (of which sand is the major material, of course) is also different; it is more vast; it is uncharted because unchartable; it is wilder, less tameable and less hospitable, less known because forever less knowable, as the sands blow away the paths and roads that form the basis of known territory. As such, Africa becomes a gripping metaphor not only for the less charted, but also for the less chartable terrains of the imagination, the wilder, less tameable and unconscious regions of art and the human mind.[16] These regions are related in Wharton's mind to sexual promiscuity and unbounded sensuality in *In Morocco*, much as Italy is often the setting, whether foreground or background, for certain kinds of passionate encounters and longings.

Wharton used light in her travel writings and fictions as a constant metaphor for imagination, but not in Enlightenment terms. Mystery, uncertainty, and darkness have their unresolvable reality too; light and dark serve each other, they act as a foreground and background; for Wharton, the one never should tyrannise over the other, as clarity and light do when they conquer darkness in Rationalism. Wharton, like Keats (and all her Romantic predecessors) never gave too much reality to 'clarity' and 'light' at the expense of mystery and the unknown. Hilda Doolittle succinctly stated the relation when she remarked that one must not flood darkness with light, so that darkness is destroyed; rather, we must enter into darkness, so that it too is experienced. This insistence imparts a powerful, often overlooked 'primitiveness' to Wharton's work and makes a Blakean statement about the nature of human experience, a statement at odds with realism, enlightenment, and rationalist simplicities of reason conquering all. In Wharton's writings, times of day have powerful metaphoric implications, for example: things look different at sunrise, sunset, twilight, in haze, and so on. Wharton described the landscape and the city or village life of Morocco using the language an art historian would use to describe painting, emphasising light and shade, tones and colours, contrasts and similarities or visual effects.[17] In the face of the virtually indescribable, Wharton resorted, time and time again, to ironic comparisons of life and landscape with paintings, frescoes, Greek vases, and other artefacts of human culture. She was clearly conscious of seeing the African world around her, whether nature or

culture, through the eyes of European art and life. This sophisticated, Jamesean consciousness of the spectacles through which she
viewed the new, unknown world liberated her to some extent, at
least, from the limitations an unconscious use of those spectacles
entails. This consciousness involved a relative detachment or an
ironic awareness of herself as a European–American sightseer,
which allowed her a more empathic, imaginative response to the
African scene. While Wharton made eminently clear that there is no
privileged or objective view, or perspective (as Henry James argued
in his prefaces and fiction), she still explored the differences between more imaginative and less imaginative views. Given her
concern for the difference between the 'mechanical tourist' and the
passionate traveller, she understandably lauded General Lyautey,
the French colonial administrator of Morocco, for his empathic,
imaginative relation to Morocco which, he avowed, arose out of his
love for the people and the place (p. 171). This love, this passion, is
the source of the 'light' associated with, or symbolic of, imaginative
acts, both in life and in art.

In addition to the landscape, it is the architecture which Wharton
most attended to in her travel book of Morocco, this guidebook-less
country of immensities and eternities, where 'the air of the
unforeseen blows on one from the roadless passes of the Atlas
[mountains]' (p. 21). Moroccan architecture became, to her mind, a
metaphor for the structures of certain types of fictions – of stories,
poems, novels – and of paintings. Perhaps it also acted as a metaphor
for art, language, and the imagination itself, as Wharton pic-
turesquely depicted courts within courts, walls within walls,
labyrinthine passageways leading to subterranean rooms which
seem to have no end, no centre and no mappable plan.[18] Elaborate
descriptions of 'gardens of forking paths' and of courts within
walls within more courts and more walls (as in, for example,
Borges' 'Man on the Threshold') abound in *In Morocco*, whether
Wharton was describing the living cities of today or the decayed
fragments of past cities now deserted. She toyed, furthermore, with
the crucial role of repetition of patterns in Arabic art and architecture, queried the relation between repetition and originality or
novelty (as had Gertrude Stein),[19] and concluded paradoxically that
much repetition in Arabic architecture and art is fantastically
imaginative and original. Wharton joked about the search for
origins both in art and history, in archaeology and anthropology,
and she concluded joyously that the origins of Arabic art and of

such peoples as the Berbers are, like imagination itself, shrouded in insoluble mysteries.[20]

Keeping in mind these techniques from *Italian Backgrounds* and *In Morocco*, one can look at a powerful story like 'Roman Fever'[21] and see many Moroccan echoes in the artistry and structure of the story, artistry which should not be neglected, since it is inseparable from the moral and social thematics. As with *In Morocco*, Wharton made the exquisite use of lighting effects, and of the backgrounds, foregrounds, and 'perspectives' central themes (as well as structural devices) from the outset of the story. Moreover, tales within tales, like courts within courts, and repetition of imagery for imaginative, novel, and metaphoric effects are evident, as is the journey, excursion, or travel metaphor. 'Setting', that realist 'prop', is not swept away so much as used ironically, intertwined with the thematics, narrative strategies, and emblematic images to comment on the possibility of truth, objectivity, and facts, as well as to comment on the nature of history, the past, and the present and how they become meaningful only from limited points of views. More precisely, life, history, art, and nature have different meanings, truths, or interpretations depending on the perspective. In 'Roman Fever', an 'event' from the past is reinterpreted from the point of view of the present, and present revelations and 'lights' change that event drastically for both women. Wharton's serious surface tone and overt subject matter is infused with a strong, covert irony, which makes it possible for her to use devices from a comedy of errors game without jarring with the story's sense of decorum. Phoney letters, unanticipated replies, unintended trysts, sexual trespasses, illegitimate daughters legitimised hurriedly, all these Shakespearean elements are exploited. Yet the contrasting 'loftiness' of the setting mirrors the loftiness of the present scene (and theme) of past passion, while underlying the loftiness is a theme of pettiness, deceit, and even humour, a recognition, that is, of the folly of all human endeavour, of the need for the presence of wit at all times, especially in art. For art delights through its sheer 'craftiness', however, serious the theme.[22]

The reader encounters the two main characters, two American ladies, on a lofty terrace of a Roman restaurant. They lean on its parapet and glance, first at each other and then at the splendour of the scene before them. For the duration of the story, the ladies remain on the terrace, Rome spread out at their feet, while a series of revelations unfold. These 'lights' completely change their understanding of a past event which they were involved in some twenty years earlier in Rome, an event which led to the mystery for Mrs Slade of Grace Ansley's delightful daughter, Barbara, a substantial and concrete outcome. Neither Grace Ansley nor Alida Slade is spared pain, as 'the truth' comes out that Barbara is the offspring of a long-past, passionate encounter between Grace and Mrs Slade's husband-to-be, engineered (by mistake of course) by Mrs Slade herself, in an effort to deflect Grace, her rival, by exposing her to Roman fever. The Roman fever under question turns out to be, in part, sexual passion fulfilled, to Mrs Slade's horror. If this account of the story suggests a commitment on Wharton's part to objective fact, to truth without perspective, one had better look again. For, as in *In Morocco*, the truth, like the past, like the origins of the Berbers, and so on, is shrouded in mystery. For Wharton forces upon the reader numerous unanswerable questions, and an inevitable wonder as to why, for example, the two women married as they did. Why did Delphin Slade meet Grace in secret in the coliseum, make love to her, yet marry the other woman? As soon as we ask the meaning of 'the facts', mystery sets in, and facts without meanings are idle things. Why, Mrs Slade asks, did Grace do what she did? Does this event change her view of her whole marriage over the last twenty-five years? She cries to Grace at the end of the story: 'After all, I had everything; I had him for twenty-five years. And you had nothing but that one letter that he didn't write' (p. 24). Grace replies, 'I had Barbara', throwing into doubt the meaning of Mrs Slade's entire married life, while, admittedly, clarifying the fact that the supposedly aborted tryst between Grace and Delphin took place after all. Did Grace and Delphin continue the affair later? Or if not, did they love each other nevertheless? Did Delphin ever love Grace or was it simply sexual passion? None of these questions are answered. Wharton's story leads us to question both the value of facts without meanings and the possibility of facts or determinate meanings. Both women's views and certainties about a past event are demolished in the present, and both are left wondering about the meaning of what happened.

Wharton made use of a number of amusing and delightful artistries in the process of leading both characters and readers to this shattering of illusions and substitution of certainty for doubt, ironically in the very process of apparently clarifying the past. Placing the women on the hotel terrace functions as a metaphor for establishing a view or perspective, just as a narrator must be established by an author. This blatantly Jamesian technique of staging the entire drama on a balcony overlooking the outspread city is an ironic emblem both of establishing narrative perspective and a metaphor for the relation of the present as a view or perspective on the past event central to the story. Present and past are indeed blurred, as their simple relation is questioned in the person of Barbara, the enigmatic daughter – so much more beautiful and vivacious than Mr and Mrs Slade's Jenny – and the product of that passionate and illicit past union. The past lives on very much in Barbara's being.

The notion of perspective, point of view, 'stylization', and inter- pretation of events is established both by the dramatic setting of the story and by the thematics. Throughout part I of the story, know- ledge of the other person and self-knowledge are explicit themes, so much so that by the end of this first section the narrator concludes: 'So these two ladies visualized each other, each through the wrong end of her little telescope' (p. 14). As the hours pass, revelations abound, and how the women view each other and themselves is left uncertain after the shattering of the earlier 'visualizations'. Earlier, for example, Alida Slade and Grace Ansley are made to reflect on 'how little they know each other' (p. 12), yet some very precise 'notions' emerge nevertheless. Mrs Ansley is seen by Mrs Slade as 'poor Grace', yet also as 'good-looking, irreproachable, examplary' – this of the very woman whose passion led to pregnancy, a hurried marriage, and an illegitimate daughter! Much more space, however, is given by the narrator to Alida Slade's view of Grace Ansley than vice versa, though Grace is said also to pity Alida:

Sometimes Mrs Ansley thought Alida Slade was disappointed; on the whole she had had a sad life. Full of failures and mistakes; Mrs Ansley had always been rather sorry for her .... (p. 14)

None of this view is substantiated by Alida's sense of her own great success as Delphin's wife, though in general she comes off worse for seeming incorrigibly egotistical and confident in contrast to Grace's modesty. Throughout the first part of the story, these views are presented in an extremely comic tone by a poker-faced narrator.

A further technique of Wharton's involves the artistic device of recreating the past in the present via the character's interpretations. That is, they both keep remarking on how like the present afternoon and evening is to their previous visit to Rome, indeed, to the very night of the fateful meeting between Grace and Delphin. Moonlight – a full moon – is the means of identifying present and past, as well as numerous comments from the two women about this evening bringing back memories: 'It's so lovely here; and so full of old memories, as you say' (p. 15); 'and here we sit ... and it all brings back the past a little too acutely' (p. 17). Related to this technique of bringing the past alive into the present is the use of ironic statements replete with implications if the reader knows the whole story – very like Sophocles's use of ironic prognostication in his tragedies. The most substantial and ironic occasion of such a Sophoclean irony occurs when Mrs Slade narrates the story within the story of Grace's Aunt Harriet, who is said to have sent her sister out to the Forum ostensibly to gather a night-blooming flower, but actually in the hopes that she would catch Roman fever and die (which she did), because they were both in love with the same man (p. 18). Gradually, the reader learns that Alida Slade did to Grace exactly what Grace's Aunt Harriet was said to have done. Shortly, it becomes evident that Alida Slade needs to confess this truth: 'I simply can't bear it any longer – !' (p. 20). This conventional device of a story within a story is used to great effect by Wharton; like Alida's false letter to Grace, it became the vehicle for Alida's scheme to harm her imagined rival. Yet in each case, the women presented the 'instrument of evil' to each other. Grace, that is, had told Alida this very story of her Aunt Harriet the summer of the event in question, and had given Alida the idea of repeating the narrated events in real life. Meanwhile, Alida's phoney letter, allegedly from Delphin, was the instrument which led to the fulfilment of the tryst. Thus, a merely incidental story within a story becomes a determining factor of actual events, just as a 'false' letter brought about the very tryst it was intended to abort. The Aunt Harriet story within the story is also a replica of the past event constituting the theme of 'Roman Fever', and revealed gradually to the reader through such self-referential devices. The 'present' narration, then, of the two mothers' revelations to each other, frames the past story of the Alida–Grace–Delphin triangle, which was brought about by and is a frame for the young Grace's story of her Aunt Harriet – a story told as if it were more a fairy-tale than a true event: 'the story of your wicked aunt' (Alida; p. 19); 'Mother used to frighten us with the story when we were children' (Grace; p. 18).

Wharton's complicated narrative strategy of frames and Chinese-box stories, through gradual revelations (which lead to a crushing consummation) at once crystalises and obfuscates through these quite Shakespearean dramatic techniques. 'Roman Fever' is an example of fine, subtle craftsmanship which repays close attention and rereading while never intruding its artifice on the reader. The gradually evolving relationship between the two women in the space of a brief afternoon provides two powerful poles of opposition, an opposition which is sharpened into blatant hostility, at least on one side. For a long-standing, continuing hatred and envy is exposed behind the façade of congenial acquaintance. This sharpening of focus about the two women's relation to each other may appear (like the apparent clarification of 'what really happened' long ago) to yield objective facts and truths which underpin a realist ideology. Yet the meanings of the 'facts' yielded is put in question, as, for example, moral discriminations become less clearly determinable. Unlike the clarity of an Ivy Compton-Burnett novel, Wharton leaves us less at ease with moral condemnation and value judgements. Alida Slade fears she herself is a monster, to have done what she did, while Mrs Ansley refuses to condemn her or absolve her. Grace does, however, attend to the meanings of Alida's revelation for her own understanding of the past and her present situation. Wharton confronts us with the puniness of moral precepts in the face of great passion, without being willing to denigrate the value of morality in the face of that passion.[23] Should Grace have gone, or shouldn't she? Did she betray her friend and her integrity? Or did she merely reject convention for the sake of fulfilling a passion which amounts, from another point of view, to a kind of personal integrity?[24] Perhaps the story suggests that, as in art, so in morality: no rules can be applied from without, or, as Wharton says in *A Backward Glance* (unconsciously borrowing from Coleridge), moral rules must come from within each situation, within the hearts and minds of the participants.

The narrator, however, presents the reader with a clear bias in favour of Mrs Ansley. From the outset of the story Mrs Slade is painted with a touch of the comic grotesque, as if a theatrical mask were being described: 'The other lady, who was fuller, and higher in colour, with a small determined nose supported by vigorous black eyebrows ... ' (p. 10). Later, the narrator describes her as 'the dark lady' (p. 10), ' ... Mrs Slade, the lady of high colour and energetic brows' (p. 10). Mrs Ansley is the 'smaller and paler one'

(p. 9). Very little more is said of their appearance after this colourful beginning by the narrator, though they each later make brief reflections on the other. Mrs Slade is 'vivid', Mrs Ansley 'slighter', and 'drawn with fainter touches' (p. 14). The clear narrative preference for Mrs Ansley as a finer moral being is the surest indications of a discernible narrative point of view, *a* perspective, as opposed to *the* perspective. Yet the 'objective facts' of the story make it harder to sustain this preference. Mrs Ansley betrayed her young girlhood friend, did she not? Consciousness of narrative authority leaves the reader freer to be aware of the power of and necessity for a point of view, one which however can shift so that we see things from other points of view. The same situation, the same moral dilemma takes on different meanings depending on the point of view. The insistence in the story on points of view is a central if covert theme. Points of view can change, leading to new interpretations of past and present, suggesting that not merely two or three points of view are available to the reader. Grace and Alida are the obvious portrayals, but there is a suggestion in the story, a powerful suggestion, that Grace and Alida are both 'pawns' of a larger structure which is much in need of scrutiny, namely, the socially patterned world which leads women into such tragic competition. The larger world is always implicit, of course, in the story, through evocation of Rome 'at their feet' and through the obvious references to the absent husband involved, to marriage, to society, to the daughters presently pursuing potential husbands, and so on.

Before turning to this social dimension, however, let us note one particularly remarkable strategy of 'Roman Fever'. For Wharton had introduced a narrative and thematic strategy which borders on the hilarious, and which threatens the seriousness and decorum of the story with its frivolity. This strategy involves the strange, colourful, and intrusive image of Mrs Ansley's knitting, which runs throughout the story, uniting the various frames and inset stories of past events. The progress of Mrs Ansley's knitting (compared to Wharton's painterly exploitation of the progress of the afternoon light on the terrace as a further unifying feature emblematic of the emotional revelations) stands out as a crafty, frivolous, witty, and nearly scandalous image, which threatens to disrupt the surface tragedy of the story with a leering jestfulness. Wharton introduced this knitting image early in the second paragraph of the story when Babs remarked to Jenny about their mothers:

... 'let's leave the young things to their knitting'; ... 'oh, ...
not actually knitting –'. 'Well, I mean figuratively', rejoined the
first.   (p. 9)

Figuratively and literally, it turns out, however, as, shortly after,
Mrs Ansley guiltily takes out her knitting, not to put it away again
until the end of the story. Knitting becomes a delightfully ironic,
witty structural device both for expressing Mrs Ansley's reactions
to Mrs Slade, for charting the progress of the narrative, and for
being a rhetorical figure suggestive of meanings on a number of
levels. First, the knitting image expresses the opposition between
the two women as the fabric of their past becomes untied and a
new pattern emerges in the present. The women are said to 'needle
each other' throughout the story. Second, the knitting is a figure for
reading, for the knitting together of the strands of a story. As such,
in the latter case, knitting becomes a domestic metaphor for fiction
writing and for acts of reading and interpretation. It also becomes
an extraordinarily apt emblem for figuration itself, that is, for the
making of figures of speech, and hence, for perception as
essentially metaphor-making.

The knitting emblem runs throughout the major part of the story
as follows, almost telling the story in its figurative way, leaving off
abruptly at the point where Mrs Slade begins her confessions and
Mrs Ansley her revelations, at the point, that is, where the pattern
of the past comes completely unravelled:

> Half guiltily she drew from her handsomely mounted black
> hand-bag a twist of crimson silk run through by two fine knitting
> needles.   (p. 10).

> She settled herself in her chair, and almost furtively drew forth
> her knitting. Mrs Slade took sideway note of this activity, but her
> own beautifully cared-for hands remained motionless on her
> knee... The long golden light was beginning to pale, and Mrs
> Ansley lifted her knitting a little closer to her eyes.   (p. 15)

> She turned again toward Mrs Ansley, but the latter had
> reached a delicate point in her knitting. 'One, two, three – slip
> two; yes, they must have been,' she assented, without looking up.
> Mrs Slade's eyes rested on her with a deepened attention. 'She
> can knit – in the face of this. How like her .... '   (p. 15)

Mrs Slade gave a hardly audible laugh, and at the sound Mrs Ansley dropped her knitting.   (p. 16)

Mrs Ansley's hands lay inert across her needles. She looked straight out at the great accumulated wreckage of passion and splendour at her feet. But her small profile was almost expressionless ... Mrs Ansley had resumed her knitting. One might almost have imagined (if one had known her less well, Mrs Slade reflected) that, for her also, too many memories rose from the lengthening shadows of those august ruins. But no; she was simply absorbed in her work.   (p. 17)

'Yes. You think I'm bluffing, don't you? Well, you went to meet the man I was engaged to – and I can repeat every word of the letter that took you there.'
While Mrs Slade spoke Mrs Ansley had risen unsteadily to her feet. Her bag, her knitting and gloves, slid in a panic-stricken heap to the ground. She looked at Mrs Slade as though she were looking at a ghost.   (p. 20)

One striking aspect of the narration of Mrs Slade's revelations is Mrs Ansley's refusal to criticise her, to see her as a 'monster', as 'horrible', as Mrs Slade sees herself to be at those times when guilt overwhelms her. The latter's only defence against this guilt is to tell herself that it is Grace who is the 'monster' (p. 22), for trying to steal her fiancé away from her (p. 22). Notably, the knitting metaphor collapses just as Mrs Slade begins her revelations about the phoney letter, her motives for writing it, and her hatred and envy of Grace then and, indeed, all through the years, concentrated now on Grace's beautiful, vivacious daughter, Barbara, who she feels puts her own daughter in the 'background'. (And how uncritically the reader is encouraged to accept Mrs Slade's assessment as if it were fact, in spite of Grace's warning that Alida 'overrates Babs'; p. 17.) Attitudes to indiscretions such as Grace committed have changed greatly since 1911, when this collection of stories appeared, and these changes mean that the balance of sympathy and of criticism has shifted in favour of Grace, while in 1911 the balance would perhaps have been more equal between the moral positions of the two women. Even so, Grace's position seems defended by the narrator as more human, based, that is, on love, passion, and acknowledged sexuality, while Mrs Slade keeps appealing to hypocritical proprieties of engagements and marriage contracts, rather than to feelings. She is positively obsessed by 'the letter', while Grace is more concerned with what 'the letter' represented, the emotion, and the love it symbolised (pp. 21–2). As such, Mrs Slade becomes a mock-representation of the literal-minded reader, confounded by the literal, ignoring the need to excavate figurative stratifications.

What seems at stake in the deeper thematics of the story is not so much moral scruples, or efforts to determine wrong-doing on the part of one or the other of the women. Rather, Wharton's story presents us with a much more profound criticism of the larger social context in which such questionable behaviour occurs, a criticism, that is, of a society whose inflexible conventions positively encourage such 'muddles' (to use a term of E. M. Forster's). Put another way, we miss another important level of criticism in the text if we remain, morally and aesthetically, at the point of judging the two women, instead of scrutinising the social constraints which turn women into competitors and enemies for the favours of men, their ultimate worth (as Alida reveals) being how attractive 'girls' are to 'men'. Both women can be seen, then, as victims of a ruthless system which relegates women to the position described, a position which brings out their worst qualities instead of nurturing their best. No doubt there are moral discriminations to be made; no doubt Alida's behaviour is deeply disturbing; but what do we do about Grace's breach of faith? Excuse it because the narrative point of view presents her as 'nicer' than Alida? If we do, we may be falling into the patriarchal trap of victimising victims, a trap which involves distracting one's criticism away from the corrupt society and towards victims precisely in order to preserve the existing privileges.[25] A more imaginative, wide view is to see both oppositional elements as within a greater whole, namely that context in which the women behave. As such, 'Roman Fever' is a model for Wharton's other writings, for many of her novels, which are more overtly critical of social, moral contexts which produce victims.

This view of the thematics has relevant consequences touched upon above for the story as a work of art, as an artefact composed of highly literary, complexly crafted structures, and formal qualities. At the outset of this chapter it was noted that thematic commentary (social and moral issues) dominates critical writings and responses to Wharton's work (and to much other literature). This imbalance, this 'neglect' of the literariness of her texts, is redressed when her work is looked at in the context of conventions of literature. To place the story in its literary context means precisely to attend to the story's conventions as well as its innovations. One can attend to this relation by examining salient aesthetic features of these texts for comparison and contrast. These features include narrative strategies, unifying structures, diction, subject matter, use of dialogue, irony, metaphor, imagery, characterisation, plot situation, descriptive techniques, settings, lighting, foregrounds and backgrounds, use of time, dramatic devices, and so on. The tendency in much criticism to neglect these aesthetic features has led to equal neglect of moral, social, and thematic features. For one of the most pressing aspects of 'Roman Fever' is its portrayal of the duality or separateness of these two aspects of literature (and of life experience) as a sham. There is no duality, no conflict, since moral and aesthetic are interdependent, knitted together throughout. The story portrays vividly the destruction and inhumanity which occurs when such qualities are separated and divided from each other.[26]

There is so much moral–aesthetic value in 'Roman Fever' that it would be foolish to single out any one aspect as uppermost, given the variousness of readers' temperaments, tastes, backgrounds, and knowledge. The consequences, however, of a powerfully drawn moral situation, a masterly dramatic development, fine use of dialogue, imagery, and complex narrative, along with a lean, spare thematics (which by suggestion and innuendo introduces social and moral issues central to life) with careful restraint in diction, tone, and imagery, leads to a consummate example of the short story. That the reader comes away with a sense of having had an aesthetically consummating and morally challenging experience *is* the moral as well as the aesthetic force of the story. Both Wharton's *In Morocco* and 'Roman Fever' subtly undermine the assumptions of realism, as their narrative strategies challenge the supposed relations between life and art, reality and fiction, history and legend. In travel writings like *In Morocco* and *Italian Backgrounds*, Wharton borrowed painterly techniques to illuminate her descriptive reversals of nature and life as 'like art', 'like statues', and 'like vases'. She revealed the origins of history to be legend and fantasy, and self-consciously portrayed her views of both landscape and foreign culture through the spectacles of her American–European sensibility. In 'Roman Fever' as in her other fiction, she added to these techniques carefully devised frameworks, perspectives, complex imagery, and Chinese-box structures of 'stories within' mirroring 'stories without' breaking through the bounds of the work of art to implicate the reader *qua* reader.

5

Style as Characterisation in Jean Rhys' Novels

Ella Gwendoline Rees Williams was born, it is thought, in 1890, in Dominica, West Indies, and died in England in 1979. Jean Rhys came to England in 1907, studying at the Perse School, Cambridge and the London Academy of Dramatic Art, before taking odd jobs as chorus girl, artist's model, and mannequin in order to earn her living after her father's death. In 1919, at the age of 29, she left for Holland, afterward living in Paris and Vienna. In 1923, Rhys was introduced in Paris to Ford Madox Ford, who encouraged her writing and helped her to publish her short stories in 1924. Four novels were published over the next fifteen years, most receiving some critical notice and some even considerable praise, but never gaining the attention of the reading public. Finally, in 1966, *Wide Sargasso Sea* won Jean Rhys an acclaim that also rescued her earlier work from obscurity. All her earlier novels, two new collections of short stories, an unfinished autobiography, and a fascinating selection of her letters were published over the next two decades.

From the first, Jean Rhys had been praised (by Ford among others) for her 'singular instinct for form' and for 'a passion for stating the case of the underdog'.[1] More recently, Francis Wyndham described her as one of the 'purest writers of our time', with a 'quivering immediacy and glossy objectivity'.[2] It is also helpful to look at the ways in which form (or 'shape', as Rhys called it), style, and subject matter influence and determine each other. Moreover, when reading Jean Rhys it is useful to keep in mind that, like so many of the writers discussed or referred to here, she was a writer concerned with developing the techniques of story-telling and of writing to the highest degree. This means experimenting with a range of literary strategies to achieve the greatest skill of which she was capable for articulating, in literary forms, the insights she had gained in living and in writing.

For Jean Rhys, writing was a means, a central means, by which one's self, one's ideas, and one's insights came into being. Moreover, because Rhys became a writer, she became a different self (with different ideas and different insights, values and beliefs) than she would have been if she had not written. Hence, Rhys, like Dorothy Richardson, for example, rejected many of the conventions of the so-called 'realist' novel, with its insistence upon alleged objectivity and the notion of language as a transparent (direct) representation or expression of an alleged objective reality, a reality independent of the perceiving, writing self.[3] Rhys argued that writing (or anything else, for that matter) was not objective in the classical realist sense; it involves selection, rearrangement, interpretation, and shaping processes, so that not only the writer's self is changed by writing. The 'thing' or experience initially written about is also transformed by the very process of writing, because it can now be seen in new and revealing ways, and in new relationships with other things. Writing can call into question everything, from higher cultural values to the most basic details of the perception of the materiality of things and their interrelations. As Henry James and Edith Wharton so eloquently showed, writing can never report or describe neutrally or objectively because it always involves interpretation.

Given the interrelation between the creation of the text (through the labour of writing) and the creation of the self (and its values and beliefs), Rhys insisted that the basis of fiction must be autobiography. Along with May Sinclair, H. D., Djuna Barnes, Stevie Smith, and others, she believed that to pretend to any other (more allegedly objective) basis was delusion or hypocrisy: 'I know that "parler de soi" is not supposed to be the proper thing to do ...[but] I feel so fiercely about that. No one knows anything but himself or herself.'[4] She admitted, moreover, that while her own writing always started out from something that had happened, the act of writing invariably involved a movement away from such relative reality or autobiography. This movement involves the matter of giving body and shape to that initial impetus or experience. The process of shaping initial experience by writing about it is the process of fiction. Moreover, Rhys explained, she found it impossible to impose shape arbitrarily upon materials; shape arose out of the interaction of the initial experience chosen and focused upon and the writer intensely, creatively attending to it. (For creative processes are nothing if not mysterious to the reason.) As Rhys modestly and humorously said, 'a novel has to have shape, and life doesn't have any; I like shape very much'.[5]

Rhys' novels and stories represent first, a continuing experiment with the possibilities of what fiction might be and what it might be able to become. In this intense preoccupation with experimentation, Rhys rivals Woolf and Mansfield. Moreover, in writing, Jean Rhys believed that her very individuality or development as an original human being was at stake – this is one of the great existentialist insights that many women writers have expressed and, recently, emphatically re-expressed. Writing influences life, and life influences writing – indeed they become inextricable, and nearly every woman discussed here has made this dynamic relation a main theme of her fiction.

One can make an art out of many things, whether writing or painting or human relationships or living 'in general'. One can make an art, for example, out of reading well, as Katherine Anne Porter humorously showed in 'The Holiday'. Whenever a high level of focus and creative activity or response is achieved, individuality is sharpened and increased. This increase in the definition or outline of individuality is always a movement away from the stultifying sameness[6] and unfocused nature of ordinary existence. Ordinary existence hems the individual into regimented patterns, set traditions, customs, and unthought-about conventions. Hence, Rhys' emphasis throughout her novels on the deadliness, the sameness of so much of life, from the ugly rows upon rows of terraced houses all over England, to the endless blank grey sameness of the sky day after day, to the sameness of the stereotyped, unindividuated human beings she encountered.

Jean Rhys' novels each represent an attempt to liberate her writing and her being into further and further realms of greater definition, originality, individuality, and innovation. Not surprisingly, then, she chose as the 'subject matter' (so to speak) of each one of her novels, a woman in various situations at various stages of life, growth, and individuality. These women (whom numerous critics have believed to be 'the same woman at different stages in her life', though her name has changed along with changes in minor detail),[7] these woman characters represent a 'congruence' in Rhys' fiction between subject matter and form, a consequence which is a prerequisite, indeed, almost a definition of art. Rhys has achieved a peculiarly intense congruence in her novels, because each new woman character (she is not the 'same woman', in any definitive sense) is a metaphor for the new achievements in style, form, and conception that each novel represents. To the extent that the reader is able to read intelligently and to recognise the congruences between characters, novels, styles, and selves in their various individualities, that reader sharpens the definition or outline of her own self – increases her own individuality and sharpens her own focus on life,[8] an insight also developed by the other women novelists discussed here.

Rhys was engaged as a writer in the search for an uncategorisable style – a style and a voice (so to speak) that would be her own. Individuality is not something one is born with or possesses automatically – one creates it. Rhys' novels and styles possess individuality to the point of distinction; they stand out from the crowd.[9] These novels enact through style (and portray through characterisation, and discuss through subject matter) this existential search for an original way of writing, living, and being. This way involves getting outside categorisation, stereotypes, and convention. Tremendous imaginative power is needed in all cases, whether of living, writing, or becoming an individual, to resist the pressures of society toward stereotyped behaviour and to achieve and realise individuality, as writers such as Willa Cather passionately insisted.

Jean Rhys' women, these metaphors for style, are 'uncategorisable' women. Are they good or bad? Are they ugly or beautiful? Are they right or wrong? Are they true or false? Are they rich or poor? Are they prostitutes or 'proper' women?[10] To break out of these categories is to put all conventional, unthought-out values into question. These uncategorisable women are the characters and the subject matter of Rhys' novels, as they were in less extreme forms in Edith Wharton's writings (see, for example, 'Roman Fever', discussed above). As such, the subject matter of her novels is also unconventional and uncategorisable. Uncategorisable subject matter, like the uncategorisable women, is battling against powerful literary (and correspondingly, social) pressures to conform by accepting rules, in the one case, and by accepting roles in the case of the women battling against the social pressures to conform. Like her women characters, Jean Rhys was unable to conform as a writer because she too was incapable of tolerating the boredom of mediocrity. As her women characters struggled with life, so Jean Rhys struggled to the death (as her *Letters* testify) with her writing, unable either in style or content to conform to the conventional novel. Rhys, much as Jane Bowles, was as incapable of spending her time and energy writing a conventional novel as her women characters are of being prudent, thrifty, or wise. The 'case for the (so-called) underdog is passionately stated' because it is the case Rhys made also for her own (so-called) underdog of a novel: her improper themes, her tarts as subject matter, or her non-realist, experimental styles.

While each one of Jean Rhys' novels is an experiment, the first two novels (*Quartet*, 1928, and *After Leaving Mr MacKenzie*, 1930) seem to represent an act of gradually consolidating a style or voice from which, as a self and a writer, Rhys, like her characters, could move forward. And forward too she did move, first, when she crashed through still more literary barriers with *Voyage in the Dark* (1934), her third novel, with all its achievements in technique – in diction, style, original use of first person narrative, experimentative use of time, dreams, memories, increased intensity of symbolism, imagery, theatrical metaphor, its constant flitting between reality, fantasy, and desire, its use of disjointed and repetitive sequences, yet within the context of a perfectly formed whole, as the end of the novel foregrounds beginnings, and the beginning foregrounds ends ('it was as if a curtain had fallen', p. 7; 'and about starting all over again ... all over again', p. 158). Meanwhile, in *Voyage in the Dark*, characters are often allowed to step out of their fictional boundaries and speak their lines to the reader, suggesting that the woman sees her life not as reality, but as a dramatisation, as something being observed by someone else. Or rather, life becomes a fiction, a dramatisation, with the main character being her own audience. Life becomes a fiction – a process of creating a self – and author, actor, and audience are all one role simultaneously. Jean Rhys, like her characters, like her readers, like Richardson, Woolf, Cather, and others, had to create not only her novels, but herself, and she is also the primary audience of her self-creation, while also being a model for her reader to learn from.

In the first two novels, Rhys had already experimented with narrative points of view (changing from third to first, omniscient to limited) and with diction, irony, imagery, and so on. By the time of *After Leaving Mr MacKenzie* (1930), she had thrown off the more conventional diction, plot techniques, narrative, and style of *Postures* (1928, also known as *Quartet* – main character: Marya), and the constraint that a too strict or literal adherence to autobiography had imposed. *MacKenzie* already marks the achievement of quiet irony, purity of diction, starkness, avoidance of sentimentality, and the remarkable achievement in characterisation (and therefore style) along with congruence of subject matter and form.[11] (Julia, utterly different from the almost conventional, rather unindividuated Marya, is characterised not primarily through action or word, but *via* Rhys' new style). As was said earlier, Anna, in *Voyage in the Dark* four years later, represents as a character yet a further development in Rhys' search for herself as an original artist with a unique style and voice.

Good Morning Midnight (1939) consolidates the gains made by 1934; but decades later, with *Wide Sargasso Sea* (1966), Rhys broke through into new achievements. Antoinette is more unlike the other women characters than anything Rhys had conceived of before, as is the technique and style of *Wide Sargasso Sea*. One way of characterising this difference would be to say that in the other novels, Rhys explored in both theme and style the (outer) limits of sanity. *Sargasso Sea* crashes through to explore the further reaches beyond sanity, and, most especially, to reveal its close blood-relation with insanity. Rhys then inverted the two, so that the sane (Rochester) is shown to be insane, while the insane (Antoinette) is shown to be a kind of sanity,[12] raising questions of the kind that come up in Stevie Smith, Gilman, and Jane Bowles.

Voyage in the Dark shares many structural, thematic, and narrative techniques with the modernist texts discussed here and with many others only mentioned in passing. Rhys made novelistic conventions serve her own ends, however, to create deeply moving and intensely original, individual novels. Each of her novels represents impressively innovative experiments in technique, and while larger, general thematic issues recur from novel to novel, the texts are notable for their uniqueness and difference from each other, as any close reading reveals. Appreciation of the particularity of each text (as well as of Jean Rhys' artistic individuality) involves careful familiarity with the detail of the texts, that is, with the way such details are shaped, structured, and then organised. Stylistic details give further uniqueness to the rich fabric of the writing (involving imagery, diction, metaphor, and so on), while layerings of narrative points of view establish alternating tones of irony, despair, hope, cynicism, and fear. Thematic details are doubtless important in themselves, but they gain in importance when appreciated additionally as vehicles for the tireless search for new forms, structures, styles, and expressions to which her novels, each in its own unique way, testifies. *Voyage in the Dark* constitutes one of Jean

Rhys' most passionate artistic achievements, as an example of a fine congruence of style, imagery, structure, thematics, and narration. The novel is organised into four major 'Parts', each of vastly differing lengths (80, 25, 34, and 4 pages each). These parts are divided into several numbered sections (nine, five, seven, and only one in Part IV). The numbered sections are also divided by blank spaces into parts of greatly varying lengths, some only a sentence or short paragraph, others several pages. In spite of this deliberate fragmentation of the novel, familiar to readers today from Stevie Smith, Jane Bowles, May Sinclair, and, pre-eminently, Hilda Doolittle (whose *Her* is a similar parody of surface organisation of an even more complex hierarchy), the novel nevertheless neatly splits narratively and thematically in two, though the first half, Part I, is slightly longer than the second half, comprised of Parts II, III, and IV. If we do not respect the literal surface boundary of Part I, the novel splits thematically and narratively into two almost exactly equal portions – the dividing point being, ironically, the cruel announcement, *via* a letter, of Walter's 'break' with Anna and the devastating effect upon her (p. 72 out of 143 pages of text). The exact mid-point of the novel is the break, then, by Walter, followed by a brief, confused, and ineffective effort by Anna to win Walter back. Thematically, the first half of the novel is about Anna's developing love-relationship with Walter; the second half the 'downward path to wisdom' (Katherine Anne Porter's phrase).

That the superficial organisation of the novel into innumerable fragments does not unequivocally reflect this other view of its structure as two-part is no weakness or inconsistency; on the contrary, it reflects the modernists' view of the artificiality of form and of the difficulty of determining beginnings and ends. The break with Walter at the heart of the novel suggests an ironically clichéd representation of Anna's 'broken heart': the rest of the novel charts the gradual stages of the breaking of her spirit, hence the division of the second half into three parts. In Part II, Anna makes a desperate effort to recover herself; in the process she re-encounters Laurie, the 'tart' who stays by her to the end, and meets, contrastingly, the 'respectable' Ethel, who claims to give Anna a chance – by hypocritically exploiting her in Part III and then kicking her out. In the very brief, four-page Part IV, Anna is dying from an abortion (but the publisher persuaded Rhys to change the ending to make it more ambiguous, suggesting possible recovery, though only for 'more of the same').

This novel, just as Rhys' others, articulates the themes discussed in more 'respectable' contexts by Edith Wharton or Katherine Mansfield: namely, through characterisation it exposes the falsity of many social categorisations used as modes of exploitation and privilege. People become like the cats and dogs glimpsed in the novel (and in Katherine Mansfield's 'Bliss' – see below), preying on each other with few traces of conscience or compassion, thus dehumanising themselves as they treat others inhumanely by putting money before everything else. Only the 'tarts' are portrayed as generous, either in spirit or with money. The novel is feminist in a sophisticated sense: it exposes the destructive, insane, and irrational effects of patriarchal social arrangements, while exposing many women to be as sexist and vicious as men. There is no idealisation, no sentimentalising of the female sex, as, for example, landladies are portrayed 'evicting' Anna with scorn and contempt. Her friend, Ethel – the hypocrite of hypocrites (whose profession is to pose as a proper, professional masseuse, luring men in for a manicure and 'innocent' massage, only, however, by tantalising them with the hope of sex) – later throws Anna out with outrageous accusations rooted in unmitigated jealousy. And, earlier in the novel, Anna's stepmother Hester rejects her as a nuisance and a burden, after a queenly, pompous speech about having done more than her duty (though Uncle Bo accuses Hester of robbing Anna of her inheritance from her father). In criticising social hypocrisies, Rhys, much in the way of Jane Bowles, constantly mocked labels; words such as good, bad, 'gentleman', 'lady', 'tart', 'that sort of girl', are all problematised:

> Is that me? I am bad, not good any longer, bad. That has no meaning, absolutely none. Just words. But something about the darkness of the streets has a meaning.   (Anna: p. 49)

Rhys problematises all categories and evaluations; everything is questioned. Words cease to have meaning as the novel raises questions but fails to allow any clear answer to emerge: 'Was Anna "in love" with Walter?' Is this the gradual story of her becoming a 'prostitute'? Did her stepmother 'steal' Anna's inheritance; is she a 'thief'? Does it matter? Was Walter really a 'cad' or did he 'just' fall out of love? What were Ethel's motives? And so on. Rhys painted such a complete and complex figure for each one of these characters that we see too much to write them off totally (only Vincent is an exception.) By such complexity of characterisation, the novel makes a point crucial to all Rhys' texts. It transcends the folly of allocating blame entirely to individuals, and depicts them, instead – 'losers' and 'winners' alike – as caught up in the social machinery of sex, money, and power which manipulates them like puppets. Many of the apparently irrelevant details of imagery, events, and theme throughout the story are designed painstakingly to construct this more imaginative point of view, but in a different way from the realist's objectivisation. People are, in part at least, puppets, if not entirely – and this fine balance between personal responsibility and social pressure creates a clarity of vision which is one of Rhys' major strengths, as it is in Wharton's writings and Mansfield's stories. Nearly every character is balanced on this double-edged life situation, including Anna. Life is a theatre; we play roles, yet within those pre-written texts we have, potentially, at least, some freedom.

The three-page hallucination at the end of the novel (presented in italics – which were occasionally used more briefly elsewhere to suggest 'direct access' to Anna's mind) describes in detail a masquerade which occurred in Anna's childhood as part of a West Indian festival. The masquerade becomes a terrible metaphor for life as a whole, unifying previous theatrical elements in the novel (and in other Rhys novels), such as emphases upon make-up, costumes and clothing, roles people play, almost in the language of Faulkner's *The Sound and the Fury* (1931) as we read, for example, about

> ... a mask. Father said with an idiot behind it I believe the whole damned business is like that ... – it ought to be stopped some- body said it's not a decent and respectable way to go on it ought to be stopped.   (p. 156)

(The combined hallucination–memory Anna experiences, while dying of the botched abortion, has a racist commentary by Hester and Uncle Bo, another theme delicately woven into the narrative, as Hester, early on, after insinuating that Anna's mother was coloured, goes on to reject Anna as 'like that'.) Rhys grasped the opportunity, like other modernists, of reversing the notion that 'art is like life and a representation of it', and ties the 'life is a masquerade' metaphor to the irony that Anna's first job was as a chorus girl in a theatre – that was her reality, while her life became the actual tragedy or drama. Reinforcing this theatrical metaphor and inversion (and the eventual coalescence of such oppositions) are images of curtains, doors, stage lighting, rooms as scenery, clocks ticking the time away, and endless mirrors and looking-glasses described as distorting and altering our ways of seeing ourselves (a metaphor for the reading of the novel, too). The lengthily described hallucination-memory brings together many of the images in the novel, such as the road along the sea (p. 158, repeated from p. 129) which was introduced in a previous reminiscence as a metaphor for the journey of life as a 'mysterious passage':

> The road goes along by the sea ... you ride in a sort of dream, the saddle creaks sometimes, and you smell the sea and the good smell of the horse. And then – wait a minute. Then do you turn to the right or the left? To the left of course. You turn to the left and the sea is at your back, and the road goes zigzag upwards.   (p. 129, varied on p. 158)

This paragraph reinforces previous metaphors of the sea as death (carefully developed throughout the text, and closely related to Kate Chopin's, Katherine Anne Porter's, and Stevie Smith's analogy of the ocean as, ambiguously, death as well as seductive lover), a traditional literary allegory revitalised into fresh form by all these writers. For example, Anna feels Walter's rejection as a submergence, and as a ghastly drama seen from outside: 'It was like letting go and falling back into the water and seeing yourself grinning up through the water, your face like a mask' (p. 84). Yet Anna (or the narrator – the point of view is uncertain) also remarks, after she and Walter make love: 'Lying so still afterwards. That's what they call the Little Death'(p. 48). This 'thought' arises as a response to Walter's query, 'Are you asleep?' Like Chopin in The Awakening, Rhys repeatedly wove complex metaphors and images for sleep, dream, life, death, and reality, as Anna, like Edna Pontellier, becomes stupefied with tiredness as the novel progresses. Dreams, flashbacks, memories, all disrupt and fragment the smooth progression of Anna's 'voyage in the dark' (and reflect Rhys' struggle to write, too) – her experience of life as a death-in-life, while, systematically, sexuality is intertwined with these other central images. Death and love-making, death and sleep or dream, and both death and sex in the image of the sea, along with the traditional sexual metaphor (quoted above) of riding down the road of life on a horse, all these relations build up an intensely powerful complex of metaphors into a final terror:

My feet were groping for the stirrups ... I balanced myself in the saddle to grip with my knees ... I felt very sick — ... I thought I'm going to fall nothing can save me now but still I clung desperately with my knees feeling very sick. (p. 158)

.Rhys not only organised these distinct images into complex, interrelating metaphors for the structural and thematic unity of her texts. She related them in ways which both illuminate their individual meanings and suggest that meaning is itself relational. For example, death is at the centre of all the images in one way or another, because, Rhys showed, the deadening of life occurs because of repetition, of sameness, of familiarity, of routine, of habit. The latter, related themes recur (repeatedly) throughout her novels and act to reveal the death at the heart of most of life, and reveal the interdependence of oppositions like life and death. Dualities become relational in meaning, as each element is a function of the 'other'. Each one of Jean Rhys' characters is on a voyage, a mysterious and terrifying passage called life, trying to escape imprisonment into 'deadening routine', as Anna calls it, namely, ordinary, respectable life:

...it was the best way to live in the world, because anything might happen. I don't know how people live when they know exactly what's going to happen to them each day. It seems to me it's better to be dead than to live like that. (p. 64)

Yet Rhys' novels show us that this death-in-life is called 'getting on', 'succeeding', 'being respectable'. Ambiguities get out of hand, as Anna's darkness seems a kind of light, terrifying as it is, a light into knowledge of this strange world of 'real' life, while getting-on is a sleep, a death, and darkness. Real-life roles, whether labelled as prostitutes, wives, mothers, landladies, gentlemen, ladies, or whatever, are portrayed like some ghastly masquerade, a nightmare, a theatre of tragedy.

Voyage in the Dark implicitly paints a picture of ordinary life as an endless repetition, a routine re-enactment daily of pre-ordained roles, most of the lines we speak hackneyed clichés, most of our thoughts and feelings stereotyped responses. Getting on involves mounting on to a stage in a theatre where the same drama is replayed every day, every night – day and night no longer distinguishable – all the acting mechanical and unspontaneous, unreal. Curtains go up and down in the novel, and doors are opened and shut, placed at strategic points in the text (at the beginning of Part I, three times in the first few pages, at the beginning of Part II; yet, ironically, there is no 'curtain' at the end of the novel). A door covered by a curtain leads to Walter's bedroom (p. 20), which Anna opens and enters, but then leaves untouched. Door and curtains, and, indeed, windows interchange meanings and recur as symbols of entrances into the world of sexuality and life, into the world of literature and reading, allegories of the 'curtain of flesh over the veil of our desire'. Laurie Gaynor teases Anna: 'Can't you manage to keep the door shut, Virgin, you silly cow?' (p. 15). Later Anna, seeking to escape Walter's embrace, says, 'Where's the door? I can't see the door? What's happened? It was as if I were blind'(p. 32). The drawn curtain also symbolises in part Anna's own growing depression and her repeated illness from 'English' diseases of flu, of pneumonia (p. 90), and of the endemic depression of the country itself. The drawn curtain is related explicitly and repeatedly to her arrival in England throughout the novel: 'A curtain fell and then I was here ... this is England' (p. 15).

Rhys opened *Voyage in the Dark* with the ironically ambiguous sentence, 'It was as if a curtain had fallen, hiding everything I had ever known. It was almost like being born again' (p. 7). This theatrical, dramatic opening–closing of the novel creates an ambiguity of evaluation about England, about literature and about reading, which permeates the narrative from beginning to end. Part IV begins and ends with a closed door, but the image, again, is ambiguous:

> The room was nearly dark but there was a long yellow ray coming in under the door from the light in the passage.   (p. 155)

> When their voices stopped the ray of light came in again under the door like the last thrust of remembering before everything is blotted out. I lay and watched it and thought about starting all over again. And about being new and fresh. And about mornings, and misty days, when anything might happen. And about starting all over again, all over again.... (p. 159)

The novel ends 'starting all over again', but like a broken record – yet also new and fresh, 'When anything might happen' – Jean Rhys' phrase for a vital life, not the death-in-life of routine. Yet repetition, freshness, and novelty are all mixed up together. Dark rooms with closed doors and rays of light from passages, curtains falling and rising, beginnings and endings severed and ironised, then repeated in the 'middle', life as a theatre, faces as masks, people as theatrical roles, all these images revolve in a rich pattern of changing views, with no view at the centre. Anna is 'potty' (pp. 124, 77), she is becoming ill, half-mad; nerve-wracking endless clocks recur throughout the novel ticking away the time ominously, as Anna fears 'failure' (pp. 76, 81, 120), as if the 'play' (or the novel) were about to be over, her time running out. Clocks, mirrors, curtains, and doors, all function as images suggestive also of the woman's body – her biological reproductive clock, her sexual biology, her role as mirror of men. Light and dark metaphorise death and life, sex and innocence, health and illness, and madness and sanity – but no allegories are permitted, for Rhys constantly showed us the complexity of things from inside out. Sanity may be madness from another point of view, while madness may be the light of knowledge into the insanity of normality. Death may be a release into the 'light' of painlessness, while life is all dark suffering. Anna, like most of Rhys' (and Wharton's) heroines, becomes a figure who is not herself so much a victim or failure as a mirror held up to society, a reflection of the destruction that the complex of men–sex–money–power of a patriarchal society releases. Mirrors abound in the text; like doors, curtains, lights, masks, roads, the sea, journeys, passages – these loaded, interrelated images become complex metaphors and symbols not only to articulate experience, but also to reflect our values and reverse them. Mirrors and 'looking-glasses' are constantly depicted by Rhys' narrator as making things look different:

I don't like your looking-glass, I said ...
'Have you ever noticed how different some looking-glasses make you look?' I said.   (p. 33)

... – it made me look so thin and pale.   (p. 35 and see p. 25)

Just before Walter breaks with Anna, an extended dialogue occurs in front of a mirror between them. Anna adopts a pose of calm when he announces he is going away for a long time: 'I didn't say anything. I put my face nearer the glass. Like when you're a kid and you make faces at yourself' (pp. 71–2). The pose, the mask Anna adopts to hide her hurt, her fear of desertion and rejection, are part of the theatrics of life, reflected in the mirror which itself is an ambiguous, rich symbol. Drawing on the traditional metaphor of art as a mirror, Rhys' theatrical imagery and complex rhetorical figures create a level of ironic self-consciousness, like other modernist and pre-modernist writers. Novels become mirrors reflecting and distorting not only reality, but also the reader's image of herself – often into revealingly unflattering reflections of reader's attitudes and values, in order to liberate the fettered, prejudiced mind into more imaginative points of view, into glimpses of other's lives which lead to loving, humane sympathy. Dehumanising divisions between people are overcome; categories, hierarchies, and dualities are exploded as ideological constructs, as fictions, dreams, and delusions – not the realities, necessities, and hard, plain facts they purport to be. Scattered, but frequent references to reading, to books, to critically placed letters occur, letters which are 'interpreted by the characters–readers' in different ways, letters which tell lies, which distort, which tell painful truths. (The classic letter scenario of the novel is Aunt Hester's reading aloud and interpretation of Uncle Bo's letter, and her own long letter of response to his 'outrageous' lies–truths, pp. 52–6; for other letters, see Walter's (actually Vincent's) elaborate, hypocritical letter, pp. 79–81; and Ethel's 'outrageous' letter, pp. 141–3). These letters become further ironic gestures by Rhys of inviting the reader to acknowledge the meaning of entering into the novel fully, first by acknowledging the stereotyped, non-objective, non-neutral, passive point of view of unimaginative reading, then, second by entering the door into the dark room of painful knowledge about our own racism, sexism, and so on, whether through writing or reading or living imaginatively.

Apart from the mirroring of reading, writing, and interpretation which the novel's three (well-spaced), substantial letters offer (two involving devastating rejections by people of Anna, and filled with transparent rationalisations), Jean Rhys slipped into this novel (and others, such as *After Leaving Mr MacKenzie*) further modernist gestures effecting self-consciousness of the process of narration as well as of reading, interpretation, and making meaning (both of texts and of the world-as-text). Early in the novel, Anna reads a book, ironically entitled *Nana*, her own story it seems, the title written in an anagrammatical form. (The title is also a reference to

Zola's fictional tart, Nana.) Her reaction is a metaphoric description both of what happens to her later as her life (and the story) unfolds, and is also a description of the likely reader-response:

> I was lying on the sofa, reading *Nana*. It was a paper-covered book with a coloured picture of a stout, dark woman brandishing a wine-glass ... The print was very small, and the endless procession of words gave me a curious feeling – sad, excited and frightened. It wasn't what I was reading, it was the look of the dark, blurred words going on endlessly that gave me that feeling.
> There was a glass door behind the sofa. You could see into a small, unfurnished room, and then another glass door led into the walled-in garden. The tree by the brick wall was lopped so that it looked like a man with stumps instead of arms and legs. The washing hung limp, without moving, in the grey-yellow light. (p. 9)

Rhys continued this extended and elaborate irony, verging on hilarity, if we keep the Nana–Anna analogy in mind:

> Maudi said, 'I know; it's about a tart. I think it's disgusting. I bet you a man writing a book about a tart tells a lot of lies one way and another. Besides, all books are like that – just somebody stuffing you up.' (p. 9)

Self-commentary and absurdly suggestive images abound. Glass doors opening on to unfurnished rooms to further glass doors leading to walled-in gardens – such elaborate, labyrinthine imagery is suggestive of interpretive transparencies and regression of meanings (using the familiar 'door' image – but see-through!). All leads merely to fantastic similes such as trees like limbless men, an image emblematic of a narrative strategy which draws our attention not only to the role of rhetorical devices and figures of speech in the creation of meaning, but which arouses us to the irony and satire of the narrative point of view. Irony or self-criticism liberates the reader from sentimentality and nostalgia, those damaging illusions. If one scrutinises the detail of this quotation further, one sees that the 'limp washing', hanging 'without moving', is a metaphorical mockery of the tree-trunk-man metaphor. This passage

is, then, a classic example early in the novel of Rhys' metadis-
cursive gestures and her varied modes of drawing the reader's
attention to reading, meaning-making, and self-referring figuration.
In addition, lies, truths, 'stuffing you up' ('the pleasure of the text'?),
false letters, letters and cards left unanswered by Anna because she
cannot bring herself to write 'lies', and other references to books
and reading confirm Rhys' self-commentating strategy, as she
pictured Anna refusing finally not only to answer letters, but to
read at all any more – because it is her own story she is constantly
confronted with, and she cannot bear the reflection of herself in the
novels:

> Everybody says the man's bound to get tired and you read it in
> all the books. But I never read now, so they can't get at me like
> that, anyway.   ('My darling Walter ...').   (p. 64)

'My darling Walter ... ' – Anna fantasises her own romance,
which she has been doing since she first met Walter:

> This is a beginning. Out of this warm room that smells of fur
> I'll go to all the lovely places I've ever dreamt of. This is the
> beginning.   (p. 25)

Being in love with Walter has transformed England from one of
those cold, depressing, ugly places ('they're so ugly. Only you get
used to it', p. 48) to the origin of voyages into undreamt of exotic
lands (where Anna had *her* beginning) – not simply because she
gets used to the ugliness so that she doesn't 'see' it any more.
Rather, love (that metaphor, according to Shelley, for 'imagination
in personal relations') has changed her view: 'The streets looked
different from the real thing' (p. 25). Yet her hope is just a dream,
an image in a 'looking-glass', and – as Katherine Mansfield, Stevie
Smith, Kate Chopin, Djuna Barnes, and so many other women seek
to reveal – the dream can become a nightmare without something
more than romantic, sexual love to sustain it: the single outcome of
that gripping nightmare is either death-in-life, that repetitive,
replayed, re-enacted daily drama of routine social roles, or suicide.
Nana, or *Anna*; the novel is, analogically, in our own names; it is
the story of our lives that we read, the voyage of our own making,
as labels disintegrate and distinctions between tarts and ladies
vanish into the ideological delusions which alone sustain them. In a

depiction of one of Anna's many dreams, Rhys' choice of images provides metaphors for sexual analogies, labour of all kinds, and even her own process of writing the book, *Voyage in the Dark*, under the guise of Anna's narration:

> I dreamt that I was on a ship ... and tried to catch hold of a branch and step ashore, but the deck of the ship expanded. Somebody had fallen overboard ... But I was thinking, 'What's overboard?' and I had that awful dropping of the heart.
> I was still trying to walk up the deck and get ashore. I took huge, climbing, flying strides among confused figures. I was powerless and very tired, but I had to go on. And the dream rose into a climax of meaninglessless, fatigue, and powerlessness, and the deck was heaving up and down, and when I woke up everything was still heaving up and down.   (p. 141)

In this analogy of reading, writing, and living, Rhys takes the ground from under all our values and beliefs, turns our world topsy-turvy, and leaves nothing unquestioned. As with Katherine Anne Porter, life is a ship of fools on an ocean, that symbol of the lover and of death. Life is a dream (or nightmare) we mistake for *the* reality, instead of just one possible reality among many, depending on our point of view. Confused images and 'figures' of speech mark Rhys' progress as a writer trying to fight her way across a heaving deck of meaninglessness to an unobtainable, stable shore. The 'climax of meaninglessness' Anna reaches at the end of her own story (not to mention in the novel *Nana*, that repetitive 'starting all over again, all over again ... ' p. 159; is it death of the body or death of the spirit?), is prefigured in the dream quoted above.

The recuperation of the past for present uses is much more complete in *Wide Sargasso Sea* (1966) than it was even in *Voyage in the Dark* (1934). In the latter novel, Rhys had already penetrated deeply into her own past to create a new, present self – not a final self though, but a self always needing further and further definition and focus. One might reasonably designate such recuperation as the very meaning of imaginative living. *Wide Sargasso Sea* is an experiment with a new style and technique, with imagery of more depth, colour, vigour, and intensity – a different individuation, definition, and focus than anything Rhys had written before. This is not to say it was better, strangely enough. it was, however, very different. This novel is no 'better' than the old woman is better than the middle-aged woman or young woman or girl or child. Each stage of life has its value, its intelligence, its strengths, just as each novel of Jean Rhys has its own peculiar beauty and strength and value. If growth is to occur, however, if repetition and stagnation (which are for Rhys, as for Bowles, what leads to the 'less good') are to be avoided, then new strengths, new virtues, new beauties must be found as individuality keeps redefining, refocusing, and re-creating itself in new ways. Jean Rhys, like Jane Bowles or Virginia Woolf, felt no interest in writing a novel similar to previous novels; each novel, as woman character, represents a new literary form and a new self created by the writing. One of the great virtues of the earlier novels is their extraordinary restraint, a quality that is left behind in *Wide Sargasso Sea*. Where the latter is freely impassioned and openly intense, the former novels have a corresponding, if opposite virtue of incredible restraint. A different kind of confidence and technical skill, which Rhys arrived at later in life, allowed her to practice less restraint. The 'beautiful restraint' of her earlier novels is one of their greatest traits of individuality. For example, in describing the restraint in the style of *Voyage in the Dark*, Rhys remarked that it was written 'almost entirely in words of one syllable. Like a kitten mewing perhaps' (*Letters*, p. 24). She 'restrained' her narrative, too, adopting a first-person perspective, but then refusing the conventional plot development through linear time, in order to practise a restraint that involved, first, showing time to be an illusion and, second, questioning what is illusion and what truth (and see *Letters*, pp. 24, 50). Meanwhile, in *Voyage* and in *Wide Sargasso Sea*, growing up is shown, as with Stevie Smith, to be another illusion (*Letters*, p. 122), as adults are portrayed as tyrannical children or powerless victims. Rhys was questioning conventions and values at both the level of subject matter – social and psychological commentary, criticism of life and society – and at the level of artistic formulation. The result is criticism of realism, conventional subject matter, and male themes and styles.[12]

While today there is, finally, general critical acclaim for Rhys' style, somewhat more questionable is interpretation of the thematics. Numerous critical platitudes (relying on the very categories Rhys challenged) abound as to the novels' thematics. The novels are said to be about 'the limitations, dependence, and despair of some women who are victims, often by their own making', or that they are about 'self-destruction', or about 'lonely depressed women', or novels whose 'sole concern is the abject misery of certain women'

(Anne Tyler), whose 'solitary disordered lives are of their own making'.[13] Even Ford Madox Ford's comment about Rhys 'passionately stating the case for the underdog' is rather misleading. Her novels and characters are much more complex than these simplistic, labelling, categorising accounts give any inkling of, just as is her style, simple as it looks at first sight. Rhys' novels are not merely about – or even mainly about – women who simply failed to get on, except in a completely ironic sense of 'failed'. These novels are not about prostitutes, but about individuals, about women uncategorisable according to conventional categories (and all categories become conventional after a time, just as the act of categorising is a convention and not a necessity). Jean Rhys' characters fail only in the sense that her own novels failed for fifty years. They failed to be appreciated, they failed to get noticed, just as her women characters fail to be appreciated except as prostitutes, as objects of use, but not as human beings. Briefly, for example, Mr MacKenzie notices Julia: 'Suddenly he saw her not as a representative of the insulted and injured, but as a solid human being. He saw all this with great clarity, and felt appalled.' Equally quickly, MacKenzie forgets; it's too much trouble: 'he suddenly remembered that, after all, he was not in love with Julia' (p. 22). It would be too much of a bother and responsibility, he decided, to continue to see her as a 'solid human being', and not as 'a representative of the insulted and injured' (as so many critics see Rhys' characters). Hence he dropped her. Julia knew anyway, that she 'was for sleeping with – not for talking to' (p. 125).

Similarly, Jean Rhys' novels and her characters are not representatives of some class of women or some type, neither as tarts, victims, underdogs, depressed women, miserables, or whatever. As Rhys told us, through Mr MacKenzie (of all ironies!) they are 'solid human beings' – individuals, originals, not types. Neither the novel itself nor its central character is a type. Each novel, each woman, is an individual, unique case. These novels, moreover, chart the women whose successes look like failure to the conventional eye – to all of us, until we 'come to think of it', until we look more deeply and read more imaginatively. Then we see individual women (not representatives of the insulted and injured) whose success lies in escaping the dehumanised, middle-class, stereotyped housewife, mother, or even working-woman roles pressed upon women, but also often accepted by them too readily. Jean Rhys' central characters, like Willa Cather's, for example, are women who have refused to be mediocre, who have refused to play the roles assigned to bourgeois, conventional women, women whose roles have so stereotyped their responses as to have become dehumanised. Rhys' characters are better understood not as prostitutes but, if we must label, as drop-outs (of many different kinds) from a society that demands of women self-sacrifice and dehumanisation as the price of getting on, as the cost of making it. Rhys' women often prefer to sacrifice the body rather than the soul, unlike their bourgeois counterparts, of which there are examples in Rhys' novels: sisters, landladies, mothers, lady employers, even 'friends'. Doubtless, Rhys also showed us that, in certain terms, the cost is enormous of opting out of the power structure, that property–money–men manifold. She also exposed as fallacious the conventional attitude that (apparent) failure suggests evil, or being somehow in the wrong, being tainted. Thus, these women who fail to get on are those who fail to conform to mediocrity, to sameness, to an unindividuated existence. Poverty, 'degeneracy' of a kind, immorality (according to convention), eccentricity, and 'neurosis' are all the signs of failure to conform, as Edith Wharton also showed. Failure to conform looks to the conventional eye like absolute failure. A more vital reading shows a profound rejection of conformity or categorisation, in preference for an individuality, uniqueness, and originality which (in literature and in life) is itself a kind of success, whether appreciated as such by others or not. Like Rhys herself, her characters would have collapsed of the boredom of a labelled life, a conventional role, whether as kept-lover, wife, mother, working woman, or prostitute.[14]

Rhys was not feminist in the conventional, familiar sense, for she had no single 'attitude to women', but rather a variety of attitudes to individual human beings. Like Katherine Mansfield, Kate Chopin, and others, she saw that most women were as chauvinistic as men, and portrayed many women as such in her novels, from brutal landladies to cruel employers to jealous sisters, uncompassionate mothers, and propriety-ridden wives. She did choose, however, in all her novels, as did Jane Bowles, to portray the original human being (who had achieved at least some scrap of individuality) as a woman, and never as a man. The dehumanising, levelling effect of the male–money–property manifold (in which sex is related to money in so far as a woman's body is her only saleable asset, since she is rarely allowed to develop her mind or her hands as labour potential) is described by Anna in *Voyage in the Dark*, when she describes England: 'Everything was always so exactly alike – that was what I could never get used to. And the cold, and the houses all exactly alike, and the streets going north, south, east, west, all exactly alike' (p. 152). This sameness in her surroundings represents for Anna symbolically the meagre possibility before her of a way of life – she is hemmed in by regimented patterns. The variety of opportunities open to her as a woman are no more genuinely varied than the different (same?) houses on different (same?) streets. It is the sale of sex that is involved in every type of life or role open to her, whether as lover, wife, mother, or prostitute.

Rhys' novels can be said, in the words of one critic, to portray the tragedy of a distinguished mind and a generous nature gone unappreciated in a conventional, unimaginative world, a situation that is often a result of men's incomprehension of women, but also a result of other women's incomprehension, jealousy, and competition for the sex, money, praise, and prizes awarded by men.[15] Rhys' books are cogent analyses of individual women, from whom important general insights can be drawn. Rhys' novels suffered the same fate as their characters for some forty to fifty years. We can only hope that the women in real life who have been as badly misunderstood as her novels and her characters were, are gradually finding more ways to reject conventional labels and roles and to create more meaningful ways of living and developing their own individuality. The force in some men, described in *Wide Sargasso Sea*, in *Pilgrimage*, in *To the Lighthouse*, and in *Over the Frontier*, for example, that seeks to destroy women's will, independence, and identity (in order to make women serve men's emotional and sexual needs) once held such power that independent women were often driven, as Antoinette, to a *kind* of madness, or to suicide, or to appalling ill-health, while repressed women may have survived in body but were often killed in spirit. Anna speaks out a rejection of the categories that imprison, kill, or madden women, when she says: 'I am bad, not good any longer, bad', and she then concludes 'that has no meaning, absolutely none, just words' (p. 49). Similarly, Sasha Jansen, in *Good Morning, Midnight*, rejects common religion and the false, hypocritical morality upon which it is based, when she says, after the death of her baby, 'God is very cruel … A Devil, of course' (p. 116). These Nietzschean reversals of meanings and of values reveal extremely intelligent women characters of remarkable insight and extraordinarily perceptive observation, freed from the imagination-deadening, stereotyped responses of successful, mediocre, 'proper' women. Rhys' endings give the reader no hint, moreover, of any future for these 'distinguished minds and generous natures', other than a stultifying repetition of the same, except that in their small, incredibly determined ways, the only ways open to them, they continue to reject conformity and mediocrity for the sake of that precious shred of individuality, won only (in the power–money–sex complex euphemistically called society) at the price of comfort and respectability.

6

Dramatic Art in Katherine Mansfield's 'Bliss'

'Bliss', first published in 1920, embodies in fifteen short pages many of the characteristics of modernist writing, and those associated with Mansfield's stories generally.[1] It has that intimacy or nearness which Frieda Lawrence spoke of ('she can come so close'),[2] while focusing on 'spots of time' – impressionistic and epiphanic moments which lead to the indeterminacy of meaning typical of much modernist fiction. 'Bliss' characteristically emphasises interiority while apparently minimising plot and action, yet symbolically relates 'exterior' effects – settings, rooms, houses, nature – to feelings. It employs the indirect free narrative point of view, that familiar shifting between narrator and central character, Bertha Young, which Dorothy Richardson practised so adeptly in *Pilgrimage*. This shifting of point of view, which undermines the authority, objectivity, and authenticity of any one view of events, is exemplary of Mansfield's well-attested ability both to project herself into people and things (with an intense Keatsian, visionary empathy), and to assume masks and personas. She thereby effected a variety of voices suggestive of Woolf's emphasis on a multiplicity of selves, in spite of a mysteriously persistent sense of a continuous self. In each story, such multiple voices overlie the main characters' perceptions. Mansfield thus simultaneously preserved some narrative distance ('Bertha knew', 'Bertha realized' – but Bertha was often wrong!) – that critical, ironic consciousness, at the same time that she entered into her characters' (and her readers') minds. Like much of her fiction, and like much modernist fiction, this story is another instance of Mansfield's delight in drawing the reader's attention not only to content, or what is happening, but how it is being narrated, or made to happen by the author through artistic techniques. Relatedly, she raised the issue of the spectator versus the spectacle, turned her characters into both observer and observed at the same time, and pressed the analogy on the reader-spectator, as she explained in the following passage:

What a QUEER business writing is! I don't know. I don't believe other people are ever as foolishly excited as I am while I'm working. How could they be? Writers would have to live in trees. I've been this man, been this women. I've stood for hours on the Auckland Wharf. I've been out in the stream waiting to be berthed – I've been a seagull hovering at the stern and a hotel porter whistling through his teeth. It isn't as though one sits and watches the spectacle. That would be thrilling enough, God knows. But one IS the spectacle for the time. If one remained oneself all the time like some writers can it would be a bit less exhausting. It's a lightning change affair, tho'.[3]

'Bliss' is also exemplary of the characteristics most often attributed to Mansfield's style, tone, and manner. It has her familiar humour – the satire modified by pathos and compassion which she employed for her knife-like criticisms of conventional relationships and social forms of behaviour, simultaneously revealing subtleties of behaviour and feeling. In 'Bliss', as in many other Mansfield (and other modernist) texts, inconsequentials – 'tremendous trifles' – are explored as sources of revelations, while imagery and 'painting' techniques borrowed from impressionist theory and practice (such as intense detail, and particularity used symbolically) abound in these few pages. That 'special prose', which delights in detail and understatement, in apparent simplicities and lucidities hiding infinitely complex and contradictory resonances of meaning, is like Miss Fulton's slender fingers, 'so pale a light seemed to come from them'. Yet, paradoxically, that very prose of light deftness hides a play of darker forces – of isolation, and failure of communication ('she only wanted to get in touch with him for a moment'). Like impressionist paintings, Mansfield's stories seem designed explicitly to draw the reader's attention to 'the act of perception itself', not only in a general, but in a specific sense. That is, the narrative techniques draw attention not only to extraordinary moments or acts of insight and perception, but to the ordinary too, in order to reveal the nature and characteristics of various types of perception, failures as well as successes of insight, blindness as well as visionary, imaginative perception.

In acquainting the reader better with perception in its multiple characters, Mansfield created the opportunity to heighten and sharpen perceptions that otherwise might remain blunted. At the same time, perception is shown to be subjective and in need of interpretation, yet the latter too is indeterminate and indecisive. Words fail, as efforts to articulate, express, and communicate are foregrounded in 'Bliss', and their tragic consequences are explored in relation to that strongly felt, but unfulfilled need for order, truth, definiteness, and exact names of things. Mansfield's 'special prose' is especially characterised by a respect for the mystery of things – for the mystery of the workings of imagination, of the quality we call aesthetic or artistic,[4] for the mystery of the fact that nature, self-consciousness, or anything at all exists. In her strong sense of the mystery of life and art, she, like Jean Rhys, Willa Cather, and so many modernist writers, adopted a powerful literary convention for expressing this mystery of perception and existence, namely, the convention of reversing the relation between life and art, so that life is like art. Life is representative of art, and not just the other way round. Closely related to this is the literary convention (expressive of existentialist philosophies) that the life of a human being is, or at least can be, a work of art through self-development: 'Art is absolutely self development.'[5]

In 'Bliss', as in many other stories, Mansfield developed this art–life metaphor in a number of ways. Sometimes she was quite explicit: in 'Bliss', Bertha's dinner guests 'reminded her of a play by Chekhov'. Other times, she made use of the dramatic and theatrical adaptations characteristic of many of Jean Rhys' novels. Not only did she adopt, and then adapt, masks, costumes, make-up, scene-settings, lightings, entrances and exits, and other obvious theatrics. She also used mistaken identities, disguises, recognition scenes, Greek tragic-irony devices, and portrayed normal social relations as brutal encounters – as 'mere' performances, melodramas, games of power, and often horrifying deceits and deception. Characters in the stories are given transparent roles which they play, often ruthlessly, often naïvely, while the reader is shown the hypocrisies and falsities they practise on each other. This drama of life – or melodrama, at times – constitutes a public performance of propriety behind which Mansfield reveals an interior life of terrors, passions, and cruelties. That 'lack of heart' of which she complained, at the root of failures of communication and of relationships, is often at centre stage, but often also hovering over the whole or implied behind the scenes. There, her passionate social criticism of prejudice and smallness of mind, or unimaginative living, remains unobtrusive, while nevertheless colouring and lighting all her stories:

> Why do people hide and withdraw and suspect – as they do? I don't think it is just shyness ... I used to. I think it is *lack of heart*: a sort of blight on them which will not let them ever come to full flower.[6]

'Bliss' is a story of endless paradox, oxymoronic at nearly every moment. The 'light in the heart' which Virginia Woolf described, the perception Woolf was reluctant to name but to which she sought to bring her reader closer,[7] is named bliss in this story. It is named, yet shown to be beyond the scope of its name, as problems of articulation and expression of feelings and perceptions (and consequently, of language and communication) become the overt subject matter of the story: how is Bertha to express or interpret the feeling she is having? She struggles to find out its meaning. (Later, interpretation comes to the front of the stage, as Bertha struggles with the meaning of the illicit love scene in the hall, of which she is the unobserved spectator.) Mansfield portrayed Bertha as both actress and spectator: she feels, and seeks to observe and understand, her feelings. She is not one of those bestial characters of D. H. Lawrence of whom Mansfield complained, characters denied imagination, humans reduced to sexual animals. Mansfield, like Henry James before, and like so many of her contemporaries, kept the matter of meaning and interpretation at an overt level, goading the reader out of passive spectatorship, into participation in the spectacle, the play, into self-consciousness about the act of reading and writing, and of interpreting.[8]

The story 'Bliss' is spaced into five separate 'acts', which in turn are divided into several scenes. The third act is twice the length of the other acts, while the various scenes range from less than half a page to one and a half pages. Given that Mansfield's fiction (and modernism in general) is associated with a rejection of conventional plot structure and dramatic action in favour of impressionistic evocations of epiphanic moments, it may be surprising to discover just how carefully dramatically structured this story, and many other Mansfield stories, turn out to be. Like Kate Chopin and Jean Rhys, who frequently resorted to dramatic devices, and who constructed highly plotted, structured novels, Mansfield's 'Bliss' adapts conventional dramatic techniques to create a powerful fusion of drama and impressionistic narrative fiction. Such a story as 'Bliss' (not to mention many of Mansfield's other short stories), challenges the notions that modernist fiction largely dispensed with, (or even de-emphasised) plot, action, drama, structure, shape, development, and so on.[9] In this story, such devices are not rejected or even muted, but strikingly, effectively adapted: their power remains, but is used for new experiences, new purposes, and in innovative ways. Drama, plot, structure, development, action, characterisation, dialogue – these conventions are used in the service of the greater expression of the interior life, though not at the expense of social relations and externalised dramatics which provide a social-realist context. Mansfield's stories and many other modernist fictions, then, are not quite accurately described as rejecting such conventions, so much as for wrenching them away from traditional emphasis on the realistic representation of external, social, public relations, which relegate interiority to the sidelines or even into virtual non-existence. One could argue that Mansfield artfully hid the 'mechanics' of her stories, as artists need to do, according to Willa Cather and others:

[artists must] present their scene by suggestion rather than by enumeration. The higher processes of art are all processes of simplification. The novelist must learn to write, and then he must unlearn it ... to subordinate it to a higher and truer effect ... The material investiture of the story is presented as if unconsciously; by the reserved, fastidious hand of an artist, not by the gaudy fingers of a showman or the mechanical industry of a department store window-dresser ....

Whatever is felt upon the page without being specifically named there–that, one might say, is created. It is the inexplicable presence of the thing not named, of the overtone divined by the ear but not heard by it, the verbal mood, the emotional aura of the fact or the thing or the deed, that gives high quality to the novel ...[10]

According to Cather, previous fiction and drama had allowed the mechanics to obtrude too distractingly on the reader or observer, blocking the view of the inner life of characters. Modernists sought to clear the stage for the (no less dramatic) presentation of the equally real inner worlds, the worlds of Miriam Henderson, Mrs Dalloway, Professor St Peter, Anna and Sasha, Mary Olivier,

Pompey, Gilman's 'mad-woman', and others. The power of much modernist fiction seems to come not from rejecting or dispensing with conventional (even many 'realist') strategies and techniques, but from turning them to new and imaginatively stimulating ends. Modernists made possible the previously neglected dramatic representation of the world within, hardly, however, 'dispensing' with the outer world. The latter is constantly involved, even if at times sparingly; even if the interior life has centre stage most of the time, 'public' life and social relations are constantly evoked through metaphor and symbol, used indeed to reinforce and give context and meaning (however indeterminate) to the psychological realm of subjective experience. Modernists, one can argue, achieved a more comprehensive representation of human experience by seeking their emphasis, their relative unity, within the conscious-ness of a character, thus providing a powerful focus for the externalities of social relations, the latter being the evoked context for the former as centre.

Correspondingly, while the 'mechanics', the overt conventions of earlier narrative and drama, were partially hidden from immediate view (though not rejected), what has previously been hidden in more traditional, familiar literature was brought to the forefront, namely, language, on the one hand, and subjective interiority on the other. Language is no longer allowed to be neutral, objective, transparent, taken for granted in its effects and workings, treated as a tool for expressing already experienced and formulated feelings and experiences. Language is, by Mansfield, brought to centre stage along with non-authoritative, non-objective, indeterminate experi-ences, characters, and points of view. While rarely the overt subject matter, it still breaks forth systematically, noticeably disrupting the surface subject matter, as characters muse on how to express themselves, on the inadequacy of words, on failures of communica-tion, on how to interpret words, actions, people, and relations, on the difficulty of grasping any definite meaning to events, to life, to experience.[11] Language, no longer treated as a merely neutral medium of the expression of pre-existent realities, has taken on the same importance in Mansfield's stories as the materials and mediums, or tools and techniques, of impressionistic painting. Impressionistic painters foregrounded these materials and tech-niques, while subject matter became the vehicle of expression, the means for experimenting with the qualities and textures of paints, of colours, of brush strokes, of techniques of perspective, lighting, shading, and so on. The primary aim of accurate representation gave way, both in literature and in painting, to greater and more conscious attention to acts of representing. Or rather (since most artists can be seen always to have been conscious of their materials and activities *qua* artists), the spectator's attention is no longer directed away from, but explicitly directed toward the materiality of art, whether in literature, painting, or music. For Mansfield and other writers, attention to the characteristics of her medium, language, led to knowledge of human psychology and experience, since language is inextricably bound up with the human mind. Perception and consciousness are structured by language, while language is expressive of the nature of our mental make-up.

In 'Bliss', Mansfield's emphatic dramatisation of language and the interior life is staged on a firm, highly complex, structurally sophisticated, and clearly developed dramatic base, contrary to much general opinion. Act One is composed of three remarkably effective scenes, the first outside the house, the second in the dining room, the third in the nursery. Act Two moves to a 'trivial' telephone conversation redolent of failed communication, and a drawing-room scene. Act Three, nearly double the length of the other four acts, is a 'play within a play', so to speak, moving from entrance hall and the 'entrance' or 'arrival' of four different sets of guests or players at varying spaces in time, to the drawing-room, and finally ends in the dining room. This complex structure of a play within a play is reinforced by Bertha's self-conscious comparison of her 'party' of friends, her 'decorative group', to 'a play by Chekhov' (p. 104). A few sentences later, in the merged narrator–Bertha point of view, Harry's 'pose – his – something or other', is drawn to the reader's attention, while Bertha has reached an apparent pitch of spectatorship, hardly seeming to participate at all in the play. She is the audience and even the critic (though this self-watching and observation of others goes on throughout the story-play). Act Four, the shortest of the acts, comprises the moment when Bertha shares the pear-tree experience with Miss Fulton. On the basis of this shared experience, Bertha completely misinterprets relationships among Miss Fulton, Harry, and Bertha herself. Finally, in Act Five, Bertha is thrown unwittingly into the (this time) devastating role of observer of other people's actions, only moments after apparently having 'awakened' sexually for the first time in her life.

If 'Bliss' is not dramatic and action-packed in the conventional sense, it is nevertheless an intense, psychological drama which adheres, ironically enough, to the three unities of time, place, and manner, most decorously. Its development is carefully plotted, its groundwork for a shattering revelation beautifully prepared, and its exquisite shape and unity assured. Meanwhile, throughout the story-play, the pear tree appears and reappears at rare but crucial moments as an elusive symbol of art, imagination, mystery, and love – and sexuality – and their transience. The pear tree occurs as either remembered or seen; it is seen only three times in the story, in Acts Two, Four, and Five (though mentioned in Acts Two, Three, and Five), its imagistic, symbolic significance vastly increased by its eminence at the end of the story. It seems almost an emblem of Bertha's bliss and her blissful sexual awakening, while it is never-theless complicated by the sinister appearance (on Bertha's first view of it) of a 'grey cat, dragging its belly [across] the lawn, and a black one, in its shadow, trail[ing] after' (p. 100). On this occasion, Bertha experiences a 'curious shiver' and, finding the cats creepy, turns away, only to conclude, in spite of the sinister cats, that the pear tree is 'a symbol of her own life'. The cats, however, reappear right at the end of the story, in a simile equating the grey cat with Miss Fulton and the black one with Eddie Warren (p. 109). The complexities and 'darker forces' lurking within and behind life are deftly, and humorously, portrayed (cat equals seducer of husband), while the natural transience of the blossoming pear tree seems to belong to an acceptable natural cycle of life and death; there is nothing sinister in this natural process of blossom, fruit, and decay.[12] Perversity enters in with the dragging (pregnant?) cat pursued by the other cat – an imagistic, grotesque artistic representation of the shameless deceit of Harry and Miss Fulton, practised in front of Bertha to throw her off the scent of their affair. (Notably, not the affair, but the deception practised by Harry and Miss Fulton, is what the details of the story expose). The cats, moreover, seem an ironic portrayal of Mansfield's criticism of D. H. Lawrence's writing:

> Lawrence denies his humanity. He denies the powers of the Imagination. He denies Life – I mean *human* life. His hero and heroine are non-human. They are animals on the prowl. They do not feel: they scarcely speak. There is not one memorable word. They submit to the physical response and for the rest go veiled – blind – *faceless* – *mindless*. This is the doctrine of mindlessness ... here is life where one has blasphemed against the spirit of reverence.[13]

The multiple connotations of the pear tree, with its emblematic appearances and reappearances carefully spaced throughout the story, are exemplary of the modernist's use, and specifically Mansfield's use, of imagery as a unifying and structuring principle, and as a source of meaning, indeterminate meaning, that is. To Bertha, the tree is a symbol of her life (and death), to the reader it seems a symbol of Bertha's apparent sexual awakening with its 'wide open blossoms' and fruits, and with its comparison both to 'the flame of a candle' (p. 106), and to Miss Fulton ('It would be silver now', 'silver as Miss Fulton, who sat there turning a tangerine in her slender fingers ....'; p. 105). Yet, in its serenity and stillness, invoked throughout, in its perfection, its silverness, it is suggestive of some mystery beyond living things, beyond time, suggestive of a realm of stillness and eternity.[14] In this fusion of the concrete and natural with the timeless and supernatural, the pear tree becomes a symbol of imagination, art, and culture. The three scenes in which the pear tree is actually seen (as opposed to the three times it is referred to) are examples of Virginia Woolf's 'moments of being', imaginative moments charged with an intensity of feeling and insight distinct from more ordinary life.[15] These viewings of the pear tree, twice by Bertha alone and once with Miss Fulton (no one else sees it), are emblematic of imaginative experiences, visionary experiences, though the first two viewings are different in response from the final viewing by a devastated Bertha, for whom no doubt the pear tree no longer seems a symbol of her life, but of what she had naïvely thought was her life. Yet the ending of the story, asserting that 'the pear tree was as lovely as ever and as full of flower and as still', may suggest the possibility of some kind of imaginative transcendence for Bertha herself. She too could perhaps be 'as lovely as ever and as full of flower and as still', if she could transcend her despair in an act of imagination which sustains her bliss and self-worth in the face of deception and loss of her romantic illusions.

Thus, in the image of the tree, one can see a fusion of various metaphors: nature, in the form of the tree, is a symbol of an individual life lived imaginatively, just as much as it is a symbol of sexuality and sexual awakening. Through such metaphor, the relative opposition between nature and human life is overcome. Yet the pear tree also symbolises art and imagination, with its stillness, perfection, and beauty: thus art, nature, and the human are inter-related in a few deft strokes. The three actual viewings of the tree suggest intense 'moments of being'. Even the three mentionings of the tree are powerfully evocative – once it is made to be a symbol of Bertha's life, once it is compared with Miss Fulton. All experiences of the pear tree constitute imaginative revelations, or acts. Another analogy operates, however, which is suggestive of the relation between the story and the reader: the pear tree is the work of art, like the story, while Bertha and Miss Fulton are appreciative observers or readers of it (the rest of the characters ignore it, though they know it is there). The response of the two women becomes an emblem of imaginative perception in general and of imaginative reading in particular. The complex of metaphorical and symbolical connotations of the pear-tree image as a unifying, structuring, artistic principle of rich but indeterminate meaning turns out, moreover, to be emblematic of the story itself, and a centre of imagery around which turn other images which enrich the texture of the language by being emblematic of reading and imaginative perception. The most obviously relevant example of self-conscious imagery suggestive of reading analogies is in Act One, scene two, when Bertha has gained entrance to the house and finds herself in the dining room. An extended metaphor is developed by Mansfield in this scene, as Bertha begins an elaborately described process of arranging the fruit for her dinner party. The entire scene, a metaphor of artistic creation and composition, is itself a still-life composition in language. Yet it also becomes a metaphor for the spectator–reader, as Bertha is made to step back to criticise and evaluate her work, just as the reader is doing. The fruit arrangement involves, moreover, emphatic relationship to its setting, as we are told that Bertha had (admittedly fancifully), bought purple grapes to 'bring the carpet up to the table' (p. 96). The whole room, the context of the bowl of fruit, is included in Bertha's domestic artistry, the result of which is something nearly as magical as the pear tree: 'the dark table seemed to melt into the dusky light and the glass dish and the blue bowl to float in the air. This, of course in her present mood, was so incredibly beautiful … She began to laugh' (p. 96).[16]

The bowl of fruit does contain 'some yellow pears, smooth as silk' (p. 96), which link the scene to the pear-tree image. Directly after the fruit-arrangement scene, Bertha goes up to the nursery to see her baby, her own body's fruit, though a fruit of unwakened sexuality, as is later insinuated. There she has a Blakean, if muted, battle with the archetypal Blakean nurse who tries to prevent

Bertha from holding, feeding, and playing with her baby. These two scenes share with scene one, staged outside the house, the characteristic of imaginative, joyful experience, and are explicitly suggestive of the anti-realist metaphor of life as art. Outside the house, before arriving at the door, Bertha is discovered in an ecstatic state about 'nothing, simply'. She compares her fear of experiencing her joy fully (out of a sense of propriety) with an unplayed musical instrument: 'Why be given a body if you have to keep it shut up in a case like a rare, rare fiddle?' (p. 95). Later, in a brutally ironic prognostication of what is to come, she complains, 'Why have a baby if it has to be kept – not in a case like a rare, rare fiddle – but in another woman's arms?' (p. 97). Sexuality, infidelity, and jealousy lurk behind these comments, yet Mansfield seemed at pains to charge her predominant images of pear tree, fruit, baby, and fiddle with self-referential implications about artistic creation. The story is her baby, her fruit-arrangement, her (well-played) rare fiddle, and pear tree, while the analogical reference to the reader–critic–spectator as imaginative participant works at another, visible level. For, immediately, Bertha retracts her fiddle metaphor for her body: 'No, that about the fiddle is not quite what I mean' ... 'it's not what I mean because –', she breaks off, unfinished (p. 95). Yet the fiddle-image comes up again later, so that while it may not be sufficient for her meaning, it certainly has considerable force. Each of the scenes in Act One has illustrated, through powerful imagery, an imaginative experience, though in scene three it is achieved only by conflict, and in scene one the inadequacy of language is a theme on equal footing with that of 'bliss'. In the next four acts, imaginative experiences emblematic of artistic creation and imaginative reading alternate and mix with failures of imagination or sinister prognostications. Harry phones, and Bertha tries to tell her 'bliss', but he silences her with his lack of interest. In the drawing room, after the telephone scene, she sees the pear tree for the first time, but the cats slink past, prophesying despair and deceit.[17] Throughout the following acts, moments of intense feeling alternate with mediocrity, banality, and stunning deceptions, creating powerfully contrasting states of artistry in life and banality in life, the latter usually mitigated by gently satiric and humorous gestures, but always analogies of unimaginative reading responses, that 'lack of heart' expressive of a blight on human life.

The final scenes of the story chart, first, the joy of shared communion which Bertha achieves with Miss Fulton (just as she had not, contrastingly, achieved it with her preoccupied husband or her other guests, whom she watches with a mixture of fond humour and disappointment). Secondly, these last scenes chart the alleged sexual awakening, 'something strange and almost terrifying ... For the first time in her life Bertha Young desired her husband' (p. 107). Bertha further asks, in a voice merged with that of the narrator, 'Was this what that feeling of bliss had been leading to? But then – '(p. 108); she breaks off, again, and the 'party' is over. The penultimate moment of these carefully charted developments of the story is the shattering 'view' Bertha inadvertently gains of Harry (her husband) and Miss Fulton in a passionate embrace in the hallway, planning a tryst for the morrow. The fourth and final dramatic moment is the ironic pathos of her cry 'Oh, what is going to happen now?' (p. 110), as ironic an ending for a story-play, as was Jean Rhys' ending-beginning in *Voyage in the Dark*, or Woolf's *Between the Acts*.[18] This is the last word, except for the still, silent, 'unanswering' pear tree.

Throughout the story, from beginning to end, Bertha was dramatised as struggling with forces that prevented her from expressing and experiencing her joy to the full. Her body mustn't dance, run, bowl hoops, or laugh (p. 95), she mustn't laugh at the beauty of her fruit-bowl effect: 'No, no, I'm getting hysterical' (p. 96). She mustn't play with her baby or criticise the nurse in any way, though the baby's unrepressed joy helped her overcome that first constraint, at least. She mustn't try Harry's patience by sharing her efforts to describe her bliss. The censors are within and without: 'I'm absurd. Absurd!' (p. 100). She represses herself in conversation with Eddie (p. 102); later, 'she had to talk because of her desire to laugh' (p. 105), which she mustn't do too much of, she even 'had to dig her nails into her hands – so as not to laugh too much' (p. 105). Harry destroys her shared communion with Miss Fulton in their viewing of the pear tree, by 'snapping on the light' (p. 106), and later, when she becomes sexually aroused, she races over to the piano for cover. Throughout these examples of inhibition, repression, and censorship, metaphors suggestive also of literary constraints emerge. As in *The Awakening* of Chopin, Mansfield toyed constantly with the problem of literary decorum, with the pressures of literary conventions and traditions, and with the constraints or censorship by critics and readers. Both 'Bliss' and *The Awakening*, partly through their metaphors of artefacts and natural fruits, suggest a constant, clearly defined sub-text of women writers (indeed, of all innovative writers) struggling against the forces of tradition, not to mention a world of mediocrity which is often incapable of appreciating originality. That Bertha so often suppresses her joy and especially her laughter (and that her sexuality had been long suppressed, like Edna Pontelier's – even in marriage) has implications for artistic experimentation.

The close relationship between humour (or 'wit') and imaginativeness suggests an analogous struggle for freedom in artistic delights paralleling sexual and social struggles. Decorousness in art and life are not rejected, but their abuse, their tyranny over playfulness and imaginativeness, is challenged. Limits and rules are questioned, as texts depict dilemmas which raise more questions than they answer. How far can one go with laughter, with sex, with love, with creativity, with innovations, before one 'ought' to stop? Mansfield challenged artistic and literary proprieties, and, in the process, challenged, through analogies and suggestive images many social and political constraints. Moreover, her texts examined the effects of such constraints on not only women, but men. Her analyses are not simplistic; she does not portray women as victims and men as perpetrators or victors. Rather, women are shown to be as much enslaved by themselves as by society or by men (as Blake argued tirelessly), and especially by the 'insipid idea that love is the only thing in the world'. Men, moreover, are shown to suffer from the emotional immaturity and dependency that results from their own enslavement to money, success, and sexual prowess. Mansfield, like Rhys, Chopin, and Wharton, developed the realist theme of portraying the individual as inherently comprehensible only in relation to the context, the environment, the social–political–cultural world in which she lives. Each of them portrayed this relationship with different techniques which emphasised different aspects of it, while never losing sight, as many realists did, of the interdependent nature of the individual and the community. For often in realist writings we find an implicit assumption that society and history are somehow anterior to individuality and art, whereas modernists subvert this hierarchical misconception.

The failure of relationships which results from male and female immaturity is in the background and foreground of many of Mansfield's stories, just as it is in Chopin, Rhys, Woolf, Bowles, Stevie Smith, Richardson, and others. The analogous implications for artist and reader are always in view, if one only chooses to look, to 'step into the blue', 'to risk things'. If 'Bliss' is in part a dramatic

representation of peoples' lives as performances, roles, and stereotypes, and of the often stereotyped inner life these roles mask, it
also raises the question of reader's role as well as artist's. Bertha's
problem of how to liberate herself into her bliss is also the reader's
problem. How to read less constrainedly, less fearfully, how to
laugh more when we read, to dare to see the humour, satire, and
irony with which artists criticise so much that is mediocre, but
nevertheless familiar and prevalent. How to laugh at our prejudices, notions, and values, to learn imaginatively to scrutinise and
question without fear, to delight in difference? 'Bliss' is an exhorta-
tion to move from unrestrained seriousness, in art, in life, in reading, and to move toward delight, humour, desire, joy, bliss, and
laughter. Bertha's expectation at the beginning of the story is a
metaphor (as Beckett's *Godot* demonstrates) for the reader's 'waiting
for something ... divine to happen ... that she knew must happen
... infallibly' (p. 96).[19] Mistaken expectations, like characters'
erroneous interpretations, preconceived notions, or failures of
communication and inadequate expressions, form a rich texture of
self-referential thematics, in which artist and reader cannot afford
to remain spectators unconscious of their activities of perception
and reading, but must become participants responding to the
subtleties, artistry, and analogies of the story with delight. Without
such self-conscious reading, there is a tendency to become passive,
censorious moralisers who generalise and reduce to taboos the
materials, structures, and thematics of the work. Social hypocrisy
and personal deceit are a major theme of the story, then, and, they
have direct relevance to artistic issues of integrity to one's vision,
and to critical issues of genuinely imaginative reading and response.
The shared communion between Bertha and her husband's
mistress, Miss Fulton, indicates that no simple condemnation of the
affair is relevant.[20] The reason for Bertha's late awakening to
sexuality (her husband's partial responsibility for this), Bertha's
naïve illusions about love 'as the only thing in the world', her
husband's apparent immaturity and readiness to deceive, Miss
Fulton's ambivalence – her sincerity with Bertha and later
insincerity, the extent and nature of the deceit – all these issues lurk
underdetermined behind the fabric of this special prose, which is
its own reward rather than being the vehicle for any moralising or
overt, specifically ascertainable social criticism.

Such 'special prose'[21] can be characterised in a number of ways. Indeed, in the first sentence of the story the reader is shown a fine example of one of these characteristics:

> Although Bertha Young was thirty she still had moments like this when she wanted to run instead of walk, to take dancing steps on and off the pavement, to bowl a hoop, to throw something up in the air and catch it again, or to stand still and laugh at – nothing – at nothing, simply.   (p. 95)

This sentence reveals the character of self-referentiality of much modernist language, in demonstrating syntactically what it describes semantically. Bertha wants to run not walk, to dance, to bowl a hoop, and so on; and in a sense the sentence does just that linguistically. Indeed, much of Mansfield's prose strives precisely with Bertha's dilemma: 'Oh, is there no way you can express it without being 'drunk and disorderly'?' (p. 95). To some readers, modernist prose fails, for it is precisely disorderly, in bad taste, nonsense, meaningless, and unreadable. Mansfield did not entirely escape censure, though it was more for the alleged waste of her fine style on the insipidity of her themes (those being merely domestic, social relations, like Jane Austen's, instead of being exciting adventures at sea, at warfare, or in politics).

'Bliss', it was suggested, is a highly dramatic, structured story fused with modernist concerns of attending to the materiality of art (especially language, in this case) and the indeterminacy of meaning or experience, itself. At the 'heart' of the story lies an interpretive dilemma as to how to make meaning of what happened to Bertha, much less what will happen afterwards (suggestive of the 'domestic discord' at the end of Woolf's *Between the Acts*).

Ostensibly, the story is about bliss – whatever that is – and the first few paragraphs make it clear how difficult it is to describe it:

> What can you do if you are thirty and, turning the corner of your own street, you are overcome, suddenly, by a feeling of bliss – absolute bliss! – as though you'd suddenly swallowed a bright piece of that late afternoon sun and it burned in your bosom, sending out a little shower of sparks into every particle, into every finger and toe? ... Oh, is there no way you can express it

without being 'drunk and disorderly'? How idiotic civilization is! Why be given a body if you have to keep it shut up in a case like a rare, rare fiddle?   (p. 95)

The difficulty of determining the meaning of this feeling called bliss is raised again and again throughout the story. Sometimes bliss seems to be a child-like certainty that something 'divine' will happen (p. 96), sometimes it takes the form of joy in Bertha's baby's perfect body (p. 98); later it is named, 'the spring':

> How strong the jonquils smelled in the warm room. Too strong? Oh, no. And yet, as though overcome, she flung down on a couch and pressed her hands to her eyes.
> 'I'm too happy – too happy!' she murmured.
> And she seemed to see on her eyelids the lovely pear tree with its wide open blossoms as a symbol of her own life ...
> 'I'm absurd. Absurd!' She sat up; but she felt quite dizzy, quite drunk. It must have been the spring.
> Yes, it was the spring. Now she was so tired she could not drag herself upstairs to dress.

After that, it is a 'fire of bliss', a shared moment of profound (p. 100) almost sexual intimacy with Miss Fulton (p. 103); then it is the shared view of the pear tree when 'prefect understanding occurs' (p. 106). Finally, bliss is said to be an ardent awakening to sexual desire, yet Bertha herself seems disappointed with this outcome, this univocal determination, namely, that her feelings of bliss in all their various, joyous forms throughout the afternoon could be reduced to any univocal meaning, such as sexual desire (p. 108). However, a careful reading suggests that Mansfield is ironising precisely such a D. H. Lawrence reduction of everything 'blissful' to sex. Perhaps Bertha's arousal is not so much ardent passion as overwhelming jealousy, an intimation that whatever she may have (really or imaginatively) shared with Miss Fulton, her husband shares far more. Mansfield's irony on this matter verges on the cruel, as she has Bertha remark: 'I shall try to tell you when we are in bed tonight what has been happening. What she and I have shared' (p. 107). This immediately follows the 'something strange and almost terrifying' which 'darted into Bertha's mind'. Shortly after, the 'narrator' interprets this something terrifying as sexual arousal and awakening passion for Harry. The reader is left to ponder this interpretation and to ask whether, far from being sexual desire, Bertha hasn't gleaned an intimation of the sexual passion between Harry and Miss Fulton – the Miss Fulton she 'found' and perhaps for whom she herself (like her husband) felt a strong sexual attraction, quickly displaced on to Harry, out of guilt and repression. Miss Fulton seems to arouse ardent feelings without regard for the sex of the aroused one. Bertha (or is it the 'narrator'?) asks: 'What was there in the touch of that cool arm that could fan – fan – start blazing – blazing – the fire of bliss that Bertha did not know what to do with?' (p. 183). Later, this bliss becomes shared imaginative response to the overwhelming beauty of the pear tree:

> And the two women stood side by side looking at the slender, flowering tree. Although it was so still it seemed, like the flame of a candle, to stretch up, to point, to quiver in the bright air, to grow taller as they gazed – almost to touch the rim of the round, silver moon. How long did they stand there? Both, as it were, caught in that circle of unearthly light, understanding each other perfectly, creatures of another world, and wondering what they were to do in this one with all this blissful treasure that burned in their bosoms and dropped, in silver flowers, from their hair and hands?
>
> For ever – for a moment? And did Miss Fulton murmur: 'Yes. Just *that*.' Or did Bertha dream it?   (p. 106)

One can hardly do justice to the fine intricacies of the language and structure of a story like 'Bliss' by interpreting such moments as mere illusions on Bertha's part, or deceit on Miss Fulton's. The hidden as well as overt allusions to Bertha and Miss Fulton's intimacy are too powerful and too often repeated to be discounted. The difficulty of assessing 'what has happened' extends into the depths of the general situation described in 'Bliss', so much so that we cannot afford even to 'authorise' the surface narrator's overt interpretations, such as, for example, that the supercharged atmosphere created by Harry's and Miss Fulton's affair has aroused Bertha's own desire for Harry. Perhaps it has awakened her to desire, perhaps to jealousy, perhaps to fear, perhaps to all three. Perhaps Bertha is more jealous of Harry than of Miss Fulton, for his intruding on her intimacy with and love for the other woman, which she dare not admit to her consciousness. Meanwhile, the pear tree seems 'to stretch up, to point, to quiver in the bright air, to grow taller as they gazed – almost to touch the rim of the round, silver moon' (p. 106). A sexual metaphor perhaps, but not merely sexual, nor merely phallic. For the pear tree also suggests the fruiting of the womb, and as such is a complex image suggestive of male and female desire, artistic creativity, and fecundity of language to create a world of experience and art, not merely to express what is already there and known.

'Bliss' is one of Mansfield's most intricate stories. With regard to structure, we can see the dinner party as the centre-piece, around which the other elaborately designed metaphors for imaginative encounters occur, such as the flower arranging, the scene with the baby and Nurse, the meditation on fiddles and dancing at the beginning of the story, and the shared intimacy with Miss Fulton through the aesthetic appreciation of the pear tree. In terms of imagery, the pear tree is the major unifying element; recurring as it does at crucial moments throughout the story, it becomes a structural element as well as the central, unifying image. Thematic-ally, the story is unified by recurring descriptions of Bertha's experiences of bliss, brutally disrupted near the end by her devasting view of her husband passionately embracing Miss Fulton. This disruption of Bertha's bliss is exacerbated by Mansfield, as it follows excruciatingly on Bertha's own sexual awakening. She experienced 'something strange and almost terrifying', which the narrator interprets: 'for the first time in her life Bertha Young desired her husband' (p. 107). The aesthetic effect of the story, 'Bliss', upon the reader is intensified by the above mentioned structural, thematic, and imagistic congruences and unities. Nor should the power of the 'play within the story' be underestimated. As in Woolf's *Between the Acts* or Cather's *Professor's House*, such a framework–centre-piece structure has the effect of creating layers of meaning, meta-fictional viewpoints, and tends to turn the story inside-out, so that relations between art and reality are reversed as, for example, Bertha sees her dinner party as a play by Chekhov, and becomes a member of the audience of her own 'play-story'. In using the dinner-party setting as the mode for her central effect, Mansfield also drew on powerful conventional associations and connotations: parties, holidays, excursions, masquerades, circuses, theatres – all of these extraordinary events connote imaginative experience, and act as metaphors for occasions of aesthetic response, whether in writing or in reading. That is, reading a story is 'like' going to a party or on an outing; it is a kind of 'feast', symbolically speaking, in which the reader partakes actively. Mansfield thereby created a meta-fictional centre-piece of self-consciousness and self-observation: the reader, like Bertha, becomes aware of herself in the act of reading – of trying to interpret the story as Bertha is trying to interpret the characters. Characteristically self-referring, Mansfield has Bertha utterly misread the behaviour of others. This misreading is revealed, ironically, when Bertha fetches a book, thereby gaining a new 'view' of the actual situation. Earlier, during the narration of the dinner party, Mansfield's determination to use every detail of the story to effect is illustrated. The topic of conversation is a play, described so as to refer indirectly to Bertha's own play–life:

He wants to write a play for me. One act. One man. Decides to commit suicide. Gives all the reasons why he should and why he shouldn't. And just as he has made up his mind either to do it or not to do it – curtain.   (p. 104)

In May, 1908, Mansfield had written a journal entry which is profoundly instructive for reading a story like 'Bliss':

I feel that I do now realise, dimly, what women in the future will be capable of. They truly as yet have never had their chance. Talk of our enlightened days and our emancipated country – pure nonsense! We are firmly held with the self-fashioned chains of slavery. Yes, now I see that they are self-fashioned, and must be self-removed... To weave the intricate tapestry of one's own life, it is well to take a thread from many harmonious skeins – and to realise that there must be harmony. Not necessary to grow the sheep, comb the wool, colour and brand it – but joyfully take all that is ready, and with that saved time, go a great way further. Independence, resolve, firm purpose, and the gift of discrimination, mental clearness – here are the inevitables. Again, Will–the realisation that Art is absolutely self-development. The knowledge that genius is dormant in every soul – that that very individuality which is at the root of our being is what matters so poignantly.
   Here then is a little summary of what I need – power, wealth and freedom. It is the hopelessly insipid doctrine that love is the only thing in the world, taught, hammered into women, from

generation to generation, which hampers us so cruelly. We must get rid of that bogey – and then, then comes the opportunity of happiness and freedom.

Much of Mansfield's fiction is concerned with dramatic portrayals of these 'self fashioned chains', but also with hints and gestures about the means for removing them ourselves. Like Jean Rhys, Mansfield was inclined to the existentialist expression that the ultimate artistic achievement is self-development: 'Art is absolutely self-development.' Nearly all the women writers discussed here engage with the idea of individuality through imaginative activity, as either overt or covert theme. Distinctions between life and art collapse, for life becomes meaningful only as the art of self-development. Mansfield, like Cather, Bowles, and others, analysed and represented the stumbling blocks and hindrances 'taught, hammered into women' until women become their own victimisers. She portrayed the various forms which failures and successes take, in the struggle for individuality. In 'Bliss', as in other stories, sexual relations almost always seem to involve the stifling of individuality; only in friendship is success in any recognisable form portrayed.[22] The quintessential form success in self-realisation takes in Mansfield's stories is an aesthetic response – either to the beauty in nature or in works of art. Through imaginative encounters of the kind portrayed in 'Bliss', we 'weave the intricate tapestry of [our] lives' by realising the importance, Mansfield explained, of harmony. 'Bliss' is one of Mansfield's finest achievements of that harmony or proportion so admired by, among others, Willa Cather.[23]

7

The Multiple Realities of Stevie Smith

Stevie (Florence Margaret) Smith, born in Hull in 1902, lived from 1905 for the next sixty years in Palmers Green, working as a private secretary for a magazine publisher. She never married, and lived with her aunt for most of her life until she died in 1971 of a brain tumour.[1] Though perhaps best known as a writer of poems (whose accompanying sketches delighted readers), she first made her reputation with the book, *Novel on Yellow Paper*, published in 1936 to much praise. She then published two more novels, *Over the Frontier* (1938) – also about Pompey Casmilus, the character from her first novel, and *The Holiday* (1949), not to mention more than half a dozen collections of poems with drawings.[2] In both the poetry and prose, Stevie Smith explored such major issues as death and suicide, power and conflict, love, friendship, sex and marriage, loneliness, childhood, sanity versus madness, war, religion, and art. Though many readers are familiar with her novels, there seems to be a belief that Stevie Smith 'was first and last a poet, not a novelist. She didn't much like writing prose.'[3] This curious notion disintegrates under even a cursory examination of Stevie Smith's own attitudes to her work and to the boundary between poetry and prose: 'There is no very strong division between what is poetry and what is prose.'[4] A much better description of Stevie Smith (than the one quoted above, which assumes a 'strong division' between poetry and prose) would take account of the imaginative fusion of prose and poetry, which occurs not merely in the novels, but in the poetry as well. The original way in which Smith fused these two genres gives both her poetic prose and her poetry (so unusual that it threatens the very notion of genre with indefinability) qualities distinct from other authors' fusions.

Stevie Smith was often taken to be a children's poet, her illustrations to her poetry adding to the effect. No such restrictions can apply to her novels, with their demanding, innovative form. Like

William Blake, she was delighted that children could read her poetry, but like Blake she was also writing for adults.[5] Her accompanying drawings were often criticised as being irrelevant to the poem, and she had to fight determinedly with her publishers to keep her illustrations. On close scrutiny, the illustrations, as with Blake's illuminations, often offer a critical, ironic commentary on the text, which is probably aimed more at the adult reader. Her poetry, as well as her novels, shatters the illusion of children as innocent, naïve beings. Drawing on Blake's insights into the violent, sexual and sinister aspects of the child's mind, Smith wrote a revision of a poem of Blake's, called 'Little Boy Sick': 'I am not God's little lamb / I am God's sick tiger. / And I prowl about at night / And what most I love I bite ... '.[6] Stevie Smith also explored the painful socialisation children are put through, at home and at school; she wondered whether there wasn't some other way of growing up than by repression, since far from producing rational adults, the whole process seemed to her to lead to dehumanisation: the untamed 'tiger' of a child remains alive and destructive inside the adult. The brutality she portrayed in children (as described, for example, in *Novel on Yellow Paper*), while demolishing the illusion of childhood innocence, is designed to expose the corresponding brutality in adults: for Smith, adults are children playing at being grown-ups, while children and adults are animals in human form.

Stevie Smith's experiments in fiction (both in the novel and in the short story form), in her poetry, essays, and drawings, themselves have a type of violence, an intense and disruptive impatience with established forms – even with recently innovative forms – which seems to spring from a passionately intense individuality, determined to express itself in its own characteristic ways. Her literary achievements demonstrate the tremendous vitality and wit with which she sought to fashion new narrative conventions, new genres and forms, new languages and new ways of dealing with experience. The commitment to experimentation makes her one with the pre-modernists and modernists immediately preceding her, such as Jean Rhys, H. D., and Virginia Woolf, and her experiments also relate to those of contemporaries like Jane Bowles. As with many of the women writers discussed here, Stevie Smith's novels and poems are united by a common theme which has many variations and disguises, namely, the theme of daring to cross the frontier of security, familiarity, conventional roles, ordinariness, propriety, alleged sanity, logic, and rationality – in order to venture 'out in the world' (to use the title of Bowles' last, unfinished novel). These 'frontiers' exist in literature as well as in life, in personal psychology as well as social community, for men as well as women, in religion and in art. Stevie Smith explored imaginatively all these areas at once, by means of metaphor, irony, wit, and other rhetorical devices in her own, original, experimental ways. Nor did she accept the 'frontier' between writer and reader, as she cajoled and heckled her readers into joining in with her literary experiments. She dared to debate with her reader, instead of allowing her passively to acquiesce; Smith required her reader to read and respond in new ways to new forms. Thus, she ridiculed and, like Lawrence Sterne, fooled with readers' expectations and inflexibilities, openly toying with and branzenly manipulating her thematic content for whatever artistic purpose was at hand. Like Gertrude Stein, Smith cheerfully ran riot through linguistic and poetic properties and decorum to achieve her imaginative ends.

As with the works of her modernist contemporaries, Smith's texts were often accused of unreadability, due in part to her determination to expose as blurred and unreliable that alleged frontier or boundary between sense, or logic, and nonsense: what seems like sense is often, she showed, the purest nonsense. Nonsense, on the other hand, along with indeterminacy of meaning, opposition and inconsistency, chaos, and disorder may be as true to a more complete view of life and literary experience as is supposed sense, order, and rationality. Often, the familiar was exposed as true, or meaningful, or rational only because it was the familiar; thus, Smith challenged and questioned logic and rationality itself. Hence her encouragement to her readers to follow her in that 'mysterious passage' over the frontier from familiar, conscious territory into new worlds. Such worlds were exotic, strange, even frightening and dangerous, like the world of the unconscious; but such a passage or journey is the only means of broadening and opening out our experience of life, and our only means of experiencing the depths, and not just the surface of life. Journey and passage metaphors abound in Smith's fiction – conventional metaphors used with imaginative innovations – to express that idea so beloved by Edith Wharton and Jane Bowles, namely, that imaginative, artistic, and creative activity are journeys of the mind into new and unfamiliar territory, often of the uncharted, unmapped, unconscious realm. Another level of significance emerges, too, from Smith's journey images, namely, the idea of rites of passage from childhood to adulthood. This analogy occurs throughout Smiths', Bowles', Chopin's, May Sinclair's, and other modernists' writings, as they explore what such a passage means, how necessarily or gratuitously painful it is, and as they reveal how few humans manage to pass beyond mere beginnings. These authors explored how human beings perish in the tumult of psychological conflict without ever becoming genuine adults. They examined how destructive such retarded emotional development can be of imaginative, loving relationship; childishness in adults is revealed to be often the source of war, crime, violence, and selfishness. Yet Stevie Smith also asked what it means to be a genuine adult, and how one achieves such a remarkable state of being.

Stevie Smith's fiction is even more unreadable than her free-verse, prosy poetry, with its passionate commitment to exploring and exploding the delusory boundaries or frontiers between such dualities as reason or logic and nonsense, between conscious and unconscious, sanity and madness, life and literature/art, reality and dream, or inner (psychological) and outer (social, public) worlds. Like other modernists, she revealed the rich complexities, ambiguities, and indeterminacies of language as well as of experience itself: no matter how simple or factual they seem, language and experience are always in need of interpretation. Her playfulness with words, phrases, speech, and writing styles yields up the richness of linguistic experience, where denotation is mere surface and connotation endlessly inexhaustible. Wit, humour, irony, parody, and satire become major tools for the analysis of conventions in both life and art, and for the construction of innovative forms to enrich and expand life, literature, and experience. Like Jane Bowles, Smith systematically, in her poetry and prose, distorted and punned on clichés in language, in order to expose clichéd stereotyped thinking and feeling, thereby revealing the hackneyed, parrot-like, passive nature of most speech (and consequently, most feelings and thoughts). Smith also exposed clichés for the purpose of disrupting the logic and familiarity which repress unconsciousness and its more positive aspects, namely spontaneity, imaginativeness, and originality. She satirised and parodied worn-out modes of speech by writing just a little 'off beam' and off centre, to create, like Jane Bowles, a slightly grotesque and certainly illogical, surprising effect. Such unfamiliar writing disrupts the 'logic' and complacency of our thinking and our reader-responses, and jolts us into new modes of perception. Smith also used understatement and banality to shock the reader, and thereby exposed the way banal generalisations can create dehumanised responses to starvation, crime, and suffering. Stevie Smith was, then, deeply committed to the effort to open up our superficial experience of conscious life to a fuller knowledge of the unconscious life as well. Through puns, through the parodying of clichés and old metaphors, by off-centre effects, she sought to communicate the nature of the unconscious. In an essay called 'Too tired for Words',[7] she delighted in 'Freudian slips', which, she argued, were revealing of that otherwise hidden world. She decided, then, to abandon the appearance of surface, conscious, ordinary life in the language and style of her novels, as well as in their structures, for the sake of exploring the unconscious world of creativity and of destruction. Like Anaïs Nin, she emphasised the role of the dream as a source of knowledge about the nature of that unconscious realm which dominates our lives unless we learn to dominate it.

Smith rejected the historicist dichotomy between art and reality (which treats art as supplementary to, and occurring after, an independent reality) showing, in a modernist gesture, that life is a kind of art, which is as dependent on art as art is on life. Imaginative activity is the common character of both, informing basic perception as much as artistic creation, while structuring a multidimensional experience through its embodiment, language (*via* metaphors and images, and other figures of speech) into something intelligible and genuinely experienced. More than many modernist texts or other contemporary novels, Stevie Smith's writings assimilated Freud's insights into human experience and psychology, and transformed them into original forms (often taking issue with Freud implicitly, however, and often giving an unusual twist to Freudian insights). Her writings reveal psychological insights into the relationships between violence (for example, war) and repressed sexuality (or the analogous, closely related failure of emotional development from childishness to adulthood). She also explored ideas related to Freud's life and death instincts – and reality and pleasure principles – and plunged deeply into the human psyche to reveal in poetic and fictional representations the nature of the emotional conflicts existing below the surface of conscious life. Her artistic expressions of the inner life (and its relation to nature and society) offer readers some of the most original and imaginative interpretations of Freud's ideas today, as she avoided the frequent errors of many less gifted readers and interpreters of Freud. This does not mean that Stevie Smith was 'a Freudian', however. She learned from Freud while nevertheless overcoming relative dualities instead of emphasising their separateness, seeing the importance of the metaphoric and metonymic language used in Freud's discourse, while cutting through the patriarchal and phallocentric prejudices which blurred his vision.[8]

Another related aspect of Stevie Smith's writing is her powerful representation of 'sanity' and its relation to 'madness'. In her poetry and novels, this theme, like the theme of going 'out in the world' (that is growing up, for example, or becoming sane), is always present at some analogical level. Like more recent novelists such as Doris Lessing, Margaret Atwood, or Nadine Gordimer, Stevie Smith recognised the relativity of such concepts, both in the sense that they change historically, and in the sense that at any given moment in history they are problematic.[9] As Charlotte Perkins Gilman, Kate Chopin, and others had shown, Stevie Smith revealed how notions of sanity are ideologically inspired – designed, that is, to maintain the *status quo* of power, prestige, money, sex-relations, and so on. Warfare, for example, becomes a metaphor in *Over the Frontier* for the insanity of accepted social practices, since less drastic, less overtly violent practices accepted as 'normal' social behaviour are implicated in novel as well, such as the power–social relations between men and women. Indeed, one of Smith's novels, *The Holiday*, has strong undercurrents suggesting that such conventions as marriage are, like warfare, examples of battles, conflicts, and insanity. These insights relate to Blakean connotations of the 'battle between the sexes' as an insane arena of physical and mental violence not only tolerated, but created by our social arrangements. Here Smith seems to be indebted also to Jane Austen's powerfully ironic revelations of the pressures of society to conform to insane arrangements as the only means of securing freedom from poverty, ridicule, or exclusion. Much of Smith's portrayal of the complex and non-dualistic, functional relation between concepts of sanity and madness is achieved (as with her other analyses of alleged dualities) not only through the thematics of her texts and poems, but through her language, style, poetic and novelistic structures, and through vigorously expressive imagery, metaphor, and analogy. Like the human mind, her texts and poems are constructed as palimpsests, not only with layerings of meaning to express topological Freudian metaphors of conscious, preconscious, and unconscious. She also used the 'natural' richness and inevitably suggestive quality of language – along with easily available distortions of familiar words, phrases, and grammatical (syntactical and semantic) and literary forms – to 'picture' the unconscious escaping or emptying into consciousness. She thereby disrupted neat dualities and challenged the acceptability of familiar uses of language and its conventions, as these commonplaces are made to yield up the very violence (and often, obscenity) which lives within them. That is, repression and the stifling of imagination is one of Smith's constant themes, but repression in all its forms, in the domain of the sexual, in the area of literature and imagination, and in the areas of food and dress, social manners, roles, and more public, political life.

One of Stevie Smith's main literary devices in her poems and novels is to blur or challenge boundaries as anything more than relative conveniences in need on constant reassessment. Smith's primary tool is her novel use of language, as she turns logic, grammar, syntax, and meaning on their heads, getting her ideas for such inversions and distortions from her powerful sense of humour. Humour is then united with 'tragic' themes of suffering, death, abortion, illness, violence, and cruelty, to overcome that frontier, too, the one between tragedy and comedy. She constructed her novels and poems on the bedrock of a Jane Bowles-type tragicomedy. This tone of witty compassion permeates her texts, though at times a wry impatience with self-importance, dogmatism, and pedantry can bring out an acerbic edge unsoftened by tolerance. One of Smith's favourite targets of unbridled, knife-like ridicule is dogmatism, whether in art, religion, politics, or social life. Like Dorothy Richardson's Miriam, who brutally ridiculed strongly held opinions, Smith joked her readers out of certainties and complacency, showed them the many-sided nature of every issue, and reminded us that every view is, as in fiction and poetry, only a point of view, not *the* point of view. Narrative techniques involving stream of consciousness, not dissimilar to those of Mansfield and Richardson, reinforce this insistence that while subjective, personal experience may only be the starting point for reflection and interpretation, the stopping point is only a relative pause, and never a final, objective one, just as no view is ideologically neutral. While Smith's exposure of ideology in conventions of language, life, and literature takes that form of the 'off-centredness' in style of such writers as Bowles, she often (especially in the poetry) adopted Flannery O'Connor's and, earlier, Djuna Barnes' and Jean Rhys'[10] thematic use of the deformed, the maimed, or the outcast from respectable society, to deliver home to readers the O'Connor belief that each one of us is deformed spiritually and morally. Or, put another way, we are essentially isolated and alienated from communion with others, in part due to our egotism and unimaginativess (a theme Carson McCullers made central to her texts).[11] This idea of failure of communication and the resulting human apartness is explored less through characterisation (except in *The Holiday*) than through style, imagery, and language. Masks, disguises, and veils, metaphors for our stereotyped roles, hide us not only from each other, but most of all from ourselves. Stevie Smith, like Bowles, Mansfield, Barnes, and other writers, saw fear as at the source of these subterfuges: fear of the violent and powerful forces within us over which we have little control. These forces we are taught only to repress, so that we are condemned to live out our lives beneath the surface of consciousness, where such passions wreak havoc in our ordinary relations, not overtly perhaps, but no less destructively for the covert violence and resulting failure of relationships. Stevie Smith, and other modernist writers, did not believe, however, that fear alone explained the need for masks, disguises, and veils. Like Mansfield and others, she made explicitly clear her belief that the notion of any intelligible reality, that is, any single, individual self or identify behind the masks – or behind language or art – is incomprehensible.[12] It is not a question of a choice between the true self or disguises, truthful language or metaphors, the real world or fiction, the dream or the reality. We only have a choice about which mask or role we adopt, which fiction we take for truth, which madness we decide to designate sanity, which dream we name reality. Moreover, as Stevie Smith's writings indicate, we need constantly to be alert, keeping alive imaginatively to the need to adopt new views, new fictions, new masks, new dreams in order not to stagnate into dogmatists and regress into egotistical children.

Over the Frontier is Stevie Smith's second novel, in which she continued the story of Pompey Casmilus from *Novel on Yellow Paper*, published two years earlier. *Over the Frontier* is a substantial novel (260 pages),[13] divided into about forty fragments, vastly differing in length from half a page to over forty pages. These sectional fragments are often disjointed (as are Bowles' or H. D.'s) in theme, place, or time. The surface illogicality of the 'disorder' is another modernist expression of Smith's commitment to a more meaningful organisation and unity than any surface smoothness could provide, in which the 'disruption' of repressively logical forms allows unconscious, imaginative gestures to erupt through cracks in the surface texture. As in *The Holiday*, there are dream-like sequences not always distinguishable from reality; sudden, jerky, unexplained arrivals and departures seems to reflect the associative character of the mind itself when free to follow its unconscious 'dictates'. The disruption of any sustained, overt, causally sequential progression of events in the three novels by interjections from the central character or narrator challenges the reader to look for more meaningful unities of language, structure, and theme than those arbitrarily imposed by a dictating authority. Unity and meaning are often 'organised' into layers of meanings, as linear, narrative progression is sacrificed to depths, and images and themes cluster around central complex metaphors, which radiate connotations, to reflect more accurately the progression of movement of unconscious, imaginative activity. Smith thus exposed logical, causally ordered narrative as a misrepresentation of human experience, much as had Virginia Woolf and others. In this stream of consciousness form of narrative, which Stevie Smith perfected, even the literal frontier – the geographical line of literal battle demarcating friend from enemy – becomes blurred, just as is the line between reality and dream in the narrative. That humourously represented geographical boundary (a 'ditch', see below) which Pompey crosses is blurred in order that the reader should see it as a symbolic and not a real, nor a primarily geographical, boundary. Its dramatic function in the narrative is to express all the boundaries dividing the dualities mentioned above, as well as a more everyday, social one, namely, the uncertainty of the boundary between those who are our friends and those who are our enemies.

As Stevie Smith explored the nature of human relationships, whether of friendship or other love–hate relations, in her three novels and in her poetry, she revealed in each one the radical indeterminancy involved in knowing ourselves, much less in knowing others. How we distinguish friend from enemy or love from hate, much less our own motivations, becomes a theme around which the novels develop. Problems of the meaning and interpretation of characters' actions and relations to each other are overt and central in *The Holiday*, and everywhere implied in the Pompey books. Evaluations of behaviour and speech are shown to be difficult, and this indeterminancy of valuation is artistically mirrored at the level of the narrative and the reader's relation to the text. Pompey's major war activity of decoding messages is a metaphor not only for the childish game-playing involved in warfare, but for the activity of reading and interpretation. Never, however, is this code-breaking metaphor to be taken literally. There is, for the reader, no definitive message to be uncovered from the text. Indeed, for Pompey, the 'definitive' messages themselves still have to be interpreted, and are therefore not definitive. Her interpretations eventually lead her to kill, for the fascination of the game of war becomes so intense as to mesmerise her, to suspend her imaginative life. Through a process of dehumanisation, she is seduced by the power and privilege of the Army hierarchy. Later, she equates this patriarchal Army-world with social hierarchy in ordinary life, and concludes that the same seduction and dehumanisation occurs in the world of the everyday. One of the main means of dehumanisation occurs through the power of cliché, banality, and understatement. The 'familiarity' of ordinary language robs words of their power to evoke imaginative, humane response, and, Smith argued, such language becomes the rationalisation for any behaviour.

Over the Frontier falls into two major parts of similar length; in each part there are approximately twenty sections, though these narrative fragments differ in length (see above). In the first part, the action is located in England, in the second the place is somewhere indeterminate on the Baltic Coast and the situation is war. In the second part, moreover, there is a suggestion that the whole sequence may be a dream. The contrast of the forty disorderly, unruly, disproportionate parts with such a superficial mode of organisation of the novel into two parts of similar length with equal numbers of sections (and with distinct, clearly demarcated geographical locations and war–peace oppositions) is a satire on conventional, logical order and unity. The suggestion in the narrative that the second-half of the novel may not be reality but dream invites the reader to view Part I as a metaphor of consciousness and Part II as a metaphor of the unconscious. Warfare in Part II, on this rather superficial allegory, would constitute the psychological conflicts within the individual psyche, with the autonomy of the characters being blurred as well. As in Kate Chopin's *Awakening*, where Mlle Reisz and Edna can be read as a metaphor for a single, fully realised individual, Stevie Smith's novels often raise the question of the boundaries of the self and other, of individual and group, as does Jean Rhys. Virginia Woolf explored this complexity most clearly in *Mrs Dalloway* and *The Waves*, but it is also evident in Mansfield's 'Bliss'. Moreover, Jane Bowles' two central female characters, like

Djuna Barnes', threaten to merge into a single, bisexual being. This problematising of distinct individualities in all these texts leads to opposing themes of alienation and relationship, both within and without the psyche. Moreover, there is a suggestion that Pompey is willing to kill because she took her own self-identify too literally: her failure of imagination, her failure to see the 'object' of her bullet as another self, allowed this killing to occur. Such imaginative failure resulted, the narrative suggests, from the numbing game-playing and decoding of messages that stripped words of their power to arouse the mind to active thinking, instead of mere passive acquiescence. An analogous meaning, that the novel itself will be murdered – without active, imaginative participation – is implied.

Authorial intrusion of a Tristram Shandyesque-kind disrupts any possibility of establishing a fictional illusion for the reader, as we are reminded time and again, both in *Novel on Yellow Paper*, and in this novel, that we are reading a tale, told by an idiot perhaps, and possibly signifying nothing. The final paragraph of the narrative seems full of morals and messages, until we try to decode it:

> The thought and desire upon death is no salve for my mood, is but a cipher, an ignis fatuus, a foolish gesture, a child's scream of pain. Not self-violence upon the flesh, not a natural death, has promise of release. Power and cruelty are the strength of our life, and in its weakness only is there the sweetness of love. (p. 272)

The 'cipher, an ignis fatuus, a foolish gesture' seems to describe the final enigmatic sentence as well, which signifies – not in any logical sense – but in its extraordinary positioning of oppositions and contraries, dualities which are merged into each other. This merging of dualities (a theme throughout Smith's writing involving specific dualisms as well as the nature of relationship itself and duality itself), suggests the interdependence of opposites upon each other, constituting a denial that they exist fundamentally as separate from each other and therefore in need of logical relation. This foolish assumption is at the basis of most of the history of western philosophy, with its endless permutations and elaborations about the 'problem' of the relation of mind to body, of consciousness to nature, of language to thought, of language to reality, of the senses to the intellect, of the individual to society, of sanity to madness, of illness to health, of the unconscious to the conscious, of man to woman, of art to life, of human to divine, and so on. Stevie Smith's novels and poetry attack the 'reality' of these dualisms, and show them to be interdependent oppositions, or functions of each other. There is no problem of how to relate them, since it is the faculty of 'reason', the faculty of logic, or analysis reflecting on experience, which divided experience into dualities in the first place. For the faculty of synthesis (as Shelley called the imagination), these dualities are only relative, only functional, and not absolute; they are interdependent functions of each other, unified in experience, but divided into separate identities only upon reflection.

The arbitrariness of the precisely dualistic structure of Stevie Smith's novel represents this interdependence, as Part II takes on the quality of an unconscious realm interdependent with Part I, and is revealed to Pompey by her arduous and much dreaded journey into the realm of war and conflict (like Mrs Copperfield, who despaired of going to Panama, and then found herself enormously liberated into a *demi-monde* of 'undreamed'-of experiences). The result of Pompey's initial journey away from the familiar (home, consciousness, convention, London) into the strange and the un- known is none other than a self-knowledge achieved after arduous expeditions 'behind the line' and 'over the frontier', numerous expeditions undertaken at night, in the winter, confronting illness, leading up to the act of homicide, which shatters Pompey's com- placency, her certainty that she, somehow, is superior to the others, more moral, more humane. This painful self-knowledge of what Pompey is capable of 'wakes her up' (the metaphor of sleeping and waking, of dreaming and imagination, is as prevalent here as in Chopin's novel, or Keats' poetry), not only to the underworld within herself, that *demi-monde* of Rhys and Bowles, of Barnes and Porter, but also to an imaginative community with the man she killed. On the final page, Pompey complains bitterly of the hypocrisy of justifying homicide in the name of nationalism, chastened that she should have shown herself to be so childish as for a moment to have been taken in by such corruption, while the equation between warfare (authorised killing) and childishness is complete. Her journey is a journey down as well as a journey 'out in the world'; thus the novel reunites itself structurally and thematically. From a two-part structure it changes into a unity of oppositions, by means, of course, of metaphor – that 'primary vehicle of imagination'. Part II becomes a metaphor for an unconscious realm, for adulthood, and it is a psychological 'quest' for self-knowledge, just as are the old fairy-tales and folk legends which Stevie Smith so often referred to in her poems.

The endlessly disruptive, often annoying, frequent invocations to the reader – both direct and indirect – function narratively to encourage the reader to push the analogy of Pompey's journey quest further, to prevent the reader from sustaining the 'illusion' that what is going on in the novel is happening only to Pompey. The events are a representation not only of the reader's need to engage in a journey, a quest for self-knowledge. The immediacy of the narrative disruption into the reader's complacent illusions requires a more immediate analogy than some distant project the reader might engage in someday if she can rouse herself, remembering Pompey as a model (of what not to do, in some instances). Stevie Smith's authorial intrusions, combined with her linguistic, stylistic, narrative, and thematic complexities, point the finger not merely at the reader, but at the reading – at the reading reader, drawing attention to how she is reading, responding, and participating. Such an evocation to the reader is a familiar, even conventional device, common in the eighteenth and nineteenth century novel, and evident in literature from Sanskrit to Greek plays. Stevie Smith distorted and twisted this authorial gesture for her own purposes, combining it with an unusually conversational, informal, indeed indecorous tone. She thereby created a sense of the present, a sense of immediacy which allows for no delay, no deferral of participation. The reader is drawn in by the unusual impropriety of such a confiding tone as Pompey's – this stranger to us – urged on by constant shatterings of any artistic illusion. Eventually Smith overcame the same distance between Pompey and the reader as the narrated events overcome between Pompey and her victim, the dead man. An identification occurs, or at least that is the hope, if not the expectation.

Over the Frontier is not without evident organisation, though its structure is certainly obscured by the 'drunk and disorderly' memories, dreams, and opinions that disrupt the narrative account of present events so much as to become the substance of the novel rather than digressions. Instead, plot is almost non-existent in the novel as a unifying element; only occasionally does the narrative make a step forward in terms of plot, and even then it is as likely to be a leap of months as it is a few moments. That is, external, objective events are submerged in a flood of psychological experiences, so that the reality we experience is not the external world, but Pompey's inner world. In terms of externality, the novel proceeds from a visit to a picture gallery of war paintings, through various excursions and parties to a trip to Schloss Tilssen for a cure, intrigues of war after a long journey over the frontier, a killing, and, finally, a trip to Mentz to be praised by the Archbishop and the General. At Mentz, Pompey awakens from her arrogant folly, sees herself as a figure in the war paintings of the picture gallery – and the novel comes full circle. Even this skeletal plot, overwhelmed as it is by the psychological material, is not without its ironic touches and striking consequences. That is, the plot is made up entirely of excursions; indeed, the experience of reading the novel is not unlike that of an exhausting journey. The initial excursion to the picture gallery is mentioned indirectly on a number of occasions in the rest of the novel, before being involved at the end, where Pompey's self-knowledge emerges when she sees herself in real life as one of the pompous characters in the paintings in the gallery. Moreover, the gallery and paintings provide Pompey with an opportunity for a long meditation on art – the distinction, however, between great art and what she calls art 'without inspiration, ... just so laborious and so pain-staking' (p. 61); the role of pain and torture and cruelty in literature and painting; and her doubts about the worthwhile-ness of her own writing:

> I sometimes feel there is nothing noble in this book at all, but just sadness and tears and death without glory. And perhaps it is I should quit writing, and not that Sam I was speaking of just now, that has this world weariness about him but can set out so many many pages of words that go to tell the story.   (p. 59)

This section on art and pain is framed by discussions about a young academic, Professor Dryasdust who 'covers the living limbs of the poet with the vile slime of commentary, so dull, so pompous, so without hope and so cruel in its stupidity' (p. 54). Pompey's scathing comments on 'those damned bloodsuckers the commentators' (p. 53) are a caution to her reader:

> it takes an artist to appreciate an artist and the barest of all the hangers-on artistic creation are these same commentators that are always so smart to point out what's what and how the comma got left out and the quotation misquoted. To hell with them.   (p. 54)

Some twenty pages on, after a narrative excursion about torture and art, the war between Russia and England, and the fancy-dress party where all these thoughts are taking place, Pompey berates the critic again in the form of a man 'drinking by the bar. He is fair fat famous and fifty, he is my pet aversion' (p. 72), whom she names 'Mr Low-Down on Life'. More narrative excursions occur, memories of seaside trips, rides on horses, Freud, and then, 'young professor Dryasdust' comes up again:

> He has a great deal of book knowledge, and outside of books he knows nothing. He is a clever baby, will he ever be anything more. I do not know, in a moment of irritation I guess not. Already the rime of the pedant is upon his young bones. And his pugnacity, the aggressiveness of his prejudice, it is to be heard to be believed.   (p. 89)

These references to reading, criticism, and art recur innumerable times throughout Part I, and are reinforced by repeated occasions of self-references, both to the text and to the reader and reading. Early in the text, Smith alerted the 'dear Reader' (an address used a couple of dozen times throughout the book in variations – 'gentle Reader', 'O Reader') to the extreme immediacy of her narrative style, at the same time that she indicated one of the main unifying features of the book:

> I will tell you now, as quickly and as shortly as possible I will tell you, that you will know why this book is set to anger and disturbance, and need not pity me.
> Oh Pompey, I am so sick of bloody Freddy. Pax, Reader, see me through this and then no more of it.   (p. 29)

Friendship, conflict, love, hate, and war are all interrelated themes whose interdependence is raised throughout the novel. Part I constantly refers to the break-up of Pompey and Freddy's relationship – that battle between the sexes – while Part II revolves around war between nations. At the end of the novel, the 'personal lust for power' and 'national arrogance' are exposed as coming from exactly the same spirit: 'how divide ... the springs of our being, brought forth in pain and set to its infliction?' (p. 272). This interdependence of personal relationships and large, public events of war and peace is pursued in the context of a self-consciousness on the part of the writer designed to disturb the reader's passivity as 'the veil of imaginative fiction thus rent unfriendlywise in twain' encourages the reader to a self-consciousness parallel to that of the author:

> Do you ever have the thought, gentle Reader, the thought to have an empty mind, to be like the clam that sits upon the mud in the sunlight, without the burden of this voracious consciousness that goes to eating up everything it sees and hears to make up a thought about it?
> You must be receptive to your own thoughts, said I to the great established and polished man of letters ...
> So here it was I came out with this clever idea that if you are going to write, and then why certainly you must go on writing, and above all you must be receptive to your own thoughts.
> But now I feel that you must be very careful about this clever idea, or you will go to opening a door that never never will be shut again.   (pp. 43–4)

Apart from the witty irony of the simile of the muddy clam, this passage is an apt example of Smith's Gertrude-Steinish stylistics and is self-descriptive of her narrative. When her thoughts overwhelm her Pompey compares them to 'that great wilderness of thought, coming rolling up from the deep deep sea' (p. 44), a metaphor which recurs throughout the text as a powerful Freudian image. She turns away from her upsetting inner world, to a comic description of an object in the external world, namely, a valuable Greek 'Lion Vase' which she compares to the horse in the picture gallery painting she had delighted in so much at the outset of the novel. This leads to a comical contrast of animals and humans:

> Be careful not to cross the path of this serious middle-aged lion, that is turning his head, that has this funny look upon his lion face.
> Beautiful Lion Vase, sombre and ferocious lion, so set in upon himself, so quiet and aloof. And quiet horse of my earlier picture-gallery excursion, set again in quietness upon a sombre ferocity. Ah, the animals *are* so quiet, there is no fuss up there, no fret and fume for guilt and delinquency, no mind sickness and a thought upon death.   (p. 46)

In the midst of Pompey's self-referential gestures (which are designed to include the reader) such metaphors of conscious-unconscious abound, but the narrative gestures also include innumerable authorial intrusions designed to refer to other literature either by direct and indirect allusion or by actual quotation. The powerful dimension of intertextuality woven into the narrative keeps in play a readerly consciousness of contextuality as essential for participation in the text. Pompey's most frequent reference is to Parsifal, Titurel, and the Holy Grail story, especially the life-in-death existence which she compares with her own. Other references to Paracelsus, Trismegisthus, Hardy, Pater, and others of a more improbable kind create an intertextuality which, combined with her lucubrations on painting and torture, add to the breakdown of distinctions between history–reality and art–literature.

Another major thematic unifier in *Over the Frontier* is the constant reference throughout Parts I and II to sleep, dreams, tiredness, and wakenings. As in Kate Chopin's novel, these experiences act as symbols of multiple significance. Moreover, at the mid-point of the novel, after Part I and introducing Part II, a narrative of a recurring dream occurs which turns out to prophesy the reality of Part II (pp. 134ff). Pompey calls it her 'dream-reality', and throughout Part II a deep sleep, preceding her journey over the frontier (p. 180), references to the need to be wide awake, not dreaming (pp. 162–3, 165), further sleeping (p. 229), references to tiredness, and finally criticisms of her former dream-life abound; combined with the lack of reference to external events, Part II becomes a dream-like narrative for the reader and for Pompey:

> I must give you my view of the Archbishiop quickly now before I forget, for I am slipped back, the ground has slipped from under my conceited feet, I have slipped back into my former dream life of an imperfect outward consciousness ... this dreamy maze, this heavy silent Approach–Recoil, that has in it the movements of a dance, a little difficult to follow, to see but one step at a time, to inveigle one's feet, past forgot, future unguessed, indifferently considered.   (p. 261)

References to forgetting and remembering throughout the novel add to the 'dreamy-maze', while the reference to the dance as descriptive of the novel itself connects up with the two wild dances which precede each of Pompey's journeys 'over the frontier'. In both cases, the dances are described in ways metaphorical of the nature of thought and of the novel itself. Indeed, in both the mad dances (pp. 49–50, 209–11) a whole array of separate themes and images are brought together from all parts of the novel into a whirling unity: pain, war, conflict, joy, exhilaration, images of the sea as unconsciousness and as waves of thought, the dream, spells and enchantments, sleep, deception, anger, hate and rebellion from the constraints of convention. These two passages on the dance, too long to quote, are exemplary of Smith's unifying techniques through complex metaphor, self-commentary, and interlocking of images.

One might want to challenge the notion of the novel as a two-part whole. It falls just as easily into three major parts (or indeed into more, if one sees the long picture-gallery excursion (pp. 8–18), the journey-dream excursion (pp. 120–40), and the trip to Mentz (pp. 260–end) as distinct elements). The third major part would be the journey with Tom on horseback 'over the frontier', cutting Part II (the Schloss-Tilssen sections) short by some fifty-five pages. Any division of the novel is arbitrary, though such distinctions will help the reader to find her way initially. Most of the plot-aspects of the novel involve excursions, journeys, sailings, horse rides, train trips, and passages of every possible description, relieved only by parties and dances and, finally, code-breaking, war-related activities at the end of the novel, many of which act as metaphors for reading, writing, and imaginative activity generally. Those innumerable excursions occur as memories at parties, as memories of excursions during other excursions, as narrated dreams of journeys, and as memories of excursions within other narrated memories occurring during parties and other excursions. The complexities are indescribable, as the external world fades, and Pompey is whirled into the intrigues of war and killing. Just how arbitrary is any effort to order the novel becomes evident when Pompey narrates her long-awaited crossing of the frontier into enemy territory with irony, hilarity, and understatement:

> Tom has broken into a canter to take a wide-spread ditch some yards ahead. ... But can Beau-Minon *do it*? Oh come on, come on, Beau-Minon, this is not a time to check and be so cross, to check and prance, to dance sideways and to dissipate in this absurd antic so much of your energy and mine. ... Beau-Minon responds, breaks into a canter, skims the ditch, land, pecks at the landing, and shoots me over his head... Tom... sets me in the saddle again...

'Do try and stay on, we are over the frontier now, that ditch was the frontier.' (p. 225)

'That ditch' is the famous frontier which gives the novel its suggestive title. Not even the overtly self-referential passages outdo this comical description of what it is like to read Stevie Smith's novel, and identification of reader, Pompey, and author is achieved yet again.

A related technique used to this effect of identification is the constant reference to other literature. Indeed the name of her main character, Pompey Casmilus, is introduced as a historical figure ('a great devil that laid waste the hearts of the people of Carthage'), who failed to get into the annals of literature – of those of Milton and Crashaw at least (pp. 30–1). In order to right this deficiency, *Novel on Yellow Paper* and *Over the Frontier* tell the story, at least of the namesake. Stevie Smith thus toyed with the question of the relation of art to history, another one of those illusory dualities, which she quickly dismantled by drawing her reader into the boundaries of the work of art, blurring the fine line between our life, our biography, our history, and the text, while urging us into active participation in a life of imagination. Art is experience, living experience, not some lifeless product, but a process of imaginative perception. After reading 'The Adventures of Pompey Casmilus', we will look at ourselves and our world differently. Our conception of so-called reality, not to mention nature, will be transformed by our reading of art, by our looking at paintings, by listening to music. As Edith Wharton demonstrated so vividly in her *In Morocco* and *Italian Backgrounds*, we see the landscape and architecture around us through the eyes that painting and literature have given us. Equally, history, as itself narrative, is shown by Smith to be so dependent on literary remains as to be supplemental to literature (contrary to New Historicists' notions). In addition, our reading of the interpretations of historical texts and other 'remains' is deeply influenced by the development of our artistic sensibility, our imagination, through literature, painting, music, and architecture. We see and understand and create history through the eyes of art just as we see 'Nature' or 'Society' through the vision and the imagination that aesthetic experience has strengthened and developed in us.

Stevie Smith's novels are often said to be semi-autobiographical;[14] a criticism, implicit, if not explicit, is usually intended. That is, a failure of complete imaginative transformation of personal material into artistic impersonality is the implication. This 'criticism' (so banal and inappropriate as to be hardly worthy of the name) is rarely levelled at male writers, no matter how autobiographically based their novels are (D. H. Lawrence, Malcolm Lowry, Henry Miller, and so on). As Jean Rhys and Dorothy Richardson argued, personal experience is the starting-point for any work of fiction; what distinguishes works of fiction is the shaping of selected material by means of an artistic process. Even when a woman writer like Stevie Smith writes of war and public affairs, she still cannot satisfy her male critics, who usually accuse her nevertheless of writing of mere domestic matters under a thin disguise, writing merely of love, of mere human relations ('how narrow and irresponsible of Jane Austen to make almost no reference to political conflicts and stories of the day', for example). This borderline, this genre distinction, between biography or autobiography and 'genuinely imaginative fiction' is only relative and is not indicative of classes of excellence, any more than the distinction between art and history or art and reality is. As Smith indicated, such distinction are useful for certain purposes in certain contexts, but their extension to universality or absolute status leads to abuse and prejudice. One of the great contributions such women writers as Stevie Smith made to literature and literary criticism is a determined 'blurring' of the frontier between autobiography and fiction, in order to express the insight that to divide art from life and set up hierarchies of reality can only lead to death of the imagination and of much that we value in life. When these women wrote their prose, poetry, or essays, their letters and diaries, the 'poetic prose' of Smith, they knew they were both at work and at leisure, living in the writing as their writing became more and more their lives. No absolute division between work and leisure was possible for them, as they shuffled their domestic duties or careers around their writing, and slipped their writing, as Stevie Smith described, into their busy and demanding days at home or at work.

Modernism, understood as experimental literature, gave Smith and others the opportunity to portray experience more empirically, more as she found it in her life – subjectively, if you like – instead of imposing worn-out traditional, artificial forms of order, organisation, and pseudo-objectivity on their texts. Smith often wrote in fragments of greatly differing lengths, loosely arranged, and in new and original free forms of poetry; she de-emphasised strong plot

and logical, causal development; she exploited 'stream of consciousness' techniques at times, and wrote in more stark, austere
forms at others. This reflected her experience, while the old forms
of realism and romance did not, because she had a different point
of view on life, a different experience to narrate (not the female
point of view, but her own point of view).[15] Modernism had provided her with the opportunity to express her intense originality in
forms, styles, and languages expressive of that individuality,
expressive of her new and different experience. Stevie Smith's writing testifies to the authenticity of experience from a point of view
greatly at odds with the prevailing, objective, authorised account
of the world.[16] As such, the artistic forms, structures, styles,
languages, characters, and themes that Smith, and other women
like her, forged, enrich immeasurably our knowledge of a much
larger world of experience than that provided by men writers and
readers alone, and they are the losers if they fail to appreciate the
fine, artistic quality of Smith's (or other women's) writing. Women's
experiences, and the experiences of many groups of different
people, form worlds of experience analogous to the world of the
unconscious that Pompey explores – that world of imagination,
which can be both creative and destructive. Each of us lives limited,
indeed, poverty-stricken lives, if we fail to go on the (albeit) arduous journey of educating ourselves about the new and different
points of view opening out on to new and different worlds. We
cannot afford to sit back and wait to be educated or convinced by
others of the value of their world, any more than we can afford to
ignore the world of the unconscious and of imagination, for our
very existence as *human* beings is at stake, as is our individuality.
Stevie Smith showed that we remain at the level of animals – brute
unconscious forces, stereotyped cogs in a mindless social machine –
perpetrating destruction, through warfare or other conflicts (male–
female, black–white, rich–poor, and so on), if we don't get up and
go 'out in the world', over that frontier of the conscious self, the
familiar, into new realms of multifaceted dimensions and realities.

8
Jane Bowles: That Modern Legend

Jane Bowles was born in New York in 1917 and died in Spain, in 1973, in a convent hospital. She wrote *Two Serious Ladies* (published 1943) when she was only twenty-five, a novel celebrated by writers in her own time, and exemplary of late modernist fiction. Her only play, *In the Summer House* (performed in New York in 1953), and a number of short stories (such as 'Camp Cataract' and 'A Guatemalan Idyll', 1944) collected in the volume *Plain Pleasures* (1966), not to mention part of a new novel, *Out in the World*,[1] were written before Jane Bowles suffered the cerebral haemorrhage in 1957 which made writing extremely difficult. Having lived for a time (with her husband, Paul Bowles) in a Brooklyn boarding house (where Benjamin Britten, Carson McCullers, W. H. Auden, and Gypsy Rose Lee had also boarded), she and Paul began their nomadic existence, living in Europe, Central America, then Mexico, and Ceylon, before settling eventually in Tangiers in 1947.[2]

Alan Sillitoe, John Ashberry, Tennessee Williams, Truman Capote, Sybille Bedford, and other writers have praised Bowles' writing in the highest terms. Tennessee Williams described *In the Summer House* as standing 'altogether alone ... one of those rare plays ... by which the theatre is tested', while Capote claimed to have seen three performances of it, when normally he could not 'sit through most plays once'.[3] He loved its 'thorny wit, the flavour of a newly tasted, refreshingly bitter beverage – the same qualities that had initially attracted me to Mrs. Bowles' novel, *Two Serious Ladies*'. Alan Sillitoe claimed that *Two Serious Ladies* 'is a landmark of twentieth century American literature', and praised Bowles' 'brilliant style', a prose which Robert Nye described as 'beautiful and accomplished', while Capote called Jane Bowles 'one of the really original pure stylists'. Sybille Bedford and John Ashberry were no less impressed; Bedford called attention to the 'subtlety, sharpness, and surprise of her observation, and the cool economy of her style. ... The same originality, and considerable depth, of her writing'. Ashberry summed Bowles up as 'one of the finest modern writers of fiction in any language', while Tennessee Williams argued that she was 'the most important writer of prose fiction in modern American letters'. Ashberry, like Sybille Bedford, remarked on the element of surprise in Bowles' writing, believing that surprise 'is the one essential ingredient of great art. Jane Bowles deals almost exclusively in this rare commodity'. Further, a reviewer in the *Spectator* called her a 'master [sic] of the short story form'.[4] These encomniums mitigated the less insightful American reviews Paul Bowles drew attention to in the 1989 introduction (written 1981) to *Everything is Nice*. He reported some reviewers as calling *Two Serious Ladies* 'inept' and unworthy of publication because 'chaotic, a meaningless absurdity'.[5] Chaos and meaningless absurdity are concepts used to describe the writings of James Joyce, Djuna Barnes, Henry James, Dorothy Richardson, Virginia Woolf, Stevie Smith, Hilda Doolittle, and others. Since many modernists (as other artists) set out to challenge the notions of reality as a rational, objective, meaningful order, showing the underside of such order as chaotic, and the order itself as merely convention, there may be nothing inapplicable in these adjectives. Their use as pejorative terms by uninsightful critics is, however, surprising, given the literary–historical context in which this writing occurred.

Truman Capote has written the most impressive and insightful essay on Jane Bowles available today, reprinted as an introduction to *The Collected Works of Jane Bowles*. In this extraordinarily witty, fantastically imaginative essay – itself a work of the purest artistry – he called Jane Bowles 'that modern legend', and then proceeded to add a rich dimension to that legend, demonstrating precisely how such legends are built and preserved. His amazing account of Jane Bowles is itself a remarkable fiction, making of her life an incredibly exotic fantasy-tale. Self-consciously adept at his development of the alleged legend (or did he himself create it?), Capote based his initial account of Bowles on indirect reportage 'by recent travellers to North Africa who have seen or sat with her in some dim casbah café', an account most startlingly like Shelley's 'Ozymandias': 'I met a traveller from an antique land / who said ...'. These 'recent travellers' confirm as 'true' what Capote was sure of anyway, namely that Jane is 'unchanged', is 'more or less the same as when I first knew her more than twenty years ago ... the eternal urchin'. 'A celebrated figure' already, said Capote, Jane

Bowles was a gifted linguist, speaking Arabic, French, and Spanish fluently, thus giving her dialogue the character of 'some delightful combinations of other tongues'. Capote emphasised the nomadic character of Bowles' life in her twenties, until she settled in Tangiers to become an exotic figure flitting between the dull modernity of a Westernised Tangiers, and the 'medieval puzzlement of alleys and alcoves', where she had a native house with tiny rooms furnished in Morrish style,

> illuminated by intricate lanterns and windows that allow the light of the sea skies and views that encompass minarets and ships and the blue-washed rooftops of native tenements receding like a ghostly staircase to the clamorous shoreline.   (p. vii)

Capote's delightful embellishment (or creation) of a Jane Bowles legend made her into a figure of speech – a metaphor, that is, for imagination itself – an embodiment of imaginative, artistic activity, her life being 'figured' as an exotic adventure on magical, unknown shores. She herself, that imaginative 'wight' and eternal urchin, unchanged for twenty years, is the embodiment of imagination and originality with her

> mischief-shiny, just a trifle mad eyes, her original voice (a husky soprano), her boyish clothes and schoolgirl's figure and slightly limping walk, … appealing as the most appealing of non-adults, yet with some substance cooler than blood invading her veins, and with a wit, an eccentric wisdom, no child, not the strangest wunderkind, ever possessed.

Capote's description of Bowles is remarkable in capturing something of the magical character of her writing, unlike Paul Bowles' rather carping introduction to *Everything is Nice*, which contrasts with – but in no way contradicts – Capote's lively legend. That is, the characteristics Capote ascribes to Bowles herself and her life seem an equally apt description of her eccentric and original style and remarkably fantastic characters. Curiously, his later description of her writing is also a description of the Bowles known in the legend: 'the tragic view is central to her vision', as tragedy was central to her life, a tragic vision including a humour saturated with a controlled compassion, and involving 'the subtlest comprehension of eccentricity and human apartness'. Her depiction of 'never-realized relationships', her 'language and her themes' sought after along 'tortured paths and in stony quarries', these describe her stories, plays, and novels as well as being suggestive of her life. The boundary between her life and her art blurs just as it does with many other writers, particularly the writers discussed here, such as Jean Rhys, Katherine Mansfield, and Kate Chopin, for example. Autobiographical fiction, far from being a secondary, inferior kind of fiction, is a triumph of the fusion, through creativity, of art and life, fiction and reality, so that living itself is seen as a narrative, but a self-consciously aware narrative.

While much of Bowles' writing concentrates on the experiences of unusual women, her analysis of the social constraints that inhibit individuality, autonomy, creativity, and happiness should interest both men and women. A constant theme in all Bowles' writings is human apartness. But a related theme is the way in which men and women constrain and inhibit each other from achieving individuality. People enforce stereotyped social relationships, roles, and forms of behaviour that suffocate originality in behaviour, dress, sexual conduct, and thought. Bowles' novels exude a surrealism that arises in part from the suspension of any normal logic of behaviour between people.[6] Categories of relationships are blurred and social conventions are constantly overstepped. Bowles' characters speak and act in ways just off-centre enough so that the reader is made aware that nearly everything we say and do is a cliché or a form of game-playing. Rules are unconsciously followed when we think we are being spontaneous, original, and most ourselves. Those who fail to follow the rules are looked upon as interesting eccentrics at best, and more often as troublemakers, degenerates, and outcasts with whom it is dangerous (for one's social acceptability) to become involved in any way. In du Plessix Gray's words, Bowles' fantastic 'blend of realism and the grotesque', of tragedy and compassionate comedy, of the bizarre and the familiar, is austere in its 'severe avoidance of all moralizing' (p. iv).

Jane Bowles' prose is one of the most sustained attempts ever made to render transparent the literary and linguistic conventions that normally remain obscured by subject matter. Here, subject matter is an almost constant metaphoric dramatisation of the literary conventions of story-telling, characterisation, plot, creating of setting, establishment of narrative point of view, and so on. Metaphors involving dress, food, and social behaviour are endlessly varied and repeated as Bowles illuminates the inner workings of art, language, and society. Garments and clothing are used both as a traditional metaphor for language and art, and as an example of the way in which behaviour is encoded and values communicated. Social rituals involving food and drink become metaphors for artistic technique and linguistic devices. Diction, linguistic mannerisms, and conventions of ordinary speech and literary language become Bowles' subject matter, in part, as she reveals the way in which hackneyed and clichéd language leads to stereotyped, one-dimensional behaviour. Put another way, fashions or 'styles' in food, dress, behaviour, and art are closely peered at, observed, and then slightly altered. These alterations are signposts to the reader to attend not merely to the overt subject matter but also to the language in which it is garbed.

Thus, when describing Christina Goering in *Two Serious Ladies*, Bowles' comment that 'she never picked up the mannerisms then in vogue' is also self-referring (that is, referring to the writing itself), as is the comment that Christina was 'old fashioned' and wore 'the look of certain fanatics' (compare 'her ... just a trifle mad eyes' – Capote on Jane Bowles). Christina, like the author, makes up her own rules and games, and constantly cajoles others into playing them. In another passage referring to writing, Bowles punningly noted that Christina's 'games, as a rule, were very moral, and often involved God', suggesting, moreover, that our social interactions are 'ruled' by games, many of which we mistake for matters of moral or religious significance. Christina's games as a child and an adult involve repeated occasions of taking off her dress and doing dances of worship to the sun. Jane Bowles' prose takes off the 'dress' of conventional literary language or familiar 'style', and in its own dancing, mixes up categories of diction, style, and subject matter, from children's books and fairy-tales to serious adult literature. This creates a brilliantly original tone that is more than a mere surrealist pastiche or *mélange* of forms not ordinarily mixed together. Impropriety and promiscuity of language and decorum become, as in Stevie Smith, the road to sainthood and to genius. To speak metaphorically, Jane Bowles' style, like Mary's dress, 'is completely covered with mud', so that it may become 'clean and pure as a flower is'. Whether it does so or not is of course 'of considerable interest but of no great importance'. Or, put another more humorous way, literary style is merely a 'hostess gown adapted from a central European peasant costume'. Moreover, fashions and 'styles' (whether of literary language, social behaviour, or dress) change, and though Bowles' 'unfashionable' 'unstylish' prose may, like Christina, seem 'at this time [to be] very heavy and her legs quite fat', it 'may be impossible to foresee that she [it] would turn out to be a tall and elegant lady'. In *Two Serious Ladies*, Bowles spends 'a great deal of time switching the lights off and on', but she expects 'in the future to be under control'. Luckily for the reader, she never did stop switching the lights off and on, and her style is impeccable.

Two Serious Ladies began as a novel about three serious ladies, according to Paul Bowles.[7] As the novel developed, Jane is said to have deleted a large portion, namely the 'entire part dealing with Señorita Cordoba' (which was later made into three, now published, short stories, 'A Guatemalan Idyll', 'A Day in the Open', and 'Señorita Cordoba'). The novel[8] is divided into three main portions of unequal length, with two apparently totally disconnected stories, until, 191 pages on, the two main characters, who turn out to be close friends, and not mere acquaintances, meet and converse in a bar for the last eight pages of the novel. Part I, the shortest portion (some 30 pages), introduces Miss Christina Goering,[9] first as a young girl of thirteen years. By the second section (of four sections, which make up Part I), Miss Goering is a young woman living with her companion Miss Gamelon; she attends a party, sees her acquaintance Mrs Copperfield briefly, meets Arnold and his father, decides to change her life, and plans – against Miss Gamelon's wishes – to sell up everything, including her beautiful house, in order to move to a dilapidated room at a little-populated end of an island, and begin her odyssey of self-development. Abruptly, Part II begins with the adventures of a Mr and Mrs Copperfield embarking on a voyage to Panama. This part of the novel (some 87 pages, with eight sections) narrates, in a style consistent with Parts I and III, the story of Mrs Copperfield's apparently innocent adventures with prostitutes, hotel proprietresses, and other members of a Jean Rhys-like *demi-monde* in Panama, until she decides to remain behind in Panama with Pacifica, Mrs Quill, and Peggy Gladys. Part III (divided into nine sections, and totalling ninety pages) narrates the fantastic and deliberate entrance of Miss Goering into another, probably American, *demi-monde* of one-night stands, drunkenness, and brief affairs, where she is 'mistaken' as a professional prostitute at times, and at other times is seen as a potentially permanent mistress–wife, as, for example, by the character Andy. This final part of the novel

concludes with Miss Goering telephoning Mrs Copperfield to invite
her to come to the bar, which she does. Both women have partners
with them, but Ben walks out on Miss Goering unceremoniously
on the final page, and Pacifica, while remaining with her friend Mrs
Copperfield, wants to marry her boyfriend soon but cannot bring
herself to desert Mrs Copperfield, who has brought her back to a
'better' life from Panama. (Mrs Copperfield herself is planning an
imminent return to Panama.)

There exists, unquestionably, an interesting fund of thematic
content in the novel: the struggle for independence, unusual experiences, freedom from stifling conventional relationships and conventional social structures is portrayed, not to mention a kind of
Blakean–Nietzchean self-knowledge ('the road of excess leads to
the palace of wisdom'). Somewhat less overt themes about the
nature of sexuality, lesbianism, friendship, and other human
relationships are also explored, along with isolation and apartness,
and the failure of fulfilling relationships. Such themes are hardly
innovative: they are the very stuff of literature, whether modernist
or not, though some modernist writers (Jean Rhys, Djuna Barnes
and Porter) have explored more boldly, perhaps, the world of
pimps and prostitutes, of other unconventional forms of sexuality
and relationship, and the worlds of drugs and drunkenness, of
deviants, perverts, life in the circus, theatres, artists, and other
realms where unconventionality tends to prevail. Other modernists
have chosen to expose the 'deformities and debaucheries' of life in
conventional realms (Stevie Smith, H. D., Katherine Mansfield, Kate
Chopin, Charlotte Perkins Gilman, Willa Cather, Edith Wharton).
In both types of milieu, issues of relationship and apartness,
autonomy and dependence, self-fulfilment and responsibility, sanity
and madness, propriety ('morality') and debauchery are explored.
Yet while these themes may be obvious to all readers, what is less
evident is the way the authors' insights into such issues are rooted
in their specific modes of artistic representation, that is, of disunify-
ing structures, language and style, narrative techniques (use of
point of view, of time, of reality versus dream, memory, fantasy)
and characterisation (through description and dialogue). In Jane
Bowles' writings (as in many modernists' fictions) such literary,
linguistic, stylistic, or artistic issues become some of the central
themes, rooted nevertheless in the themes as stated above in more
sociological and psychological terms of discourse. For Bowles, as
for Jean Rhys, Chopin, and these other women writers, 'life' issues

and 'art' issues could not be separately or neatly catagorised as independent aspects of a dualistic world.

Bowles' search for innovative forms of literary expression and representation paralleled (as did Gertrude Stein's) her search for innovative forms and ways of living. In this her art is perfectly mirrored in her life, as they shade into each other and she lives out what she envisages in her imagination. Her 'legendary life' is no less original than her books, and, like Jean Rhys, her search for individuality as a person was inextricably bound up with her search for originality as an artist. Such a search involves growth and development in personality and in writing, and she rebuked her husband for allegedly encouraging her to overcome her writing difficulties by making her new novel, *Out in the World*, like *Two Serious Ladies*: 'I certainly have no intention of repeating myself, if that's what you mean.'[10] This hardly contradicts Capote's depiction of his legendary Jane as 'unchanged' over a period of twenty years: what was 'unchanged', he suggested, was her rare originality, her elf-like, other worldly imaginativeness, that quality of being an embodiment of rhetoricity: an image of imagination itself. Meanwhile, her imaginativeness, drenched in unusual experiences, enriched itself in its human, social and natural surroundings, fed on life, and created 'Camp Cataract', *In the Summer House* and a portion of *Out of the World*, until she was struck down by illness.

Jane Bowles' writings reveal an almost obsessional, certainly passionate interest in literary experimentation to match her life experiments. Content and styles are closely woven into a congruence that has rarely been equalled: hence the apparently extravagant praise of contemporary writers, combined with much incomprehension from readers and critics. The latter often overlook the artistic concerns of experimentation in the search for new forms (which may be preeminent for the writer), in favour of overt themes grasped in the form of 'ideas' which are couched in social, psychological, political, and romantic discourses. Incomprehension often arises when innovative forms, devised to liberate both literature and human experience from familiar conventional moulds, obscure (often deliberately) definite thematics or ideas in order to enable the reader to experience life and art in liberating and enriching ways. Jane Bowles achieved a congruence in her originality of language or style and content as she shattered literary conventions simultaneously with social ones, by depicting bizarre social relations through, in part, weirdly styled dialogue and linguistically 'off-centre' depictions of outrageous improprieties in relationships as if both such dialogue and such relationships were perfectly normal. The 'off-centredness' of her dialogue, narrative description, and depiction of characters' behaviour is achieved precisely by surprise, in two senses. First, the characters rarely react as if anything not perfectly normal had occurred; they are almost never surprised at each other's words or actions or feelings. The reader, on the other hand, is astonished, first at what the characters do and say (in such a blasé fashion); more astonishingly still, the reader is surprised at the fact that the other characters maintain the illusion of normality. Finally, the reader is shaken by the surface incongruity of the language, theme, and artistic purpose of Bowles as a 'serious' writer. Arguments among characters arise about what to do out of practical consideration or expediency, but almost never as to the impropriety or immortality of any word, act, or feeling, except, ironically, as regards the moral obligations of wealth and property. Hence, the almost complete absence of moralising in the texts. A curious universality of moral tolerance pervades Bowles' writings, as she presents life sympathetically from every character's point of view, somehow imagining herself, by means of her 'off-centre' style, in extraordinary roles and situations, and keeping their integrity and right to exist intact. Characters conflict, needs conflict, but few moral, only practical judgements, are made, as characters do and say the most surprising, unconventional things in the most unclichéd, Bowlesian language imaginable while still remaining intelligible.

The exposure of and toying with, indeed, exploiting clichés is at the centre of this element of surprise. Bowles took clichés in writing, speech, life, social relations, and literature and changed them, while still leaving them recognisable. One artistic or literary cliché transformed by Bowles is the artificial order and unity imposed on novels by means of a central plot. Bowles brazenly ignored this novelistic convention, this expectation of such an obvious, contrived form of unity, and explored the lives of two quite separate characters. While, no doubt, comparisons can be made between the two women's progress from a conventional life of decorous propriety into experiences which most securely established middle-class women seek assiduously to avoid, such thematic consideration may be more clearly illuminated by an initial examination of language, style, and structure. Structure in *Two Serious Ladies* can be described as another element of surprise, then. For after the first thirty pages of the novel (Part I) which has introduced the Goering–

Gamelon pair, the reader is shipped off (in Part II) to Panama, with two relatively new characters, Mr and Mrs Copperfield, and for over two-fifths of the novel (some ninety pages) we hear nothing of the Goering–Gamelon partnership. Suddenly, in Part III, the Misses Goering, Gamelon, and their recently acquired friend Arthur are summarily reintroduced. They, too, however, have been transported from the luxury of the upper-middle class life to a gloomy, dilapidated house on an island. For no reasons, out of pure whimsy, it seems, Miss Goering, to the enraged disbelief of Miss Gamelon, has given up respectability for adventure, even debauchery, and the last two-fifths, or ninety pages, chart her astonishing experiments with sexual license in the form of bizarre liaisons, brief flings and one-night stands with men of all types, and involvements with apparent criminals, drop-outs, and outcasts. In Part II, Mrs Copperfield had also experimented, not, however, so much with sexual flings as with friendships with other women of the Panamanian *demi-monde*. At the end of Part III, Jane Bowles ironically (in a brazen contrivance with no literary or actual life justification) brought the two women together again, just as they had been brought together at the party in Part I with the authoritative snap of the authoress' fingers. This dispensing with artistic justification, with a blunt refusal to engineer any prior cause for this union, confronts the reader with other usually hidden novelistic clichés and conventions, namely, the artificial unity, causality, and order imposed by authors behind a screen of rationale. The two central plots and character groupings of the novel have been openly, arbitrarily tied only in the last few pages and very briefly at the party in Part I. The reader is jolted into surprise both at this brazenly contrived relationship between the two women, and the flaunting of the need for a conclusion. The 'tying together' of the two themes during the party and in the final scene is a characteristic parody by Bowles of conventional expectations of narrative unity.

The final short paragraph of the novel demonstrates some of the points made above, such as the exposure of cliché, the element of surprise, the problem of definitive interpretations and the indeterminacy of meaning, as well as the parodying of structure and of unity by ironising the expectation that the ending of a novel should be some sort of culmination:

'Certainly I am nearer to becoming a saint', reflected Miss Goering, but is it possible that a part of me hidden from my sight is piling sin upon sin as fast as Mrs. Copperfield?' This latter possibility Miss Goering thought to be of considerable interest but of no great importance.   (p. 201)

Miss Goering's interpretation of her own development as spiritual progress is not exactly a complete surprise to the reader, since this has been tentatively suggested in the novel earlier, though not so uncategorically described before as the striving for sainthood (through profligacy and 'questionable' liaisons). Her friends, Miss Gamelon and Arthur, do not see it as progress toward sainthood, though Arthur's evaluation is less articulated than Miss Gamelon's. The latter's incomprehending rage is due, however, not at all to moral condemnation, but to the discomfort of poverty and isolation after a period of complete bourgeois comfort at Miss Goering's expense. What must surprise the reader is Miss Goering's view that her friend Mrs Copperfield is heading in exactly the opposite direction, since to the reader there is no such dichotomy. The reader might feel that it was Miss Goering who, with her sexual profligacy, is piling sin upon sin, while Mrs Copperfield is simply making friends, though from a rather unusual realm of social class for a woman of the middle class. This reversal of moral evaluation is one more element of Bowles' style, as it parodies the values reflected in the language of religious discourse. Such reversal also acts to structure and unify the book, as it brings the ending of the novel back to the religious preoccupations of the child, Christina Goering, introduced in the first few paragraphs.

This 'circling round' to the beginning of the novel is reinforced by a feeling of Miss Goering immediately prior to the final paragraph: 'Hope, she felt, had discarded a childish form forever' (p. 201). Clearly spiritual development, religious feeling, and morality are themes in the novel, along with the idea of self-development and personal liberation. These conventional themes, however, are treated in hilariously grotesque, bizarre style and narrative forms which seem to turn conventional notions of the meaning of such themes on their heads. Salvation through the throwing off of respectability may not be far, after all, from a genuinely Christian ideal, indeed it may be that ideal. Yet Bowles' artistic representation of spiritual development is by means of depictions associated with precisely its opposite. Miss Goering's childhood and adult 'mental struggles – generally of a religious nature' (p. 4), took the form of games, and 'these games, as a rule, were very moral, and often involved God'. One involves doing 'a dance of worship to the sun' (p. 5). Yet, paradoxically, Christina then announces: 'I'm going to show that I'd rather have God and no sun than the sun and no God' (p. 5). Another game occurs in a tower, and is described again by the little Christina as a 'very special game':

> 'It's called "I forgive you for all your sins,"' said Christina. 'You'll have to take your dress off.'
> 'Is it fun?' Mary asked.
> 'It's not for fun that we play it, but because it's necessary to play it'. (p. 6)

(Throughout the subsequent narrative, the grown-up Miss Christina Goering is motivated by the same sense of inexplicable necessity to throw away her life and enter a new realm – of apparent decadence to the reader, but of spiritual progress, to her.)

This bizarre game involves clothing the near-naked Mary in a burlap sack with two eyeholes cut in the top, submerging her in mud near a stream, and then washing the mud away with the flowing water. As she holds the mud-enshrouded Mary under the water for three minutes, Christina yells out a loud 'prayer':

> 'Dear God', she said, 'make the girl Mary pure as Jesus Your Son. Wash her sins away as the water is now washing the mud away. This black burlap proves to you that she thinks she is a sinner'. (p. 7)

The 'game' ends abruptly with Mary being sent home to clean herself up. In the course of the novel it takes on the appearance of an allegory for Miss Goering's subsequent behaviour. The 'mud and burlap bag' she covers herself with, by immersing herself in a *demi-monde* of drink and sex and bars and criminals, is the necessary admission of sin and, curiously, the means to 'salvation'. Shortly after, Bowles catapulted the reader, without further ado, into Miss Goering's adult life, introduced Miss Gamelon in a most bizarre scene of parodies of conventional speech in the rituals of the two women making each other's acquaintance, and suddenly Miss Gamelon is asked to live with Christina, which she agrees to do. Miss Goering tells her about her 'guardian angel': 'A guardian angel comes when you are very young, and gives you special dispensation ... from the world. Yours might be luck, mine is money'

(p. 12). Later, Christina decides to dispense with this guardian angel, apparently because it is making her feel too safe and impeding her spiritual self-development, since her own newly acquired prosperity and security is threatened. Her language is strewn with a mocking of moral categories of condemnation and abuse:

> '... it's a real crime against society that you have property in your hands ...
> 'I think', said Miss Goering, 'that I like it more than most people ... However, in order to work out my own little idea of salvation I really believe that it is necessary for me to live in some more tawdry place ...'.   (p. 28)

Miss Gamelon stereotypically labels her a 'hopeless lunatic', but Miss Goering proceeds with her plan, joined by yet another unknown but newly acquired acquaintance, Arnold. (Similarly, Arnold's father, again categorising people, says, 'Well, you are all crazy ... but I'm rooting for you'; p. 120). The reference to insanity, crime, and salvation are part of the challenge Bowles sets up to our habit of unthinking, reactive categorisation and condemnation of the eccentric, original, or unconventional. Part I thus ends, and we hear nothing further for the next ninety pages, when, after fantastic tales of the extraordinary characters Mrs Copperfield, Pacifica, Mrs Quill, and Peggy Gladys, we are plunged back into the characters of Part I, well-established in their new life. Christina pursues her task of games played not because they are fun; indeed, they seem to be precisely what she least wants to do, but because they are necessary:

> 'The idea,' said Miss Goering, 'is to change first of our own volition and according to our own inner promptings before they impose completely arbitrary changes on us.'   (p. 29)

In her first task of forcing herself to go out alone at night on the train, then the ferry and into the next town, Miss Goering explains in almost exactly the words used to Mary when Christina was thirteen, 'It is not for fun that I am going ... but because it is necessary to do so' (p. 124 and see p. 137). Having given up her 'very beautiful house which she had inherited from her mother' (p. 3), sold everything she owned and having forced herself, Miss Gamelon, and Arnold to live on one-tenth of her income (p. 114), she now makes her way down a road leading in the opposite direction of respectability or conventional moral 'purity'. Certainly this seems to be Jane Bowles' (Katherine Mansfield-like) depiction of the hypocrisy and deceit of conventional social life, as well as conventional literary and religious notions which assert the possibility of daily comfort simultaneously with artistic moral, religious, and spiritual purity. Like Kierkegaard, but in her own wildly bizarre, hilariously witty manner, Bowles flicked away that veil of pretence, and set her characters on a 'quest' and 'journey' for experience of every kind. On her first night, Miss Goering gets involved with a man labelled and categorised a 'disagreeable bum', Andy, who himself narrates the grotesque story (which mirrors the novel) of his own rejection of a respectable girlfriend and job for a passionate sexual affair with a legless, armless, beautiful blonde girl with syphilis (pp. 150–2). Miss Goering returns to him the next night with Arnold's father; the two men immediately sense their difference in class background, and quarrel. More labels and moral categories are used ('society lady', 'skunk': p. 152; 'pompous old monkey', 'gutter puppy', 'cheaply dressed brute'; p. 168), while the father concludes that Andy is 'clearly not the type of man I would expect to find you associating with' (p. 168). Miss Goering, for whom all these classifications and labels are 'neither here nor there' (p. 169), decides to move in with Andy. After eight days of absence from her 'home', she again meets, as pre-arranged, Arnold's father, who has decided that his own drunken adventure of leaving his wife and respectability to follow his urge to 'sail away' on a last chance bid for freedom 'is a mere chimera and that one has not the strength' to carry it through (p. 181). His son, however, he says, has involved himself with the no-longer respectable Miss Gamelon, that 'trollop he is living with' (p. 182). Miss Goering leaves him, goes to a bar, and thereupon meets a 'gangster' who believes she is a 'prostitute'. She argues with him about such a categorisation, and then promptly goes off with him to his apartment, deserting the stricken, pleading Andy with the words:

'... perhaps my manoeuvres do seem a little strange; but I have thought for a long time now that often, so very often, heroes who believe themselves to be monsters because they are so far removed from other men turn around much later and see really monstrous acts being committed in the name of something mediocre.'

'Lunatic!' Andy yelled at her from his knees. 'You're not even a Christian.' (pp. 188–9; *note the labellings of people throughout: heroes, monsters, lunatic, Christian*)

Later, the 'gangster', whom she calls her 'gentleman' (p. 200), deserts her equally summarily, as still further labellings of people are exposed by Bowles, as they were by Jean Rhys.

Throughout her adventures, Bowles has Miss Goering unconsciously maintain her habitual speech, dress, manners, and behaviour as the 'society lady' she once was. She never associates herself with the labels of trollop, lunatic, prostitute, or harlot that others call her (pp. 27, 28, 185); this incongruity between words and action adds to the effect of grotesqueness and off-centredness which dialogue and situation create, and acts as another technique for parodying the social–religious hypocrisy of 'ordinary' life, where the gap between words and actions is usually a chasm. Mrs Copperfield's adventures show the same incongruity as she explores the demi-world of Panama. Nevertheless, she is depicted as wholly without the alleged religious or moral motives of Christian Goering, simply discovering female friendship and female intimacy in a completely unexpectedly, previously unexperienced world. Having been forced by her husband, against her will, to go to Panama on a business trip, she then refuses to leave, but eventually returns with her friend (lover?) Pacifica, having deserted her outraged spouse. Her adventures in Panama are as surprising, unpredictable, and as apparently without any tangible logic in their detail for the overall development of the novel as were Christina's. As in Parts I and III, Part II is a disarray of illogical, nonsensical encounters, ludicrously funny and apparently irrelevant events, one following upon another in a disorderly 'non-sequence'. Causality is flaunted while irrelevance is raised to a logic of its own, rationality is made out to be merely the most familiar form of irrationality, narrative order is parodied as brazenly arbitrary sequences confront the reader and confound all expectations; clichéd language is exposed and ridiculed; characters reject all labels, while decorous speech and manners are mixed into incongruous scenes of violence, brawling, and drunken rape. Throughout, all these scenes are described in Bowles' accomplished, literary prose, so that incongruity increases at the surface-level of narration. Social and class boundaries are mocked as characters tumble in and out of each other's lives and the women end up making the most unexpected liaisons with other women. As Mrs Copperfield angrily explains to her old friend Christina[11] at the end of the novel when accused of having 'gone to pieces':

'True enough ... I have gone to pieces, which is a thing I've wanted to do for years. I know I am as guilty as I can be, but I have my happiness, which I guard like a wolf, and I have authority now and a certain amount of daring, which, if you remember correctly I never had before ....

... [Miss Copperfield continues] 'I feel that you have changed anyway and lost your charm. You seem stodgy to me now and less comforting. You used to be so gracious and understanding; everyone thought you were light in the head, but I thought you were extremely instinctive and gifted with magic powers.' (p. 198)

This speech of Mrs Copperfield's is characteristic of the dialogue and writing throughout the novel. Clichés are turned upside down: it is an achievement to 'go to pieces', not a failure. It is perfectly normal to have 'magic powers', and for friends to be so direct with each other, without rancour or bitterness. The out-of-the-ordinary is made ordinary, in narrative language, in speech, and in action; nearly every character, whether major or minor, sets out on a course designed to leave behind the past, the familiar, or the normal, in word and action, as completely as possible. Analogously, Jane Bowles set out to leave behind the properties and conventions of ordinary novels, literary decorum, language, style, and logic, in part in order to rend the veil of hypocrisy in artistic, social, and religious conventions which obscures insight and inhibits fresh experience, and in part in order to create a fine artistic congruence between her artistic medium and her thematics. Additionally, her disorderly, illogical sequences, her intense understatement, her depiction of apparently wholly random events (whose details have no integral relation to other events happening to her characters), her frequent use of stories and narrations within the narration told by her characters, and the many other devices discussed above, lead to a magical surrealism designed to liberate the reader from constraining, unconscious expectations, into a fresh and novel world of reading (and living) in a surprisingly exhilarating way.

'Camp Cataract'[12] shares many of the characteristics of *Two Serious Ladies*, a story Truman Capote described as a 'comic tale of doom' told with 'controlled passion', 'that has at its heart, and *as* its heart, the subtlest comprehension of eccentricity and human apartness.' Similar in theme, language and style to *Two Serious*

Ladies, with a heroine set on escaping her humdrum life, it adds another twist to Bowles' structural innovation: unlike the double, virtually unrelated narratives of the novel, Bowles' finest short story steals in two unrelated, contradictory endings, stolen in so unobtrusively as completely to confuse the reader on a first reading. Bowles' 'forking paths' offer these possible conclusions. First,

> Sadie knew then that this agony she was suffering was itself the dreaded voyage into the world – the very voyage she had always feared Harriet would make. That she herself was making it instead of Harriet did not affect her certainty that this was it.   (p. 100)

Ironically, this (shattering? exhilarating?) realisation comes in the midst of a small clearing in a forest, where Sadie has dragged Harriet, and where Harriet leaves her in a rage, penetrating 'father into the grove' away from her sister Sadie, who, having come to Camp Cataract to lure Harriet back to the 'security' of home, falls prey to the spell of going 'out in the world … just the two of us' (p. 100).

This first 'ending' continues (to speak oxymoronically), and involves a (dreamed? fantasised? or real?) seduction scene with the 'make-believe' Indian who mans a souvenir booth. This seduction scene acts as a 'second stage' to the first ending, quoted above, as it follows from the 'first stage of this first ending', though such dual 'stages' seem completely contradicted by the Indian in the alternative, second ending. The second stage of the first ending suggests the possibility of yet a second ending constituted by a suicide in a state of hallucination about the lover who is also the make-believe Indian. The third version, or ending (or is it only the second ending?) verges on a complete mystery as it ends the whole story with the sentence:

> When Beryl returned her face was dead white; she stared at Harriet in silence, and even when Harriet finally grabbed hold of her shoulders and shook her hard, she would not say anything.   (p. 105)

Ironically, her story ends, 'she would not say anything', a typically self-referring sentence, for Bowles herself will also say nothing; only vague insinuations of accident or suicide hover. To complicate matters, a remark the 'Indian' makes in the second ending seems to refer to the second stage, the seduction scene, of the first ending. Yet both endings in that case must have occurred simultaneously. The Indian says, insinuatingly '"that woman's got impulses", he added with a broad grin' (p. 105). Thus the two contradictory endings coalesce in the reference to a seduction, coming together in a narrative copulation that generates total indeterminacy. Truman Capote was certainly making an outrageously ironic understatement when he innocently remarked of 'Camp Cataract' that it was 'to my mind the most complete of Mrs Bowles' stories and the one most representative of her work .... This story alone would require that we accord Jane Bowles high esteem'. 'Most complete' with its inconsistently consistent alternative endings – it certainly is, alongside their indeterminate meanings. Version one ends with seduction, or is it hallucination, leading to an 'accidental' leap into the waterfall and possibly (surely?) death. Version two suggests suicide or accident or anything, literally anything else you can imagine.[13] These indeterminate 'forking paths', these complexities and possibilities are the very heart of modernist texts, but rarely so finely realised: they are certainly representative of Bowles' best work.

'Camp Cataract', like *Two Serious Ladies*, is, thematically, about Bowles' favourite human experience, 'going out in the world', an experience which suggests growing up, the creation of an original individuality, the overcoming of conventional restraints in life (family, society) and art, the exploration of the unconscious, and other metaphors. For Bowles, as for Stevie Smith, growing up and becoming an original self is not something that just happens to people through time: it is achieved only through conflict, struggle, courage, and immense labour. This labour is also a part of the arduous process of becoming an original artist, of overcoming the imprisoning conventions and expectations of the literary tradition. Decorum and even duty must be breached, as Bowles showed in her play, *In the Summer House*,[14] where the struggle for autonomy leads to deaths and conflicts on a tragic scale. Many of Jane Bowles' stories explore the theme of parent–child relations, but her play is a powerful analysis particularly of the mother–daughter dynamic and its deadly effects. 'Camp Cataract' articulates more generally the imprisoning effects of the family institution, and of siblings. And in *Two Serious Ladies*, Miss Goering symbolically leaves her ancestral home (and patriarchal society) for personal self-discovery, of a shocking kind to the reader.[15] In all cases, Bowles' characters are involved in journeys of self-discovery and self-development.

They seek out the shocking, the unexpected, because they see this as the path to wisdom, downward inevitably from the point of view of polite society. Her characters often seem to be seeking those 'moments of being' of Virginia Woolf, where experience is deepened and intensified beyond the deadening ordinariness of everyday life, and in this they share much with Rhys' characters who reject the sameness and monotony of polite society.

Like Miss Goering, Mrs Copperfield journeys away from patriarchy too, but she moves into exploration of relations with women. These relations are more emotional than overtly sexual, but Bowles' novel implies that even these can be radically subversive acts, as Djuna Barnes' *Nightwood* and H. D.'s novels had already shown. Bowles, Barnes, and H. D. all challenged the notion of D. H. Lawrence that 'sexual difference is absolute'; this duality (at the root of all western life and thought) is rejected also by Virginia Woolf's *Orlando*, for example. These writers not only rejected the absoluteness of sexual difference; they redefine woman's sexuality as itself a multitude of possibilities, of forms of behaviour in need of exploration. There is no simple choice for women between two dichotomies of heterosexual identity or a lesbian role. Life offers a ceaseless transformation of sexual forms of behaviour and identity, as different people are shown by these writers to bring out different selves and responses from a character.

H. D. saw Freud's psychoanalytic project in analysis as a quest for the hidden life – that endlessly explorable inner country – and she transformed this into a quest for spiritual identity in such novels as *Her* (1981) and *Bid Me to Live* (1960), and in much of her poetry. May Sinclair, in *Mary Olivier: A Life* (1919), and in *The Life and Death of Harriett Frean* (1920), took up this theme: in the latter novel, she portrayed a spiritual death in life which resulted from acquiescence in respectability and the mediocrity of life dominated by unconscious social conventions. Bowles' characters are involved in an urgent effort to escape such burial, as is Mary Olivier, or Miriam Henderson, though their routes are entirely different; hence, Bowles never portrayed the spiritual independence of a Miriam or a Mary. H. D. used freer linguistic and ideational categories than did Bowles for overcoming the spiritually deadening, inflexible structures and logical schemata of conventional realist writing; Bowles challenged the latter in a way more akin to Stevie Smith's style with her 'off-centre' parodies of clichéd, stereotyped language. All three writers used similarly fragmented narrative structures, however, though

Smith and H. D. share much in their use of stream of consciousness. These writers also share with Gertrude Stein a language which is intensely self-conscious and deliberately draws attention to linguistic principles of operation. Bowles and Rhys particularly strip their language of any pretentions, while H. D., Stevie Smith, and Djuna Barnes, for example, use more allusiveness and richly textured language. Some of Bowles' language verges on the denuded, childish language of Gertrude Stein, as Bowles too played with language and let it play with her. Bowles' language represents a rejection of the serious and decorous tone of much male writing. Her unauthorised, arbitrary description of stereotyped responses and her incessant mockery of categories, especially those which apply to people and emotions, constitute a sustained attempt by Bowles to liberate herself, her characters, and her readers from the powerfully unconscious assumptions which determine our ways of seeing the world and responding to it, whether emotionally, aesthetically, morally, or intellectually. Bowles has an almost Wittgenstein-like respect for language as a complex of 'forms of life', of modes of behaviour and response to the world involving games, codes, and rules which are all as much conventions, and therefore subject to change, as are fashions in food and styles of dress. Bowles experiments with these rules and games and codes in such a way as to reveal that language games inform our social roles and interactions, our political relations, and our access to power structures. Her analysis of our lives as language users shows that our moral and aesthetic values as well as our perception of 'facts' can change radically if we allow ourselves to become aware of the extent to which linguistic conventions of unexamined categories, logical syntax, and unconscious dualisms inhibit imaginative, individual response and condemn us to a stereotyped existence. Bowles' art is the narrative of life's endless possibilities, and of her own life as the living narrative of art's possibilities.

Conclusion: The 'Voice of Silence' Speaks

In one of Isak Dinesen's tales, a story-teller remarked to the listener: 'The divine art is the story .... In the beginning was the story ... where the story-teller is loyal, eternally, unswervingly loyal to the story, there, in the end, silence will speak ... We, the faithful, when we have spoken our last word, will hear the voice of silence ...' ('The Cardinal's First Tale', in *Last Tales*). The wedding guest who heard Coleridge's ancient mariner's narrative had precisely the same reaction: 'He went like one / that hath been stunned / And is of sense forlorn ....' Flannery O'Connor was quoted in the Introduction as saying that stories of any depth tell the tale, in an endless variety of disguises, of the mysterious passage past the dragon of St Cyril; it requires, she continued, considerable courage at any time, in any country, not to turn away from the story-teller. In these several authors, several major themes have arisen, which express much of the interest of the present study, namely, literary conventions involving ideas of silence, mystery, journeys and passages, disguises, and the need for courage and loyalty in reading and responding to literature. We could argue, along with Eudora Welty, for example, that every fiction has as its plot the conflict between life and death, however much it may be told with variations and originality. Put another way, every story involves a search, an errand of search, rather – a hunt, a quest.

All these terms referring to familiar literary conventions imply a journey, a passage, or some kind of travelling, whether in the world or the psyche. Both conflict and search or journey involves what we could term another fictional convention, namely encounters; indeed, to use a term from Greek tragedy, we could call encounters 'recognition scenes'. The encounter could be said to be an encounter with 'Reality' – what Virginia Woolf called 'moments of being', what James Joyce called 'epiphanic moments', or what sometimes is referred to by the phrase 'spots of time'. Socrates and Plato described such moments as intimations of self-knowledge: works of art become looking-glasses (sometimes cracked ones) or mirrors in which the audience is offered the rare opportunity to gain a perspective on itself and view itself in a new way, in all its strengths and weaknesses, its insights and failures of insight, as did the convention of the Greek chorus or the similar, carefully crafted techniques of Sanskrit dramatists some fourteen hundred years ago.

More recently, writers as diverse as Nadine Gordimer, O'Connor, or Katherine Mansfield have argued explicitly that change, transformation, or revelation is another central literary convention in fiction. Change can be portrayed through dramatic action, but also through psychological awakening, another familiar code, but in all cases, transformation usually involves a change in the relation of a character to 'Reality' – a change of impression or perception, an increment in awareness. Alice Walker, in speaking of O'Connor's conventions, said that essential to her fiction is a moment of explosive revelation, usually at times of extreme loss or crisis. The individual character, Walker explained, is shown to come face to face with his or her limitations. She or he comprehends for a moment the frontiers of her own inner country. This action O'Connor called spiritual growth; we might risk naming it moral transformation, and it is a sub-theme as well as a main theme of many works of art. Yet we should also be alert for the tale which sets up a quest, an encounter, or a possibility of change, and then charts the *failure* of a character to respond. In this case, we often view ourselves in the mirror the story holds up to us, too: that is, as often as not, failure of communication between author and reader is a metaphor hidden behind the surface narrative. The author could be said to be narrating the tale of the anticipation of failure of communication as much as its partial, occasional success.

In such cases especially, it takes great courage not to turn away from the story-teller, as she unfolds the blindness and prejudice which can inhibit audience response. Loyalty from the reader is as essential as loyalty from the writer: if we remain loyal to the tale, no matter how painful its truths – its reflections of our visage – we may open ourselves to the transformations, changes, and increments of insight that the characters are apparently described as experiencing or, also, missing. In this way, the plot of every work is not only the conflict between life and death, so to speak, but between the writer and the reader, and indeed between aspects of the reader's own self: stories and novels, then, can narrate passages which are journeys for writer and reader, as well as characters; the quests, hunts, and searches described and referred directly to the characters in the text are metaphors indirectly for the errands of search and quests invoked in reading and seeking to make meaning of what is read.

The encounters in all stories and novels are, conventionally, emblematic of the reader's and writer's encounters with the text itself, while every fictional character's behaviour becomes a potential analogy for reading response, whether as model or anti-model.

Novels and stories, have, in a manner of speaking, a tendency to set up oppositions and tensions – which are not by any means resolved. Sometimes tales move from one opposition to another as they proceed to develop, oppositions of character, action, or even of plot; through oppositions in imagery, situation, theme, metaphor, and manner, tales weave a design. Often the reader discovers that these oppositions turn out to be aspects of a single unity: two or more opposing characters may be two sides of a conflict in a single psyche. Two opposing situations may unfold as metaphors for a single, complex event seen from different perspectives. Gradually, the structures and patterns of texts will reveal themselves to the reader who is awake to the tendency of tensions to be integrated, in critical ways, in artistic productions. Sometimes separate plots will be seen as mirror images of each other, or an apparently unrelated happening will reveal itself to be emblematic of the whole story. Parts seemingly opposed to a whole collapse into uneasy, transient unities, depending on readerly response. Endings are transformed abruptly into beginnings, while beginnings are arbitrarly exposed as finalities.

Tensions at the structural level of a text often involve self-conscious metaphors about art and story-telling – the latter becomes the covert theme of fiction, which seems (and is!) about something else entirely. In this way the reader constantly catches glimpses of her or himself in the looking-glass that is the tale, but only if we can overcome the paralysing distance between art and reality at a conscious level. This chasmic distance can be vaulted by imaginative reading, with the sudden but repeated realisation that the events described in the text are happening to the reader right now, in the process of reading, as Beckett's *Godot* or Sophocles *Oedipus Rex* exemplified. This conscious realisation is achieved when the underlying metaphorical description of perception glimmers from behind the surface thematics. The sub-text of every fiction is perception itself, we might argue – that is, reading, writing, interpretation, and the making meaning of texts, words, language, experience. All readers have to press their imagination to new efforts in order to arouse themselves to the vision that the characters in each fiction are not only models and anti-models for us in our lives. More immediately and more effectively, they shine out as models of us as readers – passive readers, alert readers, recalcitrant readers, naïve readers: every type of reading and response may be mirrored – represented – as these works of fiction parody, ironise, and metaphorise the experiences of coming face to face with the 'Reality' that is ourselves – in all its disguises and variations.

'Reality' comes to leer at characters and they are rarely prepared to bear it: life threatens, death threatens, and however small and intimate the situation used to convey this confrontation, large, complex situations are usually implied and symbolised. Characters and their encounters, quests, journeys, and recognitions 'connect us with the vastness of our secret life, which is endlessly explorable' (Eudora Welty). But when the plot of fiction is closest to becoming congruent with the form, then the work is at its highest level of artistry. We have looked already at a number of works which achieve just this extraordinary congruence, by means of revitalised, yet surprisingly familiar conventions, and this is art at its intensest.

One example of such congruence through these familiar but revitalised conventions is when a text tries to narrate the experience of life being imprisoned within the word. Language is foregrounded as the reader is shown the harmony between the medium – style – and the message – content, so that the 'meaning' of the tale is not crystallisable from the artistic whole. Hence, in part at least, arises the 'silence' at the end of the story mentioned earlier. Put in more aesthetic terms, the reason, confronted with the imagination, is at its most reasonable when it admits its appreciation for the limits of its own nature: it merges itself into an imaginative reason instead of remaining reason in its logical, discursive, and deductive form. As imaginative reason, it seeks out the intricacies and patterns of the artefact without trying to dissolve the silence and mystery, the tension and vastness of life and reality, into 'comprehensible' propositional forms. The imagination can 'divine', in some symbolic sense of that word, what the senses and intellect operating according to the conventions of familiar logic, cannot encompass, anymore than we can explain the meaning of a joke or a metaphor without losing the wit of it. Something like this may be what Forster implied in his final chapter of *Aspects of the Novel*, when he discussed the 'fiction of prophecy' which involves a universal struggle or contest – perhaps that life and death conflict – a contest which reaches out into infinity from individuality, he said, and which always implies more that it can say, because it reaches down into the depths of the mysteries of life.

One of the main aspects of fiction is the role of surprise in the plot, which adds to suspense and increases curiosity. Stories are often written so as 'not to comply with what may be expected'. Hence the incredible range of experimentation we find in fiction writers, who leave no conventions untouched. Time, space, order, structure, language, style, action, theme, characterisation, imagery, plot – everything is pulled and stretched toward some human truth. To be 'unswervingly loyal to the story' – as we noted at the outset – means, for a writer, to act inevitably toward the truth in sight, whatever unexpected ways and means must be used to achieve it. The author's desire not to swerve away from the unexpected, not to give in, not to comply with the reader's expectations is one source of originality and of beauty in art. Yet, to the insensitive eye, such beauty often looks monstrous, ugly, unacceptable, even morally offensive. As intelligent readers, we must be sharply alert for these very feelings and responses within ourselves, for apparent uglinesses are often going to turn out (upon examination) to be not flaws in the work of art, but the very nexus of originality and artistic achievement of a fine writer. This transformation from ugliness to beauty is one way of describing the mysterious passage of the reader which leads to the voice of silence. According to Flannery O'Connor, for example, imagery and technique will often look wild, ugly, or grotesque to a reader because of the discrepancies a prophetic writer seeks to combine: namely, the visible world with the deeper, invisible world shining with implications and meanings. Prophetic writers reach down into the depths of the concrete world to touch hidden unities and patterns obscured by surface details and concrete individualities, though the latter are most certainly the means, by tactful selection, which every writer must use to reach (though not exactly to illuminate) depths. For to touch, explore, and experience profound reaches is not to illuminate them by the light of reason. It is rather to accustom oneself to the surrounding strangeness or darkness, while respecting its resistance to clear description or comprehension by the often enlightening, but equally often reductive, intellect.

Monstrous, ugly, and grotesque writing occurs because one of the truths a prophetic writer seeks to tell the reader is the revelation that what is accepted as natural and commonplace is itself often perverse, grotesque, and monstrous, such as war, or social relations, or poverty. Hence the need for that 'courage' if the reader is to be able to face a dose of such disturbing reality. As readers of fiction, we can be alert to the conventions mentioned above for enriching and deepening our response to the immediacy of every tale – to the particularity of every story, which makes it, in a sense, a living thing with an individuality which must be grasped by the reader's imagination, if the imaginative dimensions of fiction are to be 'encountered'. The tendency of most art is to reach out and grab the reader, to drag her right into the midst of the action and thematics of the work. Such active participation in this drama – in the revelation, change, or transformation, that spiritual and moral growth which the characters and readers experience (or fail to experience) – explodes the already nearly exhausted myth that the reader is an objective spectator of independently constituted characters, actions, and meanings which we passively observe and receive from the author. The reader is wholly implicated in any act of interpreting, which is why so many works of art have as their own overt and central thematics the interpretation of the meaning of characters' actions and intentions. That is, characters are dramatised agonising over the moral, aesthetic, and personal actions of other characters, seeking interpretations, while involved in the very making of those interpretations. Any objectivity or authoritative position is shown to be a fantasy and an unsustainable ideology. Hence, the emphasis in many tales on views, sightings, perspectives, and gazes.

This idea of even the central characters' point of view being under scrutiny in every story (thus implicating the reader as viewer, too) takes us to the next major convention of story-telling under consideration, namely the point of view of the narrator. Particularly in twentieth century fiction, and certainly in the texts discussed in this study, but also in other times and countries, the narrative point of view is often indeterminate, often parodied, or often split into meta-fictional levels of discourse by means of irony, framework techniques, or self-conscious, self-referring devices. Tales are embedded within tales, for example, or the apparent objective narrative authority is undermined by a partly hidden level of irony. Narrative point of view is ironised by placing the characters on a balcony, as in 'Roman Fever', or by emphasising point of view tirelessly as in Woolf's *Between the Acts*. As has been shown above, authors draw the readers' attention to the conventions of story-telling by innumerable devices, often, for example, by disrupting conventions usually thought of as sacred. Hence Jane Bowles unobtrusively steals in alternative endings to her 'Camp Cataract' story which actually seem to work, yet are totally inconsistent with each other when the reader looks closely! Endings of stories are further undermined by insinuations that things are really only beginning now. 'Then the curtain rose. They spoke', is one typical example of an ending which disrupts neat conclusions. Other stories end with phrases like 'starting all over again', or they begin with the 'falling of the curtain'.

Another central convention of art which acts as a bridge between narrative techniques and thematics is the use of the 'extraordinary' to initiate revelations and reversals. I mean, the convention of the holiday, the play, the party, the circus, the theatre, the masquerade, to intensify the illusion and draw the reader more deeply into the questioning of normal, everyday life as itself a circus, a dream, as grotesque and theatrical. Questions about the nature of the self are posed, as masks, disguises, and roles are shown to be a part of the theatre or circus that is everyday life. These conventions are used to 'strip the veil of familiarity' from normality, to reveal its cruelty, perversity, and unnaturalness. Such conventions thus act to question the very relation between reality and illusion, between life and art, history and fiction, truth and lie. The barriers between these oppositions are broken down in the thematics of many works, as outings, excursions, journeys, holidays, parties, theatricals, and circuses turn into revealing metaphors of confrontations with reality. Such techniques bring the reader face to face with the problem of reading and making meaning, and the boundaries of the work of art expand to include the perceptual, interpretive acts of the audience. The themes, then, of communication and of language (and their failure) are always a covert if not an overt subject matter of fiction. The mystery of shaping human experience into words which both imprison and liberate confronts us with that 'Reality' of which we can bear so little. As Katherine Anne Porter expressed it, 'Is it not almost the sole end of civilised education of all sorts to teach us to be more and more highly, sensitively conscious of the reality of the existence, the essential being, of others, those around us so very like us and yet so bafflingly, mysteriously different?'

Notes

Notes to Chapter 1: Introduction

1. Flannery O'Connor, *Mystery and Manners: Occasional Prose* (London: 1972) p. 35.
2. *Art as Experience* (1934) Ch. 2.
3. Edith Wharton, *In Morocco* (London: 1927) p. 21.
4. See below, Chs 7 and 8 for Smith and Bowles. Atwood's *Surfacing* uses the image of the passage for innumerable metaphoric journeys – into the unconscious, into death, into the birth of individuality from stereotyped roles. Rachell Ingall's *Binstead's Safari* (1983) is an astonishingly effective example of the same, as is Doris Lessing's *Briefing for a Descent into Hell* (1971) and *Memoirs of a Survivor* (1974). Less centrally, Barnes' *Nightwood* (1937) combines the journey with the quest and the search. These are but three of, literally, hundreds of examples in twentieth-century women's writing of the effective use of this ancient convention.
5. Percy Bysshe Shelley, 'Defence of Poetry' (not published until 1840).
6. As early as *The Golden Notebook* (1962), Lessing was questioning the adequacy of realism to do justice to experience through fiction. That novel is an extraordinarily radical experiment in structure which anticipates her later novelistic challenges to realism, from *Briefing for a Descent into Hell* (1971) to *Memoirs of a Survivor* (1974) and finally to the 'science fiction' of the last decade. Built into the structure of *The Golden Notebook* is a critique of traditional realism, which involves more than mere alterations to the basic ideology of language as a transparent medium, and fiction as a representation of some objective reality. Lessing argued in her preface to a later edition of *The Golden Notebook* that the changing nature of human experience creates a need for new fictional forms. Lessing's innovative fragmentation of structure in the novel includes a parody of the inadequacy of a realist novel, *Free Women*, to say anything and an exploration of the absurdities of trying to report neutrally and objectively the world around one through diaries or newspaper cuttings. Through the thematic struggle of Anna for a new kind of experience, meaningfulness, both in life and literature, is shown to inhere not so much in ideas or plots or events, but in openness and flexibility of form in writing and of response in living.
7. Eudora Welty, in *The Eye of the Story: Selected Essays and Reviews* (London: 1987), p. 94, gave an apt definition of such congruence:

> it is when the plot, whatever it is, is nearest to becoming the same thing on the outside as it is deep inside, that it is purest. When it is identifiable in every motion and progression of its own with the

189

motions and progressions of the story's feeling and its intensity, then this plot is put to its highest use.

8. For Wharton's parodic use of the knitting metaphor, see 'Roman Fever', in *Roman Fever and Other Stories* (London: 1983) and see discussion below, Ch. 4.

9. I mean such texts as *Between the Acts* (1941), which constantly raises the question of the relationship of these dualities both directly and through its repeated use of metafictional devices, Young's *Miss MacIntosh, My Darling* (1965), a kind of 1960s Joycean epic novel which takes as its central theme the fantastic nature of reality, and numerous texts of Carter, Lessing, and Erdrich, such as *Love Medicine* (1983).

10. John Dewey, *Experience and Nature* (1925), Ch. 5.

11. Exposure of duality in the formal (as well as thematic) structure of novels occurs in, for example, Ellen Glasgow's *The Sheltered Life* (1932), with her alternating narrative point of view from youth to age, mixed with a Faulkner-like stream of consciousness. Or compare Woolf's *Mrs Dalloway* (1925), which overcomes duality through characterisation, while *Pilgrimage* (1915–67), works at the narrative level by rejecting both subjective and objective points of view for a fusion of the two in Miriam's self-other transcendence. May Sinclair attacked duality through her narrative use of time in *Mary Olivier* (1919).

12. See especially *Voyage in the Dark* (Harmondsworth: 1987) and *After Leaving Mr MacKenzie* (Harmondsworth: 1982).

13. William James, in *Pragmatism* (1907) and *The Meaning of Truth* (1909).

14. See especially Edith Wharton, *Italian Backgrounds* (1905) for constant references to conceptions of nature as the product of cultural assumptions.

15. Isak Dinesan, in, for example, *Seven Gothic Tales* (Harmondsworth: 1988, originally published in 1934) and *Last Tales* (Harmondsworth: 1986, originally published 1957).

16. An expression from Shelley's *Defence of Poetry* (written in 1820, published first in 1840 by Mary Shelley).

17. Nadine Gordimer, introduction to *Some Monday for Sure* (London: 1976).

18. In *Miss MacIntosh, My Darling* (New York: 1965). For an interesting discussion of this all-too little known epic novel, see Miriam Fuchs, 'Marguerite Young's *Miss MacIntosh, My Darling*: Liquescence as Form', in *Breaking the Sequence: Women's Experimental Fiction*, ed. E. G. Friedman and M. Fuchs (Princeton, NJ: 1989), pp. 188–98. And see S. Shaviro, 'Marguerite Young's Exorbitant Vision', in *Critique: Studies in Contemporary Fiction*, xxxi, 3 (Spring 1990) pp. 213–22.

19. For example, Janet Frame's *Scented Gardens for the Blind* (1982) and Bessie Head's *A Question of Power* (1974).

20. See especially Welty's first novel, *The Robber Bridegroom* (1942), for the most sustained example of the appropriation of fairy tale for modern purposes.

21. Flannery O'Connor, 'Some Aspects of the Grotesque in Southern Fiction', in *Mystery and Manners* (London: 1972), pp. 36–50.
22. Ellen Glasgow, 'Preface', *The Sheltered Life* (1932).
23. See especially, 'Proceed from the Dream', in *A Woman Speaks* (London: 1982), pp. 115–47.
24. Carson McCullers, 'The Flowering Dream', in *The Mortgaged Heart and other Essays* (Harmondsworth: 1985).
25. Angela Carter, unpublished interview.
26. Flannery O'Connor, *op. cit.*, p. 50.

Notes to Chapter 2: Excavating Meaning in Willa Cather's Novels

1. Sarah Orne Jewett (1849–1909), who wrote the beautifully crafted novel *The Country of Pointed Firs* (1896; London: 1897), which anticipated modernist impatience with the emphasis on plot and enumeration in realist writing, with its meditative, lyrical evocation of the 'power of place'. See Cather's essay 'The Best Stories of Sarah Orne Jewett', in *On Writing*, foreword by S. Tennant (New York: 1968) pp. 47–59.
2. For further biographical information see Phyllis C. Robinson, *Willa: The Life of Willa Cather* (New York: 1983); David Stouck, *Willa Cather's Imagination* (Lincoln, Nebraska: 1975), and many other earlier memoirs by, for example, Edith Lewis and Elizabeth Sergeant. For a bibliography of Cather's works, see Joan Crane, *Willa Cather: A Bibliography* (1982).
3. Michel Foucault, *Archaeology of Knowledge* (London: 1972), first published 1969 as *L'Archéologie du Savoir*, where Foucault explicitly questioned, moreover, the unexamined conventions and assumptions involved in the writing of history, as had Cather implicitly in many of her novels.
4. See Flannery O'Connor, *Mystery and Manners: Occasional Prose* (London: 1972), especially 'Some Aspects of the Grotesque in Southern Fiction', pp. 36–50, and 'The Nature and Aims of Fiction', pp. 63–86, as, for example, when she wrote: 'The beginning of human knowledge is through the senses, and the fiction writer begins where human perception begins ... the world of the fiction writer is full of matter' (p. 67).
5. Coleridge's Pythagorean view compares with Cather's naturalistic philosophy: 'The very powers which in men reflect and contemplate are in their essence the same as those powers which in nature produce the objects contemplated' (*The Philosophical Lectures*, ed. K. Coburn (London: 1949)).
6. See especially 'The Novel Démeublé', in *On Writing*, foreword by S. Tennant (New York: 1968), pp. 33–44.
7. To use Antonia Byatt's metaphor, Cather saw human beings as 'forms of energy' rather than as characters in any realist sense. See

Byatt's preface to *A Lost Lady* (London: 1980; first published 1923) p. xiv. Eudora Welty argued that Cather's art relied on the intensity of the passion, especially as expressed in the formal unity of the novels and in the characterisation. See 'The House of Willa Cather', in *The Eye of the Story* (London: 1987) pp. 41–60.

8. 'On the Art of Fiction', in *On Writing*, *op. cit.*
9. See Coleridge, who stated the necessity in art and in writing for compression: 'A little *compression* would make it a beautiful poem. *Study Compression!* –' (*Collected Letters*, ed. E. L. Griggs (Oxford: 1956), vol. I, p. 351). Many more elements of a 'Romantic' aesthetic are evident in Cather's theories about art and writing.
10. 'On the Art of Fiction', in *On Writing*, *op. cit.*, p. 102.
11. 'The Novel Démeublé', in *On Writing*, *op. cit.*, pp. 41–2.
12. Compare this with Katherine Anne Porter's stories, for the importance of using memory creatively and of not living in the past or the future, but in the present.
13. See *The Letters and Journals of Katherine Mansfield: A Selection*, ed. and introduced by C. K. Stead (Harmondsworth: 1977) p. 192:

> We only live by somehow absorbing the past – changing it. I mean, really examining it and dividing what is important from what is not (for there *is* waste), and transforming it so that it becomes part of the life of the spirit and we are *free of it*. It's no longer our personal past, it's just in the highest possible sense our servant ... no longer our master.

14. The *Kingdom of Art: Willa Cather's First Principles and Critical Statements 1893–96*, ed. B. Slote (Lincoln, Nebraska: 1976), p. 76.
15. And see Antonia Byatt, preface to *A Lost Lady* (London: 1980; first published 1923), who argued that for Cather 'passion' (in the Coleridgean sense of imaginative energy) was valued over everything else.
16. William Blake, letter to Dr Trusler, 23 August 1799: 'To the Eyes of the Man of Imagination, Nature is Imagination itself'.
17. Another 'Romantic' principle, both English and German. See Coleridge's *Biographia Literaria*, Ch. 12, on self-consciousness, and see Friedrich Schlegel, Ludwig Tieck, and Jean Paul Richter for similar arguments.
18. A central argument of modern critical theory and of romanticism. See, for example, Paul de Man, *Allegories of Reading* (London: 1979) and Barbara Johnson, *The Critical Difference* (Baltimore: 1980).
19. See Cather's contemporary, John Dewey, *Art as Experience* (1934) or *Experience and Nature* (1929), for a thorough discussion of this distinction between intelligent and inchoate experience, between excellence and mediocrity.
20. See, for example, J. H. Randall III, 'An Interpretation of My Ántonia', in *Willa Cather and her Critics*, ed. James Schroeter (Ithaca and London: 1967), pp. 272–322, which certainly seems to bear out de Man's ideas about 'blindness and insight'.

21. Kate Fulbrook, in *Free Women* (Brighton: 1990), discussed this issue only briefly and in passing in her chapter on Willa Cather. This theme of the power and destructive nature of fantasies is taken up by Chopin and Rhys, amongst others; see the relevant chapters below, which show all these authors deeply committed to exposing such illusions in order to liberate both men and women from the damaging consequences.

22. See Antonia Byatt, preface to *A Lost Lady, op. cit.*, who indicated the importance to an understanding of Cather's art of an awareness of her experiments in narrators, points of view, and limited personas. And see James Schroeter, *op. cit.*, pp. 20–4, who also discussed briefly narrative personas in *My Mortal Enemy, The Professor's House,* and *A Lost Lady*. Neither discussed it in relation to *My Ántonia,* however.

23. This is part of the meaning of Sophocles' Oedipus plays: a socio-logical/psychological analysis of the merging of wife–mother roles and how destructive such a merging is for the emotional maturation of both men and women, as each remains trapped in an infantile stage of emotional non-development.

24. See numerous essays in James Schroeter, *op. cit.*, for this stubborn blindness of Cather's readers to appreciate her narrative strategies and stylistic innovations. For example, see the essays of J. W. Krutch, Mary McCarthy, and, finally, Edmund Wilson, who attacked Cather's rejection of realist props as idealist and contrary to the social realist novels he preferred.

25. For the destructiveness of 'muddles' in human relationship, see E. M. Forster, especially *Howard's End*, but also *Passage to India*.

26. 'On the Art of Fiction', *op. cit.*, p. 103.

27. See Barbara Johnson, *The Critical Difference, op. cit.*, on a similar process in Melville's *Billy Budd*.

28. For example, J. H. Randall, *op. cit.*

29. Like Wharton, Cather was fascinated by the fictionalization of the past by historians, as is evident especially in *The Professor's House*. Both her own novels and those of Wharton's (see the relevant chapter below) are saturated with insights that act as powerful commentaries on the blindness of the 'New Historicist's' naïve treatment of history as the reality to which literature is a supplement. On the contrary, most of the writers discussed here, not to mention Virginia Woolf, Richardson, Barnes, Stein, May Sinclair, and other modernists, were deeply impressed by the dependence not only of 'history' on artefacts and literature for its 'traces'. They were also impressed by the interdependence of autobiography, fiction, and history.

30. In this sense, Cather's novels constitute a kind of existentialist statement, like the writings of Kierkegaard, Coleridge, and Sartre, for example. See Kierkegaard's *Diary* (New York: 1960) p. 109: 'You must become perfected … when you are not becoming perfected … you must at once confess [that] it is my own fault. I myself am the only obstacle to my becoming perfected'. This is almost a direct commentary on such novels as *The Song of the Lark*, but is a hidden

theme of all Cather's novels, with their implicit, if not explicit, emphasis upon mediocrity versus excellence and the individual's responsibility, which, while it occurs in a social context of restrictions and opportunities, is still a vital portion of self-development.

31. 'The Novel Démeublé', p. 41. This compares with many of Flannery O'Connor's later statements in *Mystery and Manners*, for example, on the central role of understatement (p. 79) and on the need for the symbolic mode, which involves concrete details accumulating meanings by operating on several levels of depth, beyond (but through) the literal level. This increases the story's richness of meaning in every direction, she argued (pp. 71–2): 'fiction pushes its own limits outwards toward mystery; meaning only begins at depth'.

32. See Kate Fulbrook, *Free Women, op. cit.*, pp. 33–56, who seemed disturbed by Cather's emphasis on naked energies of a Dionysiac, Nietzschean kind.

33. Compare Thea's D. H. Lawrence insistence, in *The Kingdom of Art, op. cit.*, p. 88: 'You can't know it with your mind. You have to realize it in your body, somehow; deep. It's an animal sort of feeling'.

34. Another favourite metaphor in modern critical theory; see Johnson, for example, on frames and framing, *The Critical Difference, op. cit.*

35. 'Identity' was one of the great issues of modernist writing, as it still is today. Virginia Woolf may have most systematically revealed the artificiality of borders between and around people, showing how we all flow into each other and into our environment, to the extent that individuality is a figure of speech not to be taken too literally. Compare Nietzsche, in *The Will to Power* or Shelley, in 'A Defence of Poetry', who both argued that the notion of individuality is as much a metaphor as is society.

36. Though at the same time it itself has integrity, as it charts what Cather called the 'tragic necessity' of human relationships, since they can never be wholly satisfactory. See the essay 'Katherine Mansfield', in *Not under Forty* (New York: 1936). See also Antonia Byatt's preface to *The Song of the Lark* (London: 1982; first published 1915) p. xvii, where she describes Thea as realising that the family is the artist's natural enemy.

37. Cather's Outland story anticipates much of the criticisms engendered recently by the five hundredth anniversary of Columbus's discovery of America, the implication clearly being that it was a disaster for the indigenous peoples.

38. In *Howard's End* and in numerous other of Forster's novels and prose writings.

39. They also suggest Cather's sophistication about what is involved in naming, in classifying, in categorising – all involving, that is, metaphor-making, with words understood as meaningful not refer-entially but relationally, as metaphors within a figurative discourse of reverberating, limitless connotations, not denotations primarily.

40. See my *Sources, Processes and Methods in Coleridge's 'Biographia Literaria'* (Cambridge: 1980) for further discussion, and see 'Kant and Romanticism', *Philosophy and Literature* (1989), pp. 42–56.

41. See Shelley's 'Defence of Poetry', on the idea that literal language is a 'dead metaphor'.
42. Coleridge practically defined imagination as the faculty of 'humanising nature', in his Shakespearean criticism.
43. Compare J. Schroeter, *op. cit.*, pp. 20–2, about the notion of landscape as character, much as it functions in some of Thomas Hardy's novels, especially in Cather's *Death Comes for the Archbishop*; and see his comment:

> '[that novel is] surely the most experimental ... the author throws out all the ordinary sources of appeal – plot and story, surprise, characterization in the usual sense of the term, social criticism and the play of ideas, wit ... instead of these, the author takes what may be the slightest resource at the writer's command – simply what might be called 'scene', the power of establishing with words the feel of the place – and elevates this to the unifying principle of the book'. (p. 24)

44. The 'recognition scene' is also an emblem of figuration itself: to see something different as, now, like, is a description of figuration. Compare Nietzsche's 'Gleichmachen', or appropriation.
45. See Schroeter, *op. cit.*, pp. 22–4 and see Rebecca West, 'The Classic Artist', in Schroeter, *op. cit.*, pp. 62–71. West described *Death Comes for the Archbishop* as 'the feat of making a composition out of the juxtaposition of different states of being' (p. 63). She also compared Cather to D. H. Lawrence (p. 67) and praised Cather on her great sympathy for artists doing different things from herself.
46. As the 'obtrusion of the moral', as Coleridge described it, into the 'pure imaginativeness' of 'The Ancient Mariner' at the end of the poem.

Notes to Chapter 3: Kate Chopin: Ironist of Realism

1. For further biographical material see Emily Toth, *Kate Chopin* (London: 1990) and Per Seyersted, *Kate Chopin: A Critical Biography* (Baton Rouge: 1969). For background, see L. Ziff, *The American 1890s: Life and Times of a Lost Generation* (London: 1967). And see Priscilla Allen, 'Old Critics and New: The Treatment of Chopin's *The Awakening*', in *The Authority of Experience*, ed. A. Diamond and L. R. Edwards (1977) pp. 224–38, for useful critical background. More generally, note Helen Taylor's excellent *Gender, Race, and Region* (London: 1989). And see Anne G. Jones, *Tomorrow is Another Day: The Woman Writer in the South, 1859–1936* (Baton Rouge: 1981). Willa Cather's review of *The Awakening* is reprinted in *The World and the Parish: Willa Cather's Articles and Reviews, 1893–1902*, ed. W. M. Cullin (Lincoln, Nebraska: 1970) vol. II, pp. 693–4.

2. Two decades later, Dorothy Richardson was undergoing a similar dissatisfaction with realism; see Kate Fulbrook, *Free Women* (London: 1990) pp. 114–15 and Elaine Showalter, *A Literature of their Own* (Princeton: 1977) pp. 253–5, on Richardson's repudiation of realism.

3. Chopin anticipated modernist challenges to realist order, with their parodying of structure, specifically by reversals of beginnings and endings or by ironizing definitive conclusions. For such writers as Djuna Barnes, Virginia Woolf, May Sinclair, and others, experiments in structure, unity, and order were designed to reveal the arbitrariness of order and especially of determinate endings, whether in art and fiction or in life. In *Pilgrimage*, Miriam remarks, 'It did not matter. Nothing was at an end. Nothing would ever come to an end again' (vol. III, p. 129); later, she complains of a friend, 'He had never for a moment shared her sense of endlessness' (vol. III, p. 304).

4. Chopin also anticipated modernists' fascination with death portrayed as ambiguous or even as a positive experience. For Djuna Barnes, death is represented as a fortuitous release from a universe of meaninglessness. In Rhys' *Voyage in the Dark*, a comparable ambiguity in Anna's death by abortion is notable (in part due to Rhys' publisher, who apparently protested at the pessimism of a more definitive account).

5. The decadence of realism itself is a theme of some modernist writing as it ironises and undermines the presuppositions and unexamined assumptions of realism. Djuna Barnes' *Nightwood* is as different from Chopin's text as any book could be, yet it shares with it this curious reversal, of seeing realism itself as the decadent ideology, along with many of the assumptions that go unchallenged in it, such as love as possession. Like Chopin's *Awakening*, Barnes' *Nightwood* has as its central theme the futility of possessive love, whether heterosexual or lesbian, while its shadowy character, Robin, eludes any clear gender classifications.

6. The edition used here is Penguin, 1983. See also Per Seyersted's *Complete Works of Kate Chopin*, 2 vols (Baton Rouge: 1969).

7. Katherine Mansfield, *Letters and Journals*, ed. C. K. Stead (Harmondsworth: 1977) pp. 35–6.

8. See Otis B. Wheeler, 'The Five Awakenings of Edna Pontellier', *The Southern Review*, **11** (1975) pp. 118–28, for a discussion of Chopin's recurring metaphors of sleep, dream, and awakening.

9. Unlike Rhys, Richardson, Cather, Wharton, and others, Chopin played down the cruelty of women towards each other.

10. See R. Sullivan and S. Smith, 'Narrative Stance in Kate Chopin's *The Awakening*', *Studies in American Fiction*, **1** (1973) pp. 62–75, for a quite different account.

11. Patricia S. Yaegar, 'A Language Which Nobody Understood: Emancipatory Strategies in *The Awakening*', *The Novel*, **20** (1987), explores Chopin's use of liberation themes.

12. For further discussion of death, see C. G. Wolff, 'Thanatos and Eros: Kate Chopin's *The Awakening*', *American Quarterly*, **25** (1973) pp. 449–72.

13. See Emily Toth, 'Kate Chopin's *The Awakening* as Feminist Criticism', *Louisiana Studies*, **15** (1976) pp. 241–51, and Jane P. Thompkins, *'The Awakening*: An Evaluation', *Feminist Studies*, **3** (1976) pp. 22–9, for analysis of specifically feminist themes of the novel.

14. And Cixous, for that matter, both of whose texts tend to reconstruct a metaphysical account of essential femininity, in spite of declarations to seek to avoid idealist, essentialist definitions.

15. Sandra M. Gilbert, 'The Second Coming of Aphrodite', *Kenyon Review*, **5** (1983) pp. 42–56, also in the Penguin, *The Awakening* (Harmondsworth: 1983), pp. 7–33.

16. Susanne Wolkenfeld, 'Edna's Suicide: The Problem of the One and the Many', in *The Awakening*, ed. M. Culley (New York: 1976) pp. 218–24.

17. But see Wendy Martin's stimulating collection of essays in *New Essays on The Awakening* (1988) and *Louisiana Studies*, **xiv**: 1 (Spring 1975), 'Special Kate Chopin Issue'.

18. As Showalter argued (*op. cit.*, p. 255) regarding Dorothy Richardson, women must be shown how to stop betraying their own experience, to stop seeing it – and themselves – as men see it.

19. For further secondary literature on Chopin see Gilbert's extremely full bibliography in the Penguin edition of *The Awakening* and see also M. Springer, *Edith Wharton and Kate Chopin: A Reference Guide* (Boston: 1976). Edmund Wilson, in *Patriotic Gore* (London: 1963) was one early 'revivor' of Chopin's fiction.

Notes to Chapter 4: The Attack on Realism: Edith Wharton's *In Morocco* and 'Roman Fever'

1. Marilyn French, introduction to *Roman Fever and Other Stories* (London: 1983) p. 8.

2. See, for example, Kate Fulbrook, *Free Women* (Brighton: 1990), Ch. 1, pp. 11–32 and see M. L. Lyde, *Edith Wharton: Convention and Morality in the Work of a Novelist* (1959), G. Walton, *Edith Wharton: A Critical Interpretation* (1971), and Carol Wershaven, *The Female Intruder in the Novels of Edith Wharton* (1982). For a study aimed more at Wharton's craft, however, see, for example, P. Vita-Finzi, *Edith Wharton and the Art of Fiction* (London: 1990).

3. See *The Writing of Fiction* (London and New York: 1925), for Wharton's own pithy comments on realism and the modern needs of the post-1900 novel writers. They are comparable to Flannery O'Connor's comments in *Mystery and Manners* (London: 1972) that realism of fact can limit rather than broaden a novelist's approach and that there are deeper kinds of realism than sociology, history, and psychoanalysis (p. 38). O'Connor further noted that all novelists are fundamentally seekers and describers of the real, but the realism of each depends on their views of the ultimate reaches of the real. For her, the real reaches into the depths beyond the visible – into the mystery of life, the unexpected, the unknown (pp. 40–1).

4. 'Autres Temp's, in *Roman Fever, op. cit.*, pp. 201–38.
5. *Italian Backgrounds* (London and New York: 1905).
6. As, for example, in James' *The Golden Bowl*, which is a very long meditation on life as art, on artificiality, and on the question of perfection and 'flaws' in works of art. The cracked bowl becomes a powerful metaphor for James' view of his own fiction (and of art in general) as he debunked the myths of purity and perfection, of wholeness and seamless unity, and of univocal meanings and determinate significances. See also the prefaces, for further reflections on the inadequacy of conventional notions of art as a supplement to reality and on language as a transparent medium, the notion of narrative as objective and point of view as allegedly neutral.
7. *The Writing of Fiction, op. cit.*, p. 16 and see further, pp. 20–4.
8. Like Kate Chopin's fiction, the analogy of each central female character to the artist/writer is overt: the oppression of women by social patriarchy, which Wharton's novels are said to portray, directly reflects the oppression of women writers by a male literary tradition, with its imprisoning and tyrannizing conventions of theme, form, and style. Part of Wharton's ambivalent relationship with realism involved her ironizing of such a pre-eminently male tradition of objectivity, neutrality, and transparency. 'Angel at the Grave' is a good example of Wharton's constant analogy between social and literary patriarchy. See also Kate Fulbrook, *Free Women, op. cit.*, pp. 11–31, for some brief discussion of this, but not any systematic insights into Wharton's innovations and the extent of her rejection of realism, as is argued here.
9. On the cultural preconceptions about Italy dominating British thinking at the time, see, for example, Kenneth Churchill, *Italy and English Literature 1764–1930* (London: 1980), John Pemble, *The Mediterranean Passion* (Oxford: 1988), and of course see John Ruskin, J. A. Symonds, and Swinburne. Vernon Lee also had a considerable influence on Wharton with her *The Spirit of Rome* (London: 1906), not to mention her fiction and other prose writings.
10. As did Roland Barthes some decades later with *The Pleasure of the Text*.
11. *Italian Backgrounds, op. cit.*, p. 12.
12. Her topological metaphor no doubt anticipated Freudian metaphors, which became well-known and frequently discussed some years later, though Havelock Ellis and others were already eagerly discussed and argued over.
13. See Eudora Welty, *The Eye of the Story* (London: 1987) and Ellen Glasgow, preface to *The Sheltered Life* (London: 1981; first published 1932).
14. See Michel Foucault, *The Archaeology of Knowledge* (London: 1972), for his own challenge to historicists' pretences to a unified story or master theme for varying epoques, cultures, and social forms.
15. Wharton was also fascinated, like the Romantics, with the fragment or ruin as an image for all art – as a challenge to notions of artefacts as perfect wholes or as containing some integral, specifiable meaning. And she saw that the image of the fragment and the ruin could

be an emblem for the 'dead metaphor' that constitutes literal language, thereby overcoming any duality between ordinary and literary language. The former is just a degenerate, forgotten form of the latter, a past no longer enlivened by present understanding. But Wharton's travel writings show how profoundly certain she was of the possibility of revitalizing the past, of re-enlivening dead metaphors, as had Shelley in his poetry. She sought not to uncover or reveal determinate meanings, but an imaginative 'recovery' of the past – which constituted a reinvention of it into a new form, not a copy or 'representation' of it, but an innovation.

16.   In *In Morocco*, Wharton constantly reverted to such phrases as the 'mystery and remoteness' of Africa, that 'land of mists and mysteries', 'the air of the unforeseen blows on one', a feeling of irresistable adventure comes from a sense of the 'vast unknown just beyond'. Further, she described Africa as a 'featureless, wild land ... eternity' and spoke of the 'mysterious heart of the country', the 'torturous secret soul of the land', its 'infinite sadness', with 'death and the desert for ever creeping up to overwhelm the puny works of man'. Finally, she said she felt herself 'completely reabsorbed into the past', into the 'depths of unfathomable silence ... unintelligible past'. And so on, thus attacking the univocal determinacies of realism and enlightenment emphases on reason and definiteness as our ultimate goals, much as her contemporary, Hilda Doolittle, had done.

17.   Wharton wrote of the 'play of light' repeatedly, described otherwise 'familiar African pictures bathed in an unfamiliar haze' which 'even the fierce midday sun [could] not dispel'. She wrote of Morocco as seen by moonlight and as seen by 'late sunlight [which] lay like a gold-leaf'. All these emphases of Wharton's on the effects of light and time of day on the architecture, the people, and the landscape, functioned as metaphors, both for imagination shedding light and for imaginative seeing as a matter of perspective. Things look (are) different in different 'lights', from different social, cultural, and temperamental points of view. Thus, a further rejection of realist objectivity and neutrality, photography, and 'pure' description becomes part of the fabric of *In Morocco*, as Wharton delighted in variety.

18.   Thus, anticipating the indeterminacies of meaning, the endless ambiguities, and the dissemination of meaning emphasised in critical theory today, as against the certainties of realism and of historicism.

19.   And as did Jacques Derrida more recently, in, for example, *Glas* (Paris: 1981).

20.   Her rejection of origins and her joyous acceptance of 'insoluble mysteries' is another anticipation of modernism and of aspects of critical theory today.

21.   Written in 1934, after Wharton herself had visited Rome and become quite ill. See S. W. B. Lewis, *Edith Wharton: A Biography* (London: 1975).

22.   One could argue that a collection of short stories like *Roman Fever* shows Wharton at her wittiest, while the novels tend toward a more serious, decorous tone. While there may be some truth in this, as is

exemplified particularly by such stories as 'Xingu', this would be to underestimate the detached narrative point of view of many of her novels, which allows a considerable amount of wit and parody of realism to creep in, as happens in such semi-serious tragedies as James' own *Daisy Miller*. For its tragic ending is in marked contrast with the witty and merciless parodying of Winterbourne's double-standard narrative point of view. If the reader remains blind to that, she misses everything, as she does in *The Reef* or in *The Age of Innocence* and *The House of Mirth*, where tragic themes and content may be offset by a trenchant 'higher irony' hovering over the whole and parodying the sentimental realist reader–writer. The point of view is not limited as in James' *Daisy Miller*, so much as pseudo-universal, as in Jane Austen; and Austen and Wharton then go on to ironise *that*, as representative of the universally accepted conventions that imprison men and women in stereotyped, lifeless existences. Both Austen and Wharton criticised marriage and the family far more than their readers are willing to countenance, judging from the secondary literature about them.

23.   As Wharton does, for example, in *The Reef*, which, like Kate Chopin's *Awakening*, is a strong analysis of the fantasies about love that destroy women's lives and of the destructive effects on male–female relations of the infantile innocence in which women are kept.

24.   Kate Fulbrook, *op. cit.*, pp. 27–8, is mistaken to suppose with Marilyn French that the 'reef' upon which Wharton's characters founder is passion. On the contrary, they founder on their slavish fear of custom and convention and on their obeisance to mediocrity, much as Willa Cather depicted. Passion is one of the few sources of strength and liberation. Such misreadings suggest a fear of passion in the critic rather than the characters or author and a blindness to Wharton's courageous depictions of the role of passion as a source of energy, which liberates us from the mediocrity and the conformity which Cather, Rhys, and others detested so heartily. Wharton's texts, like Jane Austen's, are deeply critical of the social–moral arrangements which imprison men and women in untenable, choiceless dead-ends. As Charlotte Perkins Gilman showed, especially in 'The Yellow Wallpaper', non-conformity leads often to physical illness or to madness. Wharton had personal experience of this and she knew well Alice James' ghastly predicament.

25.   Jean Rhys forcefully portrayed the tendency to 'blame women' for their predicaments, at the same time that she revealed women's frequent cruelty to each other. But she also showed that the failure to examine the context in which women's actions occur is a genuine failure of imagination. Wharton's own novels are realist mainly in the sense of recognising the importance of context for individual behaviour and even for individuality itself. But she never made the mistake of the realist in imagining that there was some one context, some objective context, some neutral, true background which could provide standards for moral or aesthetic judgements; such judgements

are provisional and subject to change. Nor did Wharton make the realist error of assuming literature and art to be supplements to reality and reflections or representations of some non-literary, prior, 'Other'. Wharton, like Rhys, used context not to establish objectivity, but to enlarge the imagination by showing how innumerably many different contexts any situation entails.

27. Much as Shelley had argued, when he stated that love is simply imagination operating in social relations, in 'A Defence of Poetry'.

Notes to Chapter 5: Style as Characterisation in Jean Rhys' Novels

1. In Ford Madox Ford's preface to Rhys' first collection of short stories, *The Left Bank and Other Stories* (London and New York: 1927) pp. 7–27.
2. For Francis Wyndham on Jean Rhys, see his introduction to *Wide Sargasso Sea* (London: 1966), reprinted from *Art and Literature*, 1 (March 1964) pp. 173–7, also 'An Inconvenient Novelist', *Tribune*, 721 (15 December 1950) pp. 16–18, and 'Twenty-five Years of the Novel', in *The Craft of Letters in England: A Symposium*, ed. John Lehmann (London: 1956) pp. 44–59. See also his 'Introduction to Jean Rhys', *London Magazine*, 7 (January 1960) pp. 15–18.
3. Notable is M. C. Dawson, 'Unbearable Justice', *New York Herald Tribune Books*, 28 (June 1931) p. 7, for a review of *After Leaving Mr MacKenzie* (hereafter *ALMM*) that describes Rhys as a realist of sorts. An anonymous review 'Twice-as-Naturalism', *New York Times Book Review* (28 June 1931), p. 6, views Rhys as a follower of Flaubert. This is a fairly common account which crops up repeatedly in reviews, as is well known.
4. *Letters, 1931–66*, ed. F. Wyndham and D. Melly (Harmondsworth: 1985), p. 104, to Morchard Bishop, 5 March, 1953.
5. Introduction to *Smile, Please* (London and New York: 1979).
6. *Letters*, p. 89, to Maryvonne Moerman (Rhys' daughter), 22 October 1951.
7. See (to name only a few) G. M. Casey, *Best Sellers*, 27 (15 May 1967) p. 75; Francis Wyndham, 'Jean Rhys', *Concise Encyclopedia of Modern World Literature*, ed. G. Grigson (New York: 1963) pp. 369–70; Antonia Byatt, 'Trapped', *New Statesman*, 75 (29 March 1968) pp. 421–2; Paul Bailey, 'True Romance', *TLS*, 3893 (22 October 1976) p. 1321, as well as numerous anonymous reviewers.
8. A very few critics have rejected this misleading, now worn-out notion that the characters are the 'same' woman and such readers have begun to appreciate the differences in the characterisations, for example, Shirley Hazzard, *New York Times Book Review* (11 April 1971), p. 6 and anonymous, 'Briefly Noted', *New York*, 52 (10 January 1977) p. 98.
9. For example, P. K. Bell, 'Letter from London', *New Leader*, 59 (6 December 1976), pp. 3–5, on Rhys as 'most fiercely original'. And note S. Hynes, *New Republic*, 182 (31 May 1980) p. 28–31: 'She fits

none of the standard categories of writing women'. For Hynes, Rhys' style was her most original achievement. For A. Alvarez, Rhys was 'The Best Living English Novelist', *New York Times Book Review* (17 March 1974) pp. 6–7, with her 'pure style'. See also John Updike, 'Books ...', *New Yorker*, 56 (11 August 1980) pp. 85–9 and V. S. Naipaul, 'Without a Dog's Chance', *New York Review of Books*, **18** (18 May 1972) pp. 29–31.

10. Some critics were remarkably sure the characters were either prostitutes or drunkards, as in the *TLS*, **1518** (5 March 1931) p. 180, on *ALMM* as a 'sordid little story' and an 'episode in the life of a prostitute'. Because of the excellence of the style, the reviewer concluded that such subject matter is a 'waste of talents'. Sylvia Lynd, in 'Tales of Long Ago in New Novels', *News Chronicle*, **27630** (12 November 1934) p. 4, describes *Voyage in the Dark* as the no-longer novel story of 'the making of a prostitute'. And note John Hampson, 'Movements in the Underground', *Penguin New Writing*, 27 (April 1946) pp. 133–51 and 28 (July 1946) pp. 122–40: '(Rhys) has written several novels about the lives of prostitutes ... (who) usually become drunkards'. Francis Wyndham, in 'An Inconvenient Novelist', *Tribune*, **721** (15 December 1950), disputed this assessment, arguing that none of the usual terms of prostitute, tart, courtesan, kept woman, etc., fit Rhys' characters, presumably because the characters show the intelligence of the 'distinguished mind and generous nature' gone unappreciated.

11. Innumerable critics have agreed on these characteristic excellences of Rhys' style, noting that style is her great strength (and underestimating her characterisation, narrative structures, and complex of imagery in nearly all cases), that she writes like a poet, that her verse is beautifully balanced or poised; they speak of her spectacular economy and clarity, the simplicity, restraint, and integrity of the style, and the intensity of its effects.

12. Jane S. Southron, in 'A Girl's Ordeal', *New York Times Book Review* (17 March 1935) p. 7, writes about the novelist's satire directed at the hypocrisies of society. And note the description of *ALMM* as a book of 'spare, suggestive method ... profoundly destructive of hypocrisies – social and aesthetic subterfuges'.

13. Anne Tyler, 'Boundaries and Bonds ...', *National Observer*, **15** (11 December 1976) p. 18.

14. Most critics have interpreted Rhys' characters as unequivocal failures, for example, anonymous, 'Neurotic Women', *TLS*, **3412** (20 July 1967) p. 644, and Anne Tyler (*op. cit.*), Antonia Byatt (*op. cit.*) or Kate O'Brien, 'Fiction', *Spectator*, **162** (16 June 1939) p. 1062. Far more tentative accounts occur in some critics essays, where the characters are described merely as 'doomed heroines' who succeed in defeating themselves or as victims of depression and loneliness and so on. Sara Blackburn, in 'Women's Lot', *Book World*, 4 (5 April 1970) p. 6, shows more perspicacity when she writes of Rhys' 'intelligent ... heroines', but Lorna Sage goes furthest towards my reading when, in 'Phantom Returns', *Observer*, **9665** (31 October 1976) p. 28, she writes: 'Rhys'

life and fiction converge on each other', and continues: 'Her special people are usually wretched, but if they think of surrendering or adjusting, one thought deters them: their solitary, disorderly lives are *of their own making'* (author's emphasis). Rebecca West was one of the few writer-contemporaries of Rhys to proclaim unequivocably her excellence, in the *Sunday Times*, 5626 (8 February 1931), p. 10.

15. Francis Wyndham, in 'An Inconvenient Novelist', *op. cit.*

Notes to Chapter 6: Dramatic Art in Katherine Mansfield's 'Bliss'

1. The edition used here is *Bliss and Other Stories* (Harmondsworth: 1975).
2. Reported in *The Letters and Journals of Katherine Mansfield: A Selection*, edited and introduced by C. K. Stead (Harmondsworth: 1977) p. 14.
3. *Letters and Journals, op. cit.*, p. 199.
4. See her comment to Hugh Walpole about the miracle of creating a book: 'I mean the moment when the act of creation takes place – the mysterious change – when you are no longer writing the book, *it* is writing, *it* possesses you' (*Letters and Journals, op. cit.*, p. 190).
5. *Ibid.*, p. 36.
6. *Ibid.*, p. 130.
7. Virginia Woolf, *Moments of Being*, ed. Jeanne Schulkind (St Albans, Herts: 1978).
8. See, for example, 'Je ne parle pas français', a story with a narrative persona who draws attention to himself; his project is allegedly to create an identity as an artist, which he then parodies from the point of view of yet another observing self, which mocks that observer, in a Henry Jamesian sequence of perspectives. This quite Coleridgean self-consciousness is a familiar trait of modernism, one which it shared with German and English Romanticism, for example. One result is a Brechtian defamiliarisation, as the reader's attention is forced back upon her acts of interpretation and a more self-critical awareness.
9. See Clare Hanson, *Short Stories and Short Fiction 1880–1980* (London: 1985), in her chapter on Katherine Mansfield, and throughout the book, where she discusses the changing role of plot in fiction of 1880 to 1980. She may underestimate the dramatic quality of Mansfield's stories, in which plot is not so much lacking, as reconceptualised and realised in new and unexpected ways from realist practices.
10. Willa Cather, 'The Novel Démeublé', in *On Writing* (New York: 1968), pp. 40–2.
11. See, for example, 'A Married Man's Story', in which Mansfield attended explicitly to the problems of story-telling, as her narrator explores issues of the expression and articulation of experience and satirises realist description in his careful elaboration of the furniture in his study. Later, the married man further ironises realism and

himself and writerly fantasies, in a comment which Katherine Anne
Porter would echo later in 'The Holiday'. He wryly notes:

> why is it so difficult to write simply – and not simply only but *sotto*
> *voce*, if you know what I mean? That is how I long to write. No
> fine effects – no bravura. But just the plain truth, as only a liar can
> tell it.
> *(The Collected Stories* (Harmondsworth: 1981) p. 428)

12. Mansfield wrote:

> ... even while we live again, we face death. But through life: that's
> the point. We see death in life as we see death in a flower that is
> fresh unfolded.

Compare Eudora Welty, *The Eye of the Story* (London: 1987) p. 88.

13. *Letters and Journals, op. cit.*, p. 208.
14. As is the tree occurring at the end of Mansfield's 'The Escape' (*The
     Collected Stories op. cit.*, pp. 201–2).
15. Eudora Welty discussed Mansfield in 'On Writing', in *The Eye of the
     Story, op. cit.*, pp. 87–8, describing the impressionistic intensity of
     Mansfield's art as involving change rather than conflict *per se*. Welty
     then defined Mansfield's symbolism as involving 'one small situ-
     ation ... [but] a large, complex one is implied'. This type of symbolic
     story, 'instead of being a simple situation, is an impression of a
     situation, and tells more for being so'. Compare Cather's objections
     to realism and the need to allow significance to 'hover' over the page,
     without actually, literally being present (see Ch. 2). And compare
     also Flannery O'Connor, *Mystery and Manners* (London: 1972)
     pp. 70–3, on the symbolic as giving fiction its 'depth', indeed, its
     realism, as she saw realism.
16. Mansfield waxed eloquent in a letter to Dorothy Brett:

> It seems so extraordinarily right that you should be painting still
> lives just now. What can one do, faced with this wonderful tumble
> of round bright fruits; but gather them and play with them – and
> *become them*, as it were ... There follows the moment when you are
> *more* duck, *more* apple, or more Natasha than any of these objects
> could ever possibly be, and so you *create* them anew.   (*Letters and
> Journals, op. cit.*, p. 84)

17. Kate Chopin used systematically, in the first half of *The Awakening*, a
     similar technique, of imagery shadowing sinisterly an element in the
     text; see the chapter on Chopin above, for a detailed account of the
     two lovers followed by the 'woman in black'.
18. The final sentence of *Between the Acts* is 'Then the curtain rose. They
     spoke'. *Voyage in the Dark* begins 'It was as if a curtain had fallen,
     hiding everything I had ever known. It was almost like being born
     again'. Rhys' novel ends with the ironic statement:

> When their voices stopped the ray of light came in again under the door like the last thrust of remembering before everything is blotted out. I lay and watched it and thought about starting all over again. And about being new and fresh. And about mornings, and misty days, when anything might happen. And about starting all over again, all over again …

19. Another journal entry gives a clue to reading 'Bliss':

    > To be wildly enthusiastic or deadly serious – both are wrong. Both pass. One must keep ever present a sense of humour. It depends entirely on yourself how much you see or hear or understand. But the sense of humour I have found true of every single occasion of my life. (*Letters and Journals, op. cit.*, p. 280)

20. Eudora Welty noted that in much fiction, separate characters often represent aspects of a single personality and elucidate the nature of the conflict occurring within an individual psyche (*The Eye of the Story, op. cit.*, p. 98). Miss Fulton and Bertha Young could be similarly interpreted; indeed, 'Bliss' itself might be described as Mansfield's version of D. H. Lawrence's 'The Fox'.

21. Mansfield wrote in a letter that it was 'trembling on the brink of poetry' (*The Collected Letters of Katherine Mansfield*, ed. V. O'Sullivan and M. Scott (Oxford: 1987) vol. II, p. 343). Mansfield also described prose in general as an undiscovered country, which she wished to explore. See also 'The Art of Katherine Mansfield', by Katherine Anne Porter, in *Collected Essays and Occasional Writings of Katherine Anne Porter* (New York: 1973), pp. 47–52, for Porter's comments on Mansfield's prose style.

22. As, for example, in 'At the Bay', which charts the growing companionship between Linda and Jonathan, who is a 'failure' according to Linda's husband, Stanley.

23. See Cather's essay on Katherine Mansfield in *Not Under Forty* (New York: 1936), in which she discussed Mansfield's representation of the tragic necessity of human relationships, tragic, because they are always unsatisfactory and of the double pull in all relationship between attraction toward the other and terrible revulsion, due to fear of losing oneself by being swamped by the other. This was certainly a problem depicted by Cather in *Song of the Lark, A Lost Lady*, and other novels.

Notes on Chapter 7: The Multiple Realities of Stevie Smith

1. For further biographical information see Jack Barbera, *Stevie: A Biography of Stevie Smith* (London: 1985) or Frances Spalding, *Stevie Smith: A Critical Biography* (London, 1988). See also *Ivy and Stevie*, ed. Dick Kay (1971) and *The Poet Speaks*, ed. P. Orr (1966) for interviews.

2. For further works see *Stevie Smith: A Bibliography*, ed. J. Barbera, W. McBrien, and H. Bajan (1987).
3. Janet Watts, introduction to *The Holiday* (London: 1979), unpaginated. A number of other dubious speculations about Smith arise in this and the introductions by Watts to the other novels.
4. *Me Again: The Uncollected Writings of Stevie Smith*, ed. J. Barbera and W. McBrien (London: 1981), p. 353, in the radio play 'A Turn Outside'. And see Katherine Mansfield's description of stories as nests of poems and her comments on the relation of prose to poetry in *The Collected Letters of Katherine Mansfield*, ed. Vincent O'Sullivan, with M. Scott (Oxford: 1987), vol. I, p. 313; vol. II, p. 343.
5. Blake's response, in a letter to Dr Trusler, 23 August 1799, to children enjoying his poetry is similar to Smith's pleasure:

   But I am happy to find a Great Majority of Fellow Mortals who can Elucidate My Visions, & Particularly they have been Elucidated by Children, who have taken a greater delight in contemplating my Pictures than I ever hoped.

6. *The Collected Poems of Stevie Smith*, ed. J. MacGibbon (Harmondsworth: 1975) p. 157.
7. 'Too Tired for Words', in *Me Again*, ed. J. Barbera and W. McBrien (London: 1981), pp. 111–18.
8. Amongst modernist writers, May Sinclair and H. D. addressed themselves to Freud's writings overtly and systematically, as did Smith. H. D.'s *Tribute to Freud* (1944) is a prose testimony to the influence of Freud on some of the writing of this period.
9. *The Four-Gated City* (1969), *Surfacing* (1972), and see Nadine Gordimer's comment that rationality is merely a familiar form of the irrational, in 'Introduction', *Selected Stories* (London: 1976) p. 9.
10. See, for example, *Wise Blood* (1952), *Nightwood* (1937), and *Good Morning, Midnight* (1939).
11. As in *The Member of the Wedding* (1946) or *Reflections in a Golden Eye* (1941). For McCullers' use of the deformed and the grotesque, see *The Ballad of the Sad Café* (1951).
12. Mansfield wrote: 'True to oneself! which self? Which of my many – well really, that's what it looks like coming to – hundreds of selves?', *Letters and Journals*, ed. C. K. Stead (Harmondsworth: 1977) p. 173. Yet see also her comment on the same page on that 'mysterious belief in a self which is continuous and permanent'.
13. The edition used here is *Over the Frontier* (London: 1980).
14. See Janet Watts' introduction to the Virago editions of the novels.
15. See Mark Storey, 'Why Stevie Smith Matters', in *Critical Quarterly*, **21** (Summer 1979) pp. 31–40, on this authenticity of experience.
16. Philip Larkin's remarks on her poetry apply also to her novels, when he said that 'they are completely original, and now and again they are moving. These qualities set them above 95 per cent of present-day output,' in 'Frivolous and Vulnerable', the *New Statesman*, **28** (September 1962) p. 416.

Notes on Chapter 8: Jane Bowles: That Modern Legend

1. *Out in the World* is in Manuscript in the Humanities Research Centre, University of Texas, Austin.
2. For further biographical information, see Millicent Dillon, *A Little Original Sin: The Life and Work of Jane Bowles* (New York: 1981) and see her edition of selected letters (Santa Barbara: 1985). Bowles' letters contrast sharply with Dillon's somewhat questionable, highly interpretive biography.
3. Truman Capote, *Collected Works of Jane Bowles* (London: 1984) p. viii.
4. All these comments are repeated in Capote's edition on the jacket.
5. Paul Bowles, *Everything is Nice* (London: 1989) p. ii.
6. Francine du Plessix Gray, 'Introduction', *Two Serious Ladies* (London: 1979) p. iii.
7. Paul Bowles, *op. cit.*
8. The edition used here is *Two Serious Ladies* (London: 1979).
9. Note Bowles' parodic use of names, in this case juxtaposing two most improbable ones. Willa Cather and Katherine Mansfield were fond of giving their characters names impregnated with meaning.
10. Reported by Paul Bowles, *op. cit.*, p. ii.
11. Millicent Dillon, in 'Jane Bowles: Experiment as Character', *Breaking the Sequence: Women's Experimental Fiction*, ed. E. G. Friedman and M. Fuchs (Princeton: 1989) pp. 140–7, hints at the possibility of Goering and Copperfield being 'shades' of one character, much as the two characters Nora and Robin in Barnes *Nightwood* are or, parallelly, in *Mrs Dalloway* and *The Awakening*, not to mention numerous other examples.
12. In *The Complete Works of Jane Bowles*, ed. T. Capote.
13. Dillon, *op. cit.*, p. 143, does not seem to see these endings as equally valid; she speaks of one of them as 'the real ending', which ends definitely in suicide. This is something of an overdetermination of the text.
14. This play is a remarkable dramatic achievement and deserves to be brought to a wider public.
15. Reverberations of *The Awakening* abound, as Edna's 'downward path to wisdom' was viewed by Chopin's readers as something of a scandal.

Bibliography

Jane Bowles, 1917–73

The Collected Works of Jane Bowles, intro. Truman Capote. London: 1984; reprint of New York: 1966.
Everything is Nice: The Collected Stories, ed. Paul Bowles. London: 1989.
'In the Summerhouse'. In *The Collected Works of Jane Bowles*, intro. Truman Capote. London: 1984.
Two Serious Ladies, ed. and intro. by Francine du Plessix Gray. London: 1979; first published 1943.
'Out in the World'. MS, Humanities Research Centre, University of Texas, Austin.
Out in the World: The Selected Letters of Jane Bowles 1935–70, ed. Millicent Dillon. Santa Barbara: 1985.

Dillon, M., *A Little Original Sin: The Life and Work of Jane Bowles*. New York: 1981.
Dillon, M., 'Jane Bowles: Experiment in Character'. In *Breaking the Sequence: Women's Experimental Fiction*, ed. E. G. Friedman and M. Fuchs. Princeton: 1989, pp. 140–7.
Lakritz, A. M., 'Jane Bowles' Other World'. In *Old Maids to Radical Spinsters: Unmarried Women in the Twentieth-Century Novel*, ed. Laura L. Doan. Bloomington, IN: 1991.

Willa Cather, 1873–1947

The Song of the Lark. London: 1982; first published 1915.
My Ántonia. London: 1980; first published 1918.
A Lost Lady. London: 1980; first published 1923.
The Professor's House. London: 1981; first published 1925.
Death Comes for the Archbishop. London: 1981; first published 1927.
Not under Forty. New York: 1936.
Willa Cather on Writing, ed. S. Tennant. New York: 1968; first published 1949.
The Kingdom of Art: Willa Cather's First Principles and Critical Statements, 1893–96, ed. Berenice Slote. Nebraska: 1966.

Willa Cather: A Bibliography, ed. Joan Crane. Lincoln, Nebraska: 1982.

Brown, E. K. completed by Leon Edel, *Willa Cather: A Critical Biography*. New York: 1970.
Byatt, Antonia S., Introduction, *A Lost Lady*. London: 1980.

Byatt, Antonia S., Introduction, *The Professor's House*. London: 1981.
Byatt, Antonia S., Introduction, *My Mortal Enemy*. London: 1982.
Fulbrook, Kate, *Free Women*. Brighton: 1990.
Randall, J. H., 'An Interpretation of My Ántonia'. In *Willa Cather and her Critics*, ed. J. Schroeter. Ithaca: 1967, pp. 272–322.
Robinson, P. C., *Willa: The Life of Willa Cather*. New York: 1983.
Schroeter, James (ed.), *Willa Cather and her Critics*. Ithaca: 1967.
Schroeter, James 'Willa Cather and *The Professor's House*'. In *Willa Cather and Her Critics*. Ithaca: 1967, pp. 363–82.
Sergeant, E., *Willa Cather: A Memoir*. Philadelphia: 1953.
Slote, B. and Faulkner, V. (eds), *The Art of Willa Cather*. Lincoln, Nebraska: 1974.
Stouck, David, *Willa Cather's Imagination*. Lincoln, Nebraska: 1975.
Welty, Eudora, 'The House of Willa Cather', In *The Eye of the Story*. London: 1979, pp. 41–60.
West, Rebecca, 'The Classic Artist'. In *The Strange Necessity*. London: 1987, pp. 215–28; first published 1928; reprinted in James Shroeter, op. cit.

Kate Chopin, 1851–1904

Seyersted, Per (ed.), *The Complete Works of Kate Chopin*. 2 vols. Baton Rouge: 1969.
Gilbert, Sandra M. (ed.), *The Awakening and other Stories*. Harmondsworth: 1983.
Taylor, Helen (ed.), *Portraits*. London: 1979.

Edith Wharton and Kate Chopin: A Reference Guide, Marlene Springer. Boston, MA: 1976; updated in *Resources for American Literary Study*, **11** (1981) pp. 25–42.

Allen, Priscilla, 'Old Critics and New: The Treatment of Chopin's *The Awakening*'. In *The Authority of Experience*, ed. A. Diamond and L. R. Edwards. Amherst, MA: 1977, pp. 224–38.
Cather, Willa, review of *The Awakening*. In *The World and the Parish: Willa Cather's Articles and Reviews, 1893–1902*, ed. W. M. Cullin. Lincoln, Nebraska: 1970, vol. II, pp. 693–4.
Gilbert, Sandra M., 'The Second Coming of Aphrodite'. *Kenyon Review*, **5** (1983) pp. 42–56. Also republished in *The Awakening*. Harmondsworth: 1983, pp. 7–33.
Louisiana Studies: 'Special Kate Chopin Issue', **xiv** (Spring 1975).
Martin, Wendy (ed.), *New Essays on 'The Awakening'*. Cambridge: 1988.
Regionalism and the Female Imagination (previously known as *The Kate Chopin Newsletter*), ed. Emily Toth. Philadelphia: 1975–9.
Seyersted, Per, *Kate Chopin: A Critical Biography*. Baton Rouge: 1969.
Spangler, George M. '*The Awakening*: A Partial Dissent', *The Novel*, **3** (Spring 1970) pp. 249–55.

Sullivan, Ruth and Smith, Stewart, 'Narrative Stance in Kate Chopin's *The Awakening'*, *Studies in American Fiction*, 1 (1973), pp. 62–75.
Taylor, Helen, *Gender, Race, and Region*. London: 1989.
Thompkins, Jane P., '*The Awakening*: An Evaluation'. *Feminist Studies*, 3 (1976) pp. 22–9.
Toth, Emily, *Kate Chopin*. London: 1990.
Toth, Emily, 'Kate Chopin's *The Awakening* as Feminist Criticism'. *Louisiana Studies*, 15 (1976), pp. 241–51.
Wheeler, Otis B., 'The Five Awakenings of Edna Pontellier'. *The Southern Review*, 11 (1975), pp. 118–28.
Wilson, Edmund, *Patriotic Gore*. London: 1963.
Wolff, C. G., 'Thanatos and Eros: Kate Chopin's *The Awakening'*. *American Quarterly*, 25 (1973) pp. 449–72.
Wolkenfeld, Susanne, 'Edna's Suicide: The Problem of the One and the Many'. In *The Awakening*, ed. M. Culley. New York: 1976, pp. 218–24.
Yaegar, Patricia S., 'A Language which Nobody Understood – Emancipating Strategies in *The Awakening'*. *The Novel*, 20 (1987), pp. 98–113.
Ziff, Larzer, *The American 1890s: Life and Times of a Lost Generation*. London: 1967.

Katherine Mansfield, 1888–1923

The Collected Stories of Katherine Mansfield. London: 1945; Harmondsworth: 1981, containing: *In a German Pension*, 1911; *Bliss and Other Stories*, 1920; *The Garden-Party and Other Stories*, 1922; *The Dove's Nest and Other Stories*, 1923; *Something Childish and Other Stories*, 1924; *The Aloe*, 1930.

The Critical Writings of Katherine Mansfield, ed. Clare Hanson. London: 1987.
The Collected Letters of Katherine Mansfield, ed. Vincent O'Sullivan and M. Scott. Oxford: 1987.
The Letters and Journals of Katherine Mansfield: A Selection, ed. C. K. Stead. Harmondsworth: 1977.
Novels and Novelists, ed. J. M. Murray. London: 1920.

Berkman, S., *Katherine Mansfield: A Critical Study*. London: 1952.
Boyle, Kay, 'Katherine Mansfield: A Reconsideration'. In *Words That Must Somehow Be Said*, ed. E. S. Bell. London: 1985, pp. 52–4.
Carter, Angela, 'The Life of Katherine Mansfield'. In *Nothing Sacred*. London: 1982, pp. 158–61.
Cather, Willa, 'Katherine Mansfield'. In *On Writing*, ed. S. Tennant. New York: 1968, pp. 105–21.
Fulbrook, Kate, *Katherine Mansfield*. Brighton: 1986.
Hankin, C. A., *Katherine Mansfield and her Confessional Stories*. London: 1983.
Hanson, Clare and Gurr, Andrew, *Katherine Mansfield*. London: 1981.
Hanson, Clare, *Short Stories and Short Fiction, 1880–1980*. London: 1985.
Magalaner, M., *The Fiction of Katherine Mansfield*. Illinois: 1971.

Meyers, Jeffrey, *Katherine Mansfield: A Biography*. London: 1978.
Moore, Leslie, *Katherine Mansfield*. London: 1971.
O'Sullivan, V., Introduction, *The Aloe*. London: 1985, pp. v–xviii.
Parker, Dorothy, 'The Private Papers of the Dead'. In *The Collected Dorothy Parker*. Harmondsworth: 1973, pp. 451–2.
Porter, Katherine Anne, 'The Art of Katherine Mansfield'. In *Collected Essays and Occasional Writings of Katherine Anne Porter*. New York: 1973, pp. 47–52.
Rohnberger, M., *The Art of Katherine Mansfield*. Oklahoma: 1977.
Stead, C. K., Introduction, *The Letters and Journals*. Harmondsworth: 1977, pp. 9–20.
Tomalin, Clare, *Katherine Mansfield: A Secret Life*. Harmondsworth: 1987.
Welty, Eudora, 'Looking at Short Stories'. In *The Eye of the Story*. London: 1987, 85–106.
Woolf, Virginia, 'A Terribly Sensitive Mind'. *Granite and Rainbow*. London: 1958, pp. 73–5.

Jean Rhys, 1894–1979

After Leaving Mr MacKenzie. Harmondsworth: 1971; first published 1930.
Good Morning, Midnight. Harmondsworth: 1969; first published 1939.
The Left Bank and Other Stories. Harmondsworth: 1973; first published 1927.
Letters 1931–66, ed. F. Wyndham and D. Melly. London: 1984.
My Day: Three Pieces. London and New York: 1975.
Quartet (Postures). Harmondsworth: 1973; first published 1928.
Sleep it Off Lady. London: 1976.
Smile, Please: An Unfinished Autobiography. London: 1979.
Tigers are Better Looking. London: 1968.
Voyage in the Dark. Harmondsworth: 1980; first published 1934.
Wide Sargasso Sea. London: 1966.

Jean Rhys: A Descriptive and Annotated Bibliography of Works and Criticism, ed. Elgin W. Mellown. New York and London: 1984.

Abel, Elizabeth, 'Women and Schizophrenia: The Fiction of Jean Rhys'. *Contemporary Literature*, **20** (1979) pp. 155–77.
Alvarez, A., 'The Best Living English Novelist'. *New York Times Book Review*, 17 March 1974, pp. 6–7.
Anonymous, 'Twice-as-Naturalism'. *New York Times Book Review*, 28 June 1931, p. 6.
Bell, P. K., 'Letter from London'. *New Leader*, **59** (6 December 1976), pp. 3–5.
Bender, Todd K., 'Jean Rhys and the Genius of Impressions'. In *The Female Novelist in Twentieth-Century Britain*, ed. J. I. Biles. Atlanta, GA: 1978, pp. 43–54.
Blackburn, Sara, 'Women's Lot'. *Book World*, **4** (5 April 1970), p. 6.
Byatt, Antonia, 'Trapped'. *New Statesman*, **75** (29 March 1968) pp. 421–2.

Dawson, M. C., 'Unbearable Justice'. *New York Herald Tribune Books*, **28** (June 1931) p. 7.

Ford, Ford Madox, Preface, *The Left Bank and Other Stories*. London and New York: 1927, pp. 7–27.

Friedman, E. G., 'Breaking the Master Narrative: Jean Rhys' *Wide Sargasso Sea*'. In *Breaking the Sequence*, ed. E. G. Friedman and M. Fuchs. Princeton: 1989, pp. 117–28.

Hampson, John, 'Movements in the Underground'. *Penguin New Writing*, **27** (April 1946) pp. 133–51 and **28** (July 1946) pp. 122–40.

Hazzard, Shirley, 'Jean Rhys'. *New York Times Book Review*, **6** (11 April 1971) p. 6.

Hynes, S., 'Jean Rhys'. *New Republic*, **182** (31 May 1980), pp. 28–31.

Lynd, S., 'Tales of Long Ago in New Novels'. *News Chronicle*, **27630** (12 November 1934) p. 4.

Mellown, Elgin W., 'Characters and Themes in the Novels of Jean Rhys'. In *Contemporary Women Novelists*, ed. P. M. Spacks. Englewood Cliffs, NJ: 1977, pp. 118–36.

Naipaul, V. S., 'Without a Dog's Chance'. *New York Review of Books*, **18** (18 May 1972) pp. 29–31.

Nebeker, Helen, *Jean Rhys: Woman in Passage*. St Albans, Vt: 1981.

O'Connor, Teresa F., *Jean Rhys: The West Indian Novels*. New York: 1986.

Roe, Sue, '"The Shadow of Light". The Symbolic Underworld of Jean Rhys'. *Women Reading Women's Writing*, ed. Sue Roe. Brighton: 1987, pp. 229–64.

Sage, Lorna, 'Phantom Returns'. *Observer*, **9665** (31 October 1976), p. 28.

Southron, J. S., 'A Girl's Ordeal'. *New York Times Book Review*, 17 March 1935, p. 7.

Staley, Thomas, 'The Emergence of a Form: Style and Consciousness in Jean Rhys' *Quartet*'. *Twentieth-Century Literature*, **24** (1978) pp. 203–24.

Thurman, Judith, 'The Mistress and the Mask'. *MS*, **4** (1976) pp. 50–3.

Tyler, Anne, 'Neurotic Women'. *Times Literary Supplement*, **3412** (20 July 1967) p. 644.

West, Rebecca, 'Jean Rhys'. *The Sunday Times*, **5626** (8 February 1931) p. 10.

Wyndham, Francis, 'An Inconvenient Novelist'. *Tribune* **721** (15 December 1950) pp. 16–18.

Wyndham, Francis, 'Introduction to Jean Rhys'. *London Magazine*, **7** (January 1960) pp. 115–18.

Wyndham, Francis, Introduction. *Wide Sargasso Sea*. London: 1966.

Wyndham, Francis. 'Twenty-five Years of the Novel'. In *The Craft of Letters in England: A Symposium*, ed. J. Lehmann. London: 1956, pp. 44–59.

Stevie Smith, 1902–71

The Holiday. London: 1979; first published 1949.

Novel on Yellow Paper, or Work it out for Yourself. London: 1980; first published 1936.

Over the Frontier. London: 1980; first published 1938.

The Collected Poems of Stevie Smith, ed. James MacGibbon. Harmondsworth: 1975.
Me Again: The Uncollected Writings of Stevie Smith, ed. J. Barbera and W. McBrien, preface by J. MacGibbon. London: 1981.
Ivy and Stevie, interviews, ed. Dick Kay. London: 1971.
The Poet Speaks, two interviews, ed. Peter Orr. London: 1966.

Stevie Smith: A Bibliography, ed. J. Barbera, W. McBrien, and H. Bajan. London: 1987.

Bedient, Calvin, 'Stevie Smith'. In *Eight Contemporary Poets*. London: 1974.
Enright, D. J., 'Did Nobody Teach you?' In *Encounter* (1971) pp. 53–7.
Larkin, Philip, 'Frivolous and Vulnerable' (a review of Smith's poems). *The New Statesman*, **28** (1962) pp. 416–18.
Montefiore, Jan, *Feminism and Poetry*. London: 1987.
Rankin, A. C., *The Poetry of Stevie Smith: 'Little Girl Lost'*. Gerrards Cross, Berks.: 1985.
Spalding, Frances, *Stevie Smith: A Critical Biography*. London: 1988.
Storey, Mark, 'Why Stevie Smith Matters'. *Critical Quarterly*, **21** (1979) pp. 31–40.
Watts, Janet, Introduction to *Novel on Yellow Paper*. London: 1980.
Watts, Janet, Introduction to *Over the Frontier*. London: 1980.
Watts, Janet, Introduction to *The Holiday*. London: 1979.
Whitemore, Hugh, *Stevie* (a play about Stevie Smith). Performed in London, 1977.

Edith Wharton, 1862–1937

The Age of Innocence. Harmondsworth: 1974; first published 1920.
A Backward Glance. London: 1972; first published 1934.
The House of Mirth. Harmondsworth: 1979; first published 1905.
In Morocco. London: 1927; first published 1920.
Italian Backgrounds. London and New York: 1905.
The Letters of Edith Wharton, ed. R. W. B. Lewis and Nancy Lewis. London and New York: 1988.
The Reef. London: 1983; first published 1912.
Roman Fever and Other Stories. London: 1983.
The Writing of Fiction. New York: 1970; first published 1925.

A Descriptive Bibliography, ed. Stephen Garrison. Pittsburg: 1990.

French, Marilyn, Introduction to *Roman Fever and Other Stories*. London: 1983.
Gooder, Jean, 'Unlocking Edith Wharton'. *Cambridge Quarterly*, **xv** (1980) pp. 33–52.

Goodwyn, Janet, *Edith Wharton: A Traveller in the Land of Letters*. 1990.

Fulbrook, Kate, 'Edith Wharton: Sexuality, Money and Moral Choice'. In *Free Women*. London: 1990, pp. 11–32.

Lewis, R. W. B., *Edith Wharton: A Biography*. London: 1975.

Lyde, M. L., *Edith Wharton: Convention and Morality in the Work of a Novelist*. Norman, OK: 1959.

Trilling, Diana, 'The House of Mirth Revisited'. In *Edith Wharton: A Collection of Critical Essays*, ed. Irving Howe. New Jersey: 1962.

Vita-Finzi, P., *Edith Wharton and the Art of Fiction*. London: 1990.

Walton, G., *Edith Wharton: A Critical Interpretation*. Rutherford, NJ: 1970.

Wershaven, Carol, *The Female Intruder in the Novels of Edith Wharton*. London: 1982.

Wilson, Edmund, 'Justice to Edith Wharton'. In *Edith Wharton: A Collection of Critical Essays*, ed. Irving Howe. New Jersey: 1962.

Wolff, Cynthia Griffin, *A Feast of Words: The Triumph of Edith Wharton*. Oxford: 1977.

General

Abel, Elizabeth, *Writing and Sexual Difference*. Brighton: 1982.

Antin, David, 'Some Questions about Modernism'. *Occident*, 8 (1974) pp. 7–38.

Beauman, Nicola, *A Very Great Profession: The Woman's Novel, 1914–39*. London: 1983.

Belsey, Catherine, *Critical Practice*. London; 1980.

Benstock, Shari, *Women of the Left Bank: Paris, 1900–1940*. Austin: 1986; London: 1987.

Biles, J. I. (ed.), *The Female Novelist in Twentieth-Century Britain*. Atlanta, GA: 1978.

Doan, Laura L. (ed.), *Old Maids to Radical Spinsters: Unmarried Women in the Twentieth-Century Novel*. Bloomington, IN: 1991.

DuPlessis, Rachel Blau, *Writing Beyond the Ending: Narrative Strategies of Twentieth-Century Women Writers*. Bloomington: 1984.

Eisenstein, H. and Jardine, A. (ed.) *The Future of Difference*. Boston: 1980.

Friedman, E. G. and Fuchs, M. (ed.), *Breaking the Sequence: Women's Experimental Fiction*. Princeton: 1989.

Fulbrook, Kate, *Free Women: Ethics and Aesthetics in Twentieth-Century Women's Fiction*. London: 1990.

Gilbert, S. M. and Gubar, S., *No Man's Land: The Place of the Woman Writer in the Twentieth Century*. 2 vols. London: 1988, 1989.

Gilbert, S. M. and Gubar, S. (ed.), *The Norton Anthology of Literature by Women*. New York and London: 1985.

Hanscombe, G. and Smyers, V. L., *Writing for their Lives: The Modernist Women: 1910–1940*. London: 1987.

Hanson, Clare, *Short Stories and Short Fiction, 1880–1980*. London: 1985.

Hardwick, Elizabeth (ed.), *Seduction and Betrayal*. London: 1974.

Johnson, Barbara, *The Critical Difference*. Baltimore: 1980.
Jones, Anne G., *Tomorrow is Another Day: The Woman Writer in the South, 1859–1936*. Baton Rouge: 1981.
Kiely, Robert (ed.), *Modernism Reconsidered*. Cambridge, MA: 1983.
Kolodny, Annette, 'Some Notes on Defining a "Feminist" Literary Criticism'. *Critical Inquiry*, II (1975–6) pp. 75–92.
Kristeva, Julia, *Revolution in Poetic Language*, trans. M. Walter. New York: 1984.
Levenson, M. H., *A Genealogy of Modernism*. Cambridge: 1984.
McCallum, Pamela, 'Feminist Revisions to the Literary Canon: An Overview of the Methodological Debate'. In *The Effects of Feminist Approaches on Research Methodologies*, ed. W. Tomm. Waterloo: 1989, pp. 131–41.
McCullers, Carson, *The Mortgaged Heart and Other Essays*. Harmondsworth: 1985.
Marcus, Jane, 'Thinking Back Through our Mothers'. *New Feminist Essays on Virginia Woolf*, ed. J. Marcus. Lincoln, Nebraska: 1981.
Moi, Toril, *Sexual/Textual Politics: Feminist Literary Theory*. London: 1985.
Nin, Anaïs, *A Woman Speaks*. London: 1982.
O'Connor, Flannery, *Mystery and Manners: Occasional Prose*. London: 1972.
Parker, Dorothy, 'Part Two: Later Stories, Reviews and Articles'. In *The Collected Dorothy Parker*. Harmondsworth: 1973, pp. 373–604.
Roe, Sue (ed.), *Women Reading Women's Writing*. Brighton: 1987.
Showalter, Elaine, *A Literature of their Own*. Princeton: 1977.
Spacks, Patricia M., *The Female Imagination*. London: 1976.
Spacks, Patricia M. (ed.), *Contemporary Women Novelists*. New Jersey: 1977.
Stein, Gertrude. *How to Write*. Paris: 1931.
Stein, Gertrude. *Narration*. Chicago: 1935.
Welty, Eudora, *The Eye of the Story: Selected Essays and Reviews*. London: 1987.
West, Rebecca, *The Strange Necessity*. London: 1987.
Williams, Merryn, *Six Women Novelists*. London: 1987.
Woolf, Virginia, *Granite and Rainbow*. London: 1958.
Woolf, Virginia. *Collected Essays*, 4 vols. New York: 1966–7.

Index

Abel, Elizabeth, 211, 214
Allen, Priscilla, 195, 209
Alvarez, A., 202, 211
Antin, David, 214
Ashberry, John, 162–3
Atwood, Margaret, 2, 13, 146
Auden, W. H., 162
Austen, Jane, 6, 52, 60, 135, 146, 160, 200

Bailey, Paul, 201
Bajan, H., 206, 213
Balzac, Honoré de, 21
Barbera, Jack, 205, 213
Barnes, Djuna, 2, 4, 7–8, 11, 12, 13, 17–18, 78, 100, 114, 147–8, 151–2, 163, 168, 180–1, 193, 196
    Nightwood, 18, 180, 189, 196, 206–7
Barthes, Roland, 81, 198
Beauman, Nicola, 214
Beckett, Samuel, 134
    Waiting for Godot, 134, 184
Bedford, Sybille, 162–3
Bedient, Calvin, 213
Bell, P. K., 201, 211
Belsey, Catherine, 214
Bender, Todd K., 211
Benstock, Shari, 214
Berkman, S., 210
Biles, J. I., 214
Bishop, Morchard, 201
Blackburn, Sara, 202, 211
Blake, William, 13–14, 21, 24, 31, 86, 130, 133, 142, 146, 168, 192, 206
Borges, Jorge Luis, 11, 87, 178
Bowles, Jane, 2, 4–14, 17, 36, 56, 62, 102, 104–6, 116, 118, 133, 140, 143–4, 147–8, 150, 162–81, 188–9, 207–8
    'Camp Cataract', 178–80, 188
    Collected Works, 163, 208
    Everything is Nice, 163–4, 208

'In the Summer-house', 162, 169, 208
    'Out in the World', 143, 163, 169, 207–8
    Plain Pleasures, 162
    Two Serious Ladies, 14, 62, 152, 162–88, 208
Bowles, Paul, 162–4, 167, 207–8
Boyle, Kay, 14, 210
Brecht, Bertold, 203
Brett, Dorothy, 204
Britten, Benjamin, 162
Brontë, Charlotte, 51
    Jane Eyre, 51
Brown, E. K., 208
Byatt, Antonia, 191–4, 201–2, 208–9, 211

Capote, Truman, 162–4, 166, 169, 177, 179, 207–8
Carrington, Leonora, 6, 12
Carter, Angela, 6, 12–13, 17, 190–1, 210
Casey, G. M., 201
Cather, Willa, 2, 5–6, 8–14, 16–17, 19–50, 52, 67, 75, 78, 80, 82, 84–5, 102–3, 117, 123, 125, 136, 140, 168, 191–5, 200, 203–4, 208–10
    Alexander's Bridge, 19
    A Lost Lady, 192–3, 205, 208
    Death Comes for the Archbishop, 20, 33, 47–50, 195, 208
    My Ántonia, 20, 26–30, 33–6, 45, 193, 208
    My Mortal Enemy, 193
    O Pioneers!, 19, 33
    The Professor's House, 14, 20, 28, 30–47, 125, 138, 193
    The Song of the Lark, 20, 31–3, 36, 63, 193, 205, 207–8
Chekov, Anton, 123, 127, 138
Chopin, Kate, 5–7, 9–11, 13–14, 16, 21, 28, 36, 51–76, 108, 114, 118,

124, 132–3, 144, 146, 150, 152, 157, 165, 168, 193, 195–8, 204, 209–10
At Fault, 51
The Awakening, 51–76, 108, 132, 150, 200, 204, 207–9
Young Doctor Gosse, 51
Churchill, Kenneth, 198
Cixous, Hélène, 197
Coleridge, Samuel Taylor, 21–2, 35–6, 40, 49, 92, 182, 191–3, 195, 203
'The Ancient Mariner', 35, 182, 195
'Kubla Khan', 22
Compton-Burnett, Ivy, 92
Crane, Joan, 191
Crane, Stephen, 21
Crashaw, Richard, 159
Culley, M., 210
Cullin, W. M., 209

Darwin, Charles, 51
Dawson, M. C., 201, 212
De Man, Paul, 192
Derrida, Jacques, 7, 34, 37, 45, 199
Dewey, John, 1, 7, 189–90, 192
Dillon, Millicent, 207–8
Dinesen, Isak, 11, 182
Last Tales, 182, 190
Seven Gothic Tales, 190
Doan, Laura L., 214
Doolittle, Hilda (H.D.), 2, 4, 7–8, 12–13, 86, 100, 105, 142, 148, 163, 180–1, 206
Bid Me to Live, 180
Hermione, 105, 180
Du Plessis, Rachel Blau, 214
Du Plessix Gray, Francine, 165, 208

Eisenstein, H., 214
Ellis, Havelock, 198
Emerson, Ralph Waldo, 21
Enright, D. J., 213
Erdrich, Louise, 6, 16
Love Medicine, 190

Faulkner, V., 208.
Faulkner, William, 107, 190

The Sound and the Fury, 107
Flaubert, Gustave, 21, 201
Ford, Ford Madox, 99, 117, 201, 212
Forster, E. M., 20, 28, 80, 96, 185–6, 193–4
Aspects of the Novel, 185
Howard's End, 193–4
Passage to India, 193
Foucault, Michel, 20, 191, 198
Archaeology of Knowledge, 191
Frame, Janet, 12, 16
Scented Gardens for the Blind, 190
Freeman, Mary Wilkins, 21, 52
French, Marilyn, 77, 197, 200, 213
Freud, Sigmund, 11, 46, 80, 145–6, 180, 198, 206
Friedman, E. G., 190, 212
Fuchs, Miriam, 190, 212
Fulbrook, Kate, 193–4, 196–8, 200, 204–10, 214

Garrison, Stephen, 213
Gilbert, Sandra, 57, 72–5, 197, 209
Gilman, Charlotte Perkins, 2, 5–6, 8–9, 11, 13–15, 17, 21, 104, 126, 146, 168, 200
The Yellow Wallpaper, 126, 200
Glasgow, Ellen, 7, 16, 82, 191, 198
The Sheltered Life, 190, 198
Gooder, Jean, 213
Goodwyn, Janet, 214
Gordimer, Nadine, 11, 146, 183, 190, 206
Gubar, Susan, 214
Gurr, Andrew, 210

Hall, Radclyffe, 8
Hampson, John, 202, 212
Hankin, C. A., 210
Hanscombe, Gillian, 214
Hanson, Clare, 203, 210
Hardwick, Elizabeth, 214
Hardy, Thomas, 157, 195
Hawthorne, Nathaniel, 21
Hazzard, Shirley, 201, 212
Head, Bessie, 12, 190
A Question of Power, 190
Heidegger, Martin, 7, 11
Howe, Irving, 214

Huxley, Thomas Henry, 51
Hynes, S., 201–2, 212

Ingalls, Rachel, 2
  Binstead's Safari, 189
Irigaray, Luce, 71

James, Alice, 200
James, Henry, 21, 77–9, 84, 87, 90,
  100, 124, 163, 198, 200, 203
  Daisy Miller, 200
  The Golden Bowl, 198
James, William, 10, 190
  Pragmatism, 190
  The Meaning of Truth, 190
Jardine, Alice, 214
Jewett, Sarah Orne, 19, 21, 52, 191
  The Country of the Pointed Firs,
  191
Johnson, Barbara, 192–4, 215
Jones, Anne G., 195, 215
Joyce, James, 163, 182, 190

Kay, Dick, 205, 213
Keats, John, 1–2, 16, 86, 121, 152
Kiely, Robert, 215
Kierkegaard, Søren, 175, 193
Kolodny, Annette, 215
Kristeva, Julia, 215
Krutch, J. W., 193

Lakritz, A. M., 208
Larkin, Philip, 206, 213
Lawrence, D. H., 124, 128, 136, 160,
  180, 194–5, 205
Lawrence, Frieda, 121
Lee, Gypsy Rose, 162
Lee, Vernon, 198
Lehmann, John, 201
Lessing, Doris, 2, 4, 6, 146, 189–90,
  206
  Briefing for a Descent into Hell, 189
  The Four-Gated City, 206
  The Golden Notebook, 4, 189
  Memoirs of a Survivor, 189
Levenson, M. H., 215
Lewis, Edith, 19, 191
Lewis, Nancy, 213
Lewis, R. W. B., 199, 213–14

Lowry, Malcolm, 160
Lyde, M. L., 197, 213
Lynd, Sylvia, 202, 212

McBrien, W., 206, 213
McCallum, Pamela, 215
McCarthy, Mary, 193
McClung, Isabella, 19
McCullers, Carson, 16, 148, 162,
  191, 206, 215
  The Ballad of the Sad Café, 206
  The Member of the Wedding, 206
  *The Mortgaged Heart and Other
    Essays*, 191, 215
  Reflections in a Golden Eye, 206
MacGibbon, James, 206, 213
Magalaner, M., 210
Mansfield, Katherine, 2, 5, 8–9, 12,
  14, 28, 36, 38, 55, 57, 60–2, 101,
  106–7, 114, 118, 121–40, 147–8,
  165, 168, 175, 183, 192, 194, 196,
  203–7, 210–11
  'Bliss', 57, 60, 106, 121–40, 203–5
  The Collected Stories, 210
  Letters and Journals, 60, 196, 203–5
Marcus, Jane, 215
Martin, Wendy, 197, 209
Maupassant, Guy de, 21, 51
Mellown, Elgin W., 211–12
Melly, Diane, 201
Melville, Herman, 193
Meyers, Jeffrey, 211
Miller, Henry, 160
Milton, John, 159
Moermann, Maryvonne, 201
Moi, Toril, 215
Montefiore, Jan, 213
Moore, Leslie, 211
Murray, J. J., 210

Naipaul, V. S., 202, 212
Nebeker, Helen, 212
New Historicism, 6, 45, 82, 159
Nietzsche, Friedrich, 2, 37, 59, 67,
  71, 119, 168, 194–5
  The Will to Power, 194
Nin, Anaïs, 16, 145, 191, 215
  A Woman Speaks, 191
Nye, Robert, 162

O'Brien, Kate, 202
O'Connor, Flannery, 1, 16–17, 21,
  147–8, 182–3, 186, 204, 206, 215
  Mystery and Manners, 1, 17, 182,
    189, 191, 194, 197, 204, 215
  Wise Blood, 206
O'Connor, Teresa, 212
O'Keeffe, Georgia, 31
Orr, Peter, 213
O'Sullivan, Vincent, 206, 210–11

Parker, Dorothy, 211, 215
Pater, Walter, 157
Pemble, John, 198
Plato, 182
Poe, Edgar Allan, 21
Porter, Katherine Anne, 5, 9, 12–13,
  17, 23, 29, 101, 105, 108, 115,
  152, 168, 188, 192, 204–5, 211
  'The Holiday', 101, 204
  Ship of Fools, 115

Randall, J. H. III, 192–3, 209
Rankin, A. C., 213
Ricoeur, Paul, 45
Rhys, Jean, 2, 4–11, 13, 15, 17, 23,
  28, 55, 60, 63, 72, 99–120, 123–4,
  132–3, 140, 142, 147, 150, 152,
  160, 165, 167–9, 181, 193, 196,
  200–4, 211–12
  After Leaving Mr Mackenzie, 8, 14,
    103, 112, 190, 201–2, 211
  Good Morning, Midnight, 104, 119,
    206, 211
  Letters, 102, 116, 211
  Quartet (or *Postures*), 103, 211
  Voyage in the Dark, 8, 55, 103–16,
    118, 132, 188, 190, 196, 204,
    211
  Wide Sargasso Sea, 6, 99, 104,
    115–16, 119, 211
Richardson, Dorothy, 4, 7, 13, 17,
  32, 60, 72, 78, 100, 103, 121, 133,
  147, 160, 163, 193, 196
  Pilgrimage, 13, 32, 63, 119, 121,
    125, 180, 190, 196
Richter, Jean Paul, 192
Robinson, Phyllis C., 191, 209
Roe, Sue, 212, 215

Rohnberger, M., 211
Ruskin, John, 198

Sage, Lorna, 202–3, 212
Sartre, Jean Paul, 193
Schlegel, Friedrich, 192
Schroeter, James, 192–3, 195, 209
Scott, M., 210
Sergeant, Elizabeth, 191, 209
Seyersted, Per, 51, 195–6, 209
Shakespeare, William, 88, 92, 195
Shaviro, S., 190
Shelley, Percy Bysshe, 3, 36, 53, 85,
  152, 163, 198, 201
  'Adonais', 53
  'A Defence of Poetry', 189–90,
    194–5, 201
  'Ozymandias', 85, 163
Showalter, Elaine, 196, 215
Sillitoe, Alan, 162
Sinclair, May, 4, 7, 11, 14, 17, 55, 78,
  100, 105, 144, 180, 190, 193, 196,
  206
  *The Life and Death of Harriett
    Frean*, 180
  Mary Olivier: A Life, 55, 63, 125,
    180, 190
Slote, Berenice, 209
Smith, Stevie, 2, 4–13, 15, 17, 28, 36,
  100, 104–5, 108, 114, 116, 133,
  141–61, 163, 166, 168, 179–81,
  189, 205–7, 212–13
  The Holiday, 141, 146, 148–9, 206,
    212
  Novel on Yellow Paper, 141–2, 148,
    159, 213
  Over the Frontier, 18, 119, 126,
    141, 146, 148–61, 213
  The Collected Poems, 206, 213
Smith, Stewart, 196, 210
Smyers, V. L., 214
Socrates, 182
Sophocles, 52, 55, 158, 191, 193
  Oedipus Rex, 184, 193
Southron, Jane S., 202, 212
Spacks, Patricia M., 215
Spalding, Frances, 205, 213
Spangler, George M., 209
Spencer, Elizabeth, 11, 14

Spencer, Herbert, 51
Springer, Marlene, 197, 209
Staley, Thomas, 212
Stead, C. K., 210–11
Stein, Gertrude, 4, 6–8, 11–13, 87,
    143, 156, 169, 181, 193, 215
Sterne, Lawrence, 143
    Tristram Shandy, 151
Stewart, McEnery, 52
Storey, Mark, 206, 213
Stouck, David, 19, 209
Sullivan, Ruth, 196, 210
Swinburne, Algernon Charles, 198
Symonds, J. A., 198

Taylor, Helen, 195, 209–10
Tennant, S., 210
Thompkins, Jane P., 197, 210
Thurman, Judith, 212
Tieck, Ludwig, 192
Tomalin, Clare, 211
Toth, Emily, 195–6, 209–10
Trilling, Diana, 214
Tyler, Anne, 117, 202, 212

Updike, John, 202

Vita-Finzi, P., 197, 214

Walker, Alice, 183
Walpole, Hugh, 203
Walton, G., 197, 214
Watts, Jane, 206–7, 213
Welty, Eudora, vi, vii, 13, 24, 82,
    182, 185, 192, 198, 204–5, 209,
    211, 215
    The Eye of the Story, 13, 189, 192,
        198, 204
    The Robber Bridegroom, 190
Wershaven, Carol, 197, 214
West, Rebecca, 7, 195, 203, 209, 212,
    215
Wharton, Edith, 2, 5–15, 17, 21,
    77–98, 100, 102, 106–7, 111, 118,

133, 143, 159, 168, 193, 196–201,
    213–14
    A Backward Glance, 92, 213
    The Age of Innocence, 200, 213
    'Autres Temps', 77, 198
    The House of Mirth, 14, 200, 213
    In Morocco, 80, 82–8, 97, 159, 189,
        199, 213
    Italian Background, 77, 80, 88, 97,
        159, 190, 198, 213
    The Reef, 14, 200, 213
    'Roman Fever', 8, 80, 82–3, 88–98,
        102, 188, 190, 213
    The Writing of Fiction, 78, 197,
        213
Wheeler, Kathleen M., 194
Wheeler, Otis B., 196, 210
Whitemore, Hugh, 213
Williams, Merryn, 215
Williams, Tennessee, 162–3
Wilson, Edmund, 193, 197, 210, 214
Wittgenstein, Ludwig, 181
Wolff, C. G., 196, 210, 214
Wolkenfeld, Susanne, 73, 197, 210
Woolf, Virginia, 2, 4, 6–7, 11–13, 17,
    28, 55, 60, 62, 75, 78, 101, 103,
    116, 121, 124, 129, 132, 135, 138,
    142, 149, 163, 180, 182, 193–4,
    196, 203, 211, 215
    Between the Acts, 132, 135, 138,
        188, 190, 204
    Mrs Dalloway, 125, 150, 190, 207
    Orlando, 180
    To the Lighthouse, 62, 75, 119
    The Waves, 150
    'moments of being', 129, 182
Wyndham, Francis, 99, 201–3, 212

Yaegar, Patricia, S., 196, 210
Young, Marguerite, 6, 12
    Miss MacIntosh, My Darling, 190

Ziff, Larzer, 195, 210
Zola, Émile, 21, 113